A FOGGY DAY ON THE BRONX. S. R. GIFFORD.

Out of Town

A Rural Episode

By BARRY GRAY

WITH ILLUSTRATIONS

NEW YORK
PUBLISHED BY HURD AND HOUGHTON
459 Broome Street
1866

RIVERSIDE, CAMBRIDGE:
STEREOTYPED AND PRINTED BY
H. O. HOUGHTON AND COMPANY.

PREFATORY AND DEDICATORY.

"Do you know, Mr. Gray," asked my estimable wife early one morning, as she raised the sash and threw open the blinds of the chamber-window, in our house in Merryfield Place, "that the spring is here? Observe how balmy is the air, and see how the buds are swelling on the trees, and the grass sending forth its green blades in the courtyard. Listen to the song of that bluebird, perched upon the swaying branch of the elm, and hearken, too, to the buzzing of the early flies, enjoying the warm sunshine on the window panes. Yes, the spring is here, my dear, and we are on the verge, as the poet hath it, of the 'delicate-footed May'; and this reminds me — oh! sad anticlimax — that you have not yet obtained a house for the coming year, and that, before ten days go by, unless you do, we shall be homeless, having neither a shelter for, nor a place wherein to lay, our heads."

"I am fully aware of it, my dear," I replied; "and I have for the last month, as you are aware, travelled over the greater part of the city searching for a proper residence, without finding one. I have half-decided to look no further" —

"That would be just like you, Mr. Gray," interrupted my wife; "you would be willing to sit down quietly, with folded hands, and let the future take care of itself."

"You are very much mistaken, my dear," I said, "if you think so. What I was going to say was, that I was half-decided to look no further for a house in the city; but to get one out of town. And, if it will please you, I will do so."

My wife having expressed a decided approbation of this plan, I continued: "Your quotation, my dear, from the poet is so suggestive of the country that I wish we were there at this moment. The phrase, 'delicate-footed May,' is especially good to employ if one lives in the country, or even if he be a lounger among the city parks, and is given to frequenting that Park of parks, the Central. But if he be condemned, as most of our people are, to the purlieus of brick and mortar, and only sees the parks as he rides by in the over-crowded car, or the not less crowded omnibus, it is not so appropriate. For May, in most cases, then means 'moving time,' when the year's Lares and Penates are torn up by the roots, and the household gods are borne from place to place, and, in the midst of much dirt, confusion, and anxiety, planted afresh in some new locality to be again transferred when the next 'delicate-footed May' comes round. The approaching May promises to be unusually fraught with annoyance. Houses to be let are remarkably rare, even at greatly advanced prices, and many a family will find itself, on the first of May, without a sheltering roof."

"That is so," said my wife, "and it would not surprise me if we should be among the number."

"Persons," I continued, not heeding Mrs. Gray's interruption, "who heretofore thought they could not live out of town, will find it not only cheaper, but healthier and pleasanter, to have a house in the country; and, before the year goes round, will have come to understand and appreciate what our poet means when he says, 'The Spring is here, the delicate-footed May.'"

"Well, if you intend to get a place in the country," said my wife, "I think you had better be about it, and not wait until the first of May arrives."

"I have already been seeking a place," I replied; "and among the pleasant spots which I visited, a few days since, within an hour's ride of business, was the village of Fordham, — a quiet, unpretentious little place, nestled on and among the hills, with sundry picturesque houses, and an air of thrift pervading its people that was delightful to witness. It is poetic ground, too; for here Poe once lived, and Drake wrote charmingly of the little river, the Bronx, which flows through its precincts. Even now it is not without its literary representative, in the person of the author of the tragedy of 'Sybil,' John Savage, who dwells in a most hospitable cottage, near St. John's College. And this reminds me that there is also much classical knowledge contained in Fordham, — as those who meet and converse with the grave and dignified priests who inhabit the college will assuredly attest. It was pleasant to see those scholastic-looking men, clad in their long black cassocks, thoughtfully pacing, in the afternoon sunshine of that mild spring-day, the neatly-kept walks of the college-ground; and to hear, wafted upon the balmy air, the musical sound of the chapel bell ringing the 'Angelus.'

"In company with my friend," I continued, "I visited the little Dutch cottage where, in the spring of 1846, Poe carried his young wife, Virginia, to die, and where he passed the three remaining years of his life. It is a low-roofed dwelling, scarcely over one story in height, — for the three narrow windows over the lowly porch are only a pane of glass in width, — and has suffered no change, save such as Time has wrought, since Poe made it his home. The clumps of rare dahlias and beds of mignonette which once grew in its garden, are no longer there; but the cherry-trees, grown older by nineteen years, still throw their sheltering arms above and around it; and the descendants of the birds that used to sing to him from its leafy coverts, doubtless yet build nests in its branches. A favorite resort of the poet, which we visited, was a ledge of rocky ground a little east of the cottage, partly covered with pines and cedars, commanding a fine view of the surrounding country. 'Here,' says Mrs. Whitman, 'through long summer days, and through solitary, star-lit nights, he loved to sit, dreaming his gorgeous waking dreams, or pondering the deep problems of "The Universe" — that grand "prose-poem" to which he devoted the last and maturest energies of his wonderful intellect.'

"Filled with painful thoughts, my friend and myself turned from this humble cottage, where Edgar Poe dwelt with sorrow and remorse during the later years of his life, and, passing to the banks of the Bronx, sought, amidst its picturesque scenery, to find themes for less bitter fancies. The water rippled over its rocky bed, and along its high and sloping shores, with a musical cadence that brought peace to our minds, and seemed to say that the spring was here, even the 'delicate-footed May.'"

"But, what about a house, Mr. Gray?" my wife asked. "Did you find one that would suit our purpose?"

"Well," I replied, "I am not quite certain; though, so far as I am concerned, it is all that I would desire; but you, my dear, may think differently. I fear that you will deem it too small, and will be wanting me to put on all kinds of additions, including wings, sub-cellars and attic-stories."

"Any house will be better than none, my dear," my wife said; "and if you are satisfied with it, I think you had better purchase it, and then we can add to or take away from it, as we may desire."

"And I'll tell you what I'll do," I said, "to help pay for it. My publishers want another book of mine, and so I'll write an account of our life in the country, from spring until mid-winter, and they shall publish it under the title of 'OUT OF TOWN;' and I will dedicate it, my dear, to you, and the dedication shall run in this wise: —

'TO

MY WIFE,

WHO, THROUGH SPRING-TIME AND HARVEST, SUMMER AND WINTER, FOR MANY YEARS; IN JOY AND SORROW, SICKNESS AND HEALTH, HAS BEEN TO ME A SOLACE AND SUPPORT, MORE THAN WORDS OF MINE CAN TELL, OR DEEDS CAN VERIFY,

THIS VOLUME,

DESCRIPTIVE OF A RURAL EPISODE IN OUR JOURNEY THROUGH LIFE,
IS AFFECTIONATELY INSCRIBED.'"

FORDHAM, N. Y., *July 25th*, 1866.

CONTENTS.

CHAPTER		PAGE
	Prefatory	iii
I.	Mr. Gray goes into the Country	1
II.	Woodbine Cottage, and matters thereto pertaining	6
III.	A Poultry Convention convenes before Mr. Gray's Cottage	13
IV.	Mr. Gray buys and loses a black-and-tan Hen	20
V.	Mr. Gray and Family go a-fishing	25
VI.	Fourth of July	31
VII.	A Literary Young Lady comes to Woodbine Cottage	36
VIII.	A Night Attack	41
IX.	An Assemblage of Artist Friends	50
X.	The "Flag of Freedom" reports their Doings	56
XI.	Robbery of Mr. Gray's Melon Patch	62
XII.	Mr. Gray purchases a Goat	69
XIII.	The Goat gets into the Pound	76
XIV.	A Reminiscence	81
XV.	Three good Things at Woodbine Cottage	85
XVI.	Rev. Mr. Stricklebat makes his Appearance	93
XVII.	A Meeting around the Library Lamp	100
XVIII.	Mr. Gray takes a Lesson in Milking	109
XIX.	Lamb and Wine	114
XX.	How the little Grays celebrated the Eclipse	121
XXI.	Mr. Gray brings "Something" from Town	126
XXII.	Indian Summer	134
XXIII.	"Honest Daniel Due"	139
XXIV.	Several Thanksgiving Days	146
XXV.	Chartreuse, Billiards, and Poetry	153

CHAPTER		PAGE
XXVI.	Mr. Gray harvests his Crops . . .	161
XXVII.	The Little Folks celebrate Evacuation Day	167
XXVIII.	Mr. Gray's Indian Descent	173
XXIX.	The Day of Thanksgiving	178
XXX.	Mrs. Gray goes to an early Tea Party .	187
XXXI.	A few Trumpets are introduced . . .	195
XXXII.	Santa Claus's Visit	199
XXXIII.	Buckwheat Cakes and Sausages . . .	206
XXXIV.	My Children in Utopia — A Christmas Story	210
XXXV.	My Little Ones at Home, with more of the Christmas Story	219
XXXVI.	The Story within a Story of Christmas Times	231
XXXVII.	Another Part of our Christmas Nights' Entertainments	237
XXXVIII.	The End of my Family in Utopia . .	249
XXXIX.	Winter in Town and out of Town . .	261
XL.	The Story of the Little Quakeress . .	271
XLI.	Mr. Gray attends a Tea Party . .	283
XLII.	Mr. Gray's Youthful Days	289
XLIII.	Mrs. Gray receives a Present . . .	294
XLIV.	Woodbine Cottage goes to a Wedding .	304

OUT OF TOWN.

CHAPTER I.

I go into the Country. — My Reasons. — Choice of a Village. — Woodbine Cottage. — My Library. — Other Rooms. — Camping-out.

WHEN spring came, I resolved to move into the country. There were numerous reasons which induced me to take this step. I had become thoroughly disenchanted with town-life. Ten years spent amidst brick walls and street-flagging, without getting, in all that time, a whiff of country air, or a sight of a blade of grass, save what the city parks afforded, were as many as I cared to endure. Besides, house-rents in town had advanced enormously, and, as the little English-basement house in Merryfield Place, where I had dwelt so comfortably all these years of city-life, had been sold, and I was forced to seek another habitation, I resolved to save money by purchasing a place in the country. Other reasons, quite as important — the health of my estimable spouse and also of my little ones, and still others which I will not particularize — had weight in leading me to change my base.

Now, it is very easy to say that you will go into the country; you can make the declaration at the breakfast-table of a morning, over your coffee and rolls, as I did, and yet you are very far from having gone into the country. The country covers a great deal of ground, even that portion of it which lies directly in the neighborhood of the town in which you live, and it is not a simple affair to decide as to the particular locality wherein you will establish your *lares et penates.* If you wish to be, as I did, within easy access of the city,—I believe " within an hour's ride " is the proper phrase to employ, — you will be obliged, not only to visit a large number of "suburban retreats," but also to hold many conversations with your wife in relation to the affair. There are many *pros* and *cons* to be considered before you come to a decision. The healthfulness of the place, its society, its religious and educational advantages, its proximity and facilities for getting to town, the skill and character of its physician ; even its butcher, its groceryman, and shoemaker have to be thought of; and, not least, though last in the list, the properties of its drinking-water should be investigated before you arrive at a final decision.

I will not say that I was wise enough to attend to all these matters previous to becoming a resident of the little village which has the honor of numbering me among its inhabitants; though concerning some of these points I did inquire, and I must say that the answers I received were all highly favorable. The persons, however, whom I interrogated were, to a certain extent, interested in having me reside among them, and, therefore, were disposed to make everything appear of a rose-color. After all, it is not a bad place I selected ; and as I presume that there are very few gardens of Eden within the area of twenty miles of New York, I am contented with it. I visited a good many spots that professed to be somewhat in the Eden line, but found none that would, in any marked degree, compare with the original Paradise. It was not pleasant, either, to go among strangers; and, as I am a somewhat quiet and retiring individual, not prone to form new relations, I feared I might dwell many years in sundry of the villages I explored, without making the acquaintance of any one therein, except the ticket-agent at the railroad station. So, when a savage literary friend of mine commended the village of Fordham, where he resided, as a desirable location in which to place my household gods, I at once decided to become a Fordhamerer, and the owner of the little woodbine-clad cottage he had selected for me.

The house is small, but, as the maid-of-all-work remarked, " mighty-convenient." She declared to my wife that she could stand at the bottom of the stairs, in the hall, and sweep every room in the house without moving more than a foot either way; and, from the slight manner in which she performs this little task, I am disposed to think that she acts up to the letter of her remark.

I found it a work of much difficulty to get all of my household effects into its apartments. The main thing with me was to obtain a place for my books. So I selected the largest and best room in the house for my library, and told my wife that all the others were at her disposal. She seemed to think, however, that I had taken the lion's share, and asked me what she should do for a parlor. I advised her to take the adjoining apartment, but she said she intended that for the dining-room.

"Then the one still beyond," I said.

"Oh! that is the kitchen," she replied.

"Perhaps," I suggested, "one of the four up-stairs will answer."

"We require them all," she declared, "for sleeping apartments."

"Well, then, my dear," I replied, "I don't know what you will do. But what is the necessity of having a parlor at all?"

"Why, to entertain our friends in, when they call to see us," she replied.

"Oh! if that be all," I replied, "the library will do well enough. In fact, it is a much better place for that purpose than a parlor; for what, after all, is a parlor, with its rosewood furniture, satin hangings, and gilded ornaments, compared to a library, with its books, pictures, and oaken furniture, as a place wherein to entertain a thoughtfully inclined person? It is a pleasant place withal wherein to pass a rainy day. The patter of the rain upon the windows seems a fit accompaniment to the rhythm of the poem we may be reading; and the gusts of wind that, ever and anon, shake the casement, seem appropriate to the weird tale we are perusing. Then, again, if it be a sunny instead of a rainy day, what more delightful spot can one find to while away the hours in than this same library! When surrounded by books we never feel lonely. They are silent but agreeable companions, and in their society we may obtain both amusement and instruction. How delightful it is, too, to sit down before a package of new books! How carefully one unties the twine that binds it, and, unfolding the thick brown paper, lays bare the fresh and welcome volumes. The surroundings of a library, too, are all suggestive of interesting topics of conversation; while your parlor proper, with its collection of knicknackeries, only reminds one of the fashionable frivolities of life. Not, I own, my dear, that we are heavily burdened with expensive parlor articles, though there are the lounges, and pier-glasses, and piano, and — I declare, I don't know where we can put that piano. I am inclined to think that we shall be obliged to return it to the maker's for safe keeping until we can make room for it. Ah! I have it, my dear; I 'll build on a parlor. A wing added to the house will materially improve its appearance, and give us all the additional room we require."

Therefore it is that, until I put a wing to my cottage, we shall live without a parlor, and have to entertain our friends in the library. If more guests come than we can accommodate within the house, we can take possession of the adjoining orchard, or adjourn to the shade of the neighboring groves. One cannot do this if he lives in the town; there, if his house is ever so crowded with company, he has to make the best of it, and put up with all kind of inconveniences. But out of town, on a pinch, especially in pleasant summer weather, if one's sleeping accommodations are limited, he can swing hammocks under the trees for his friends, and, my word for it, if they like camping-out, they will enjoy it more than being cooped up in a small bedroom. Some night, when the children cry so as to keep me awake, I will abdicate my own room, and essay a lodging out-of-doors.

CHAPTER II.

Getting Settled. — Carpets. — Refrigerator. — My Heater. — Taylor's Aster-ale. — An Infernal Machine. — The Elephant. — Household Changes. — Cows, Milkmaids, and Milk. — A Wise Maiden. — Ice-men. — Bronx *vs.* Harlem. — My Exordium. — Drake's Verses. — The Majority.

IT takes a long time for a family to "get to rights" after moving into the country. The carpets, which were fitted to the rooms in your city home, seem stubbornly disinclined to take kindly to their new apartments. As a general rule, on these occasions, they are too small, though, in the present case, I will give them the credit of being much larger than is necessary. This, as my wife remarked, is a good fault; though how, if it be a fault, it can at the same time be a good one, is past my comprehension. When I said as much to my wife, she answered that, if I could not understand her meaning, I might remain in ignorance; but that to her it was perfectly clear and simple. As I before remarked, the carpets are all too large; but when I suggested the expediency of cutting them down to the proper size, my wife objected to it, on the ground that it would unsuit them for larger rooms, and, therefore, preferred to turn them under at the ends. As I purpose to live many years in this little house, and expect to wear out several carpets in the mean while, I could not fully appreciate the advantage to be derived from turning them in; but, as I have learned the wisdom of not making objections to the economies of housekeeping, I held my peace on the subject. I notice, however, a slight inequality in the surface of the carpeting in the various rooms, making a ridge-like elevation, extending across the rooms about three feet from the base-board, which does not strike me as being exactly the thing.

Fortunately, my bookcases all fitted properly into the niches wherein I desired to place them, and it was not necessary to saw off any projecting mouldings to enable them to occupy their appropriate spheres in the library. My wife found some difficulty, however, in this particular, with a bureau and a sofa, which articles seriously objected to being placed in the particular locations wherein she desired to see them. The refrigerator, too, a large, octagonal-shaped one, had to be nearly taken apart before we could get it through a certain doorway. Then, too, the heater, an immense thing that could n't be got apart, had to remain out-of-doors, upon the front piazza, for more than a month, until I could get a mason to come and make a passage-way for it into the cellar; and, after that, it required three men three hours to get it in; nor could they have accomplished it in that time had they not fortified themselves, every five minutes, with mugs of Aster-ale, a barrel of which stood conveniently at hand.

When I waggishly proposed to one of them — thinking the ale would not hold out — to go to the village saloon, and get some lager and cheese, he answered me in verse, that —

"Lager might do for burly Dutchmen,
To wash down Schweitzer cheese severe;
But give to Yankees, when they 're working,
Full mugs of Taylor's sparkling beer."

While the heater was ornamenting the exterior of my dwelling, it was a source of much interest to the small lads of the village, who assembled in squads of ten or a dozen, outside of the garden palings, and gazed at it with wondering and curious eyes. At first a report got abroad that it was a sort of infernal machine, or torpedo, — one which I had picked up off Charleston Harbor; and I noticed that persons going by the house usually gave it a wide berth, imitating, to a certain extent, the conduct of the opposites of the Good Samaritan, who passed by on the other side. But, as day by day wore on, and it failed to explode, or, in fact, go off in any way, their confidence returned, and a complete revolution, as it were, took place in their actions. They began to cast ridicule at both the heater and the owner, and the boys took to pelting it with green apples from the neighboring orchard. One man, indeed, had the audacity to ask me what I intended to do with my elephant. If he had not been a particular friend of mine, I should have knocked him down; as it was, I opened a bottle of wine for him. The next day I got the mason, as aforesaid, and had my "elephant" taken into the cellar. I count greatly upon the warming power of that "elephant" during the coming winter, and expect with it to keep my entire cottage at summer temperature.

Although we have been in our new home — which I have called "Woodbine Cottage," from the fact that a woodbine, or, after all, it may be a honeysuckle, grows about the front veranda — now nearly three months, I cannot yet honestly declare that we are quite settled. Every few days my wife makes some important change in the location of the furniture. Tables, chairs, bureaus, sofas, and bedsteads dance an irregular jig about the house. That which is my bedroom one night is the children's nursery the next. And because I eat my breakfast in the morning, before I go to town, in one room, it is no proof to me that, when I return in the afternoon, I shall eat my dinner there. Fortunately, it is not an easy matter to move bookcases, else I might expect, some day, to find my library transferred to the garret. The fact is, my wife has a liking for change. I do not mean, now, the small change which she surreptitiously extracts from my pocket-book, whenever I leave it lying loosely around, but that change which is akin to a love of novelty, and which, to say the least, is annoying to any one who, like myself, has a regard for old landmarks.

I have no doubt, however, that in course of time — if we both live so long — our furniture will, as a general thing, get into its proper place, to be disturbed only semi-annually, at the regular spring and fall house-cleanings. Though I confess, too, that I already begin to dread the time when I shall build the additions to the house — the parlor and kitchen — which I contemplate doing, and, indeed, have promised my wife to effect in the autumn. It will be very much like "moving-day" when those additions are completed; and it will be a good thing for me if I can make business which will detain me in town for a few days about that time.

Everybody in the country ought to keep a cow, — at least, every one who has a family of young children who like milk. As yet, I have only inquired for a cow. And though several respectable-looking cows did, in an independent manner, make me an early morning-call, and, opening the gate with their horns, walk into the enclosure where my youthful beets, and cabbages, and peas, and beans are growing, and eliminated their tender shoots from the parent roots, I failed to appreciate their visit, or to do them the honor of becoming their owner. On the contrary, I drove them forth with opprobrious epithets, accompanied with sticks and stones; and afterward put up a shingle sign on the fence to the effect that cows could not be pastured in my garden, and that hereafter all such trespassers would be taken to the pound, and there pounded. Since then I am happy to state that my garden-gate has remained unlifted.

The very day we took possession of our cottage, a generous procession of milkmaids, bearing huge cans of milk, came to welcome and ask us to purchase milk of them. Not knowing that my wife had already engaged milk of one of the aforesaid maidens, I entered into an agreement with another to supply us, twice a day, with the pure article; while a third, whom neither of us had engaged, but who acted upon her own responsibility, and further argued, in no unskilful manner, her right to supply us, because she had, for several years, been the sole milkmaid of the family who had occupied the house previous to our taking possession of it, also declared her intention of favoring us, daily, with all we might require. The result was that we had a superabundance of milk, and not a small part of it soured on our hands.

When my wife mentioned this little circumstance to the three milkmaids, they each declared it to be a fortunate circumstance. "For, you know, ma'am," they said, "nothing can be better than sour milk for making biscuits with."

But as my wife did not propose to live by biscuits alone, nor yet by milk, she gave the lacteal-bearing maidens to understand that, after the following day, she should only take milk from one of them. That afternoon the wisest of those three maidens — the one, evidently, who knew how to keep her lamp trimmed and burning — brought to my wife a basket containing a dozen duck's eggs, as a present. It is scarcely necessary to add that she is the favored one, now, who supplies us with milk, while the other two may be regarded as milkmaids all forlorn.

After having settled satisfactorily the matter of the milk business, another difficulty arose regarding the ice-man. It might be presumed that, taught by experience, neither my wife nor myself would have again duplicated our orders, as we did on the milk question. Owing, however, to the supposition, which each of us arrived at, that, while there might be many milkmaids, there was little probability of there being, in so small a village, more than one ice-man, and desirous, during the hot weather, of adding to the attractiveness of our well-water, and having an eye, also, to the better preservation of our meats and fancy dishes, each, unknown to the other, engaged for the season a supply of ice, to be delivered every other day. Several days elapsed before we discovered that we were in the receipt, daily, of a hundred pounds of ice. When, however, our large refrigerator began to groan under its burden, and we found that we had a larger quantity of ice on hand than was necessary, mutual explanations revealed the fact that we were obtaining more than our share of the product of the polar regions. Of course, we resolved to dispense with one of the Arctic explorers; but which of the two, became the question to be solved. My wife, for her part, advocated the retention of the Harlem River man, because she had engaged him, and, besides, she had a lingering regard for the High Bridge, which spanned it, and which structure she had more than once visited, not only with me, but with other gentlemen friends, before she was married. This, however, had no weight with me, and I strongly advocated the retention of the Bronx River man.

"A person who, evidently," I said to my wife, "possesses finer poetical instincts than he who cuts his ice in the Harlem. For, recall to mind, my dear, the fact that one of our charmingest poets, the friend of my friend Fitz-Greene Halleck, who lived in the early part of the present century, wrote most delightfully of this stream. Remember he sung, —

'The humbird shook his sun-touched wings around,
  The blue-finch carolled in the still retreat,
The antic squirrel capered on the ground
  Where lichens made a carpet for his feet.
Through the transparent waves the ruddy winkle
Shot up, in glimmering sparks, his red fin's tiny twinkle.'

Mark the phrase, my love, he used, — '*transparent wave*,' — and, of course, the ice is transparent. But you don't hear anything about the Harlem's transparent wave. No, no, my dear; it is very thick, muddy, and the ice, doubtless, is equally wanting in transparency. No poet, my love, ever wrote a line about the Harlem River, unless, perhaps, one of the early settlers, who spelt it Harlaem, may have indited something in Low Dutch concerning it. To be sure, my dear, the Bronx man charges a little more for his ice than does the Harlem man; but are we to be governed by dollars and cents? Shall we not concede something to the poetical phase of the subject? Is not the frozen 'transparent wave' of the Bronx more valuable than the ice of the Harlem, or even of the Croton? To be sure it is, and I for one, my dear, — and I believe I am the majority on this occasion, — give my entire vote in favor of the Bronx. And, with all due respect for your youthful feelings in this matter, I think I may safely declare that the Bronx man is unanimously elected to supply us with ice during the season."

And, as Mrs. Gray vouchsafed no reply, it was duly carried and recorded.

CHAPTER III.

Making a Garden. — Peas, Beans, Corn, and other Greeneries. — Spring Chickens. — Egg-nogg. — The Moral thereof. — An unexpected Poultry Show. — Barnum outdone. — Game-cocks. — An Indignant Female. — Blissful Ignorance. — Jack. — Shanghais and Bantams. — An English Rooster. — End of the Show. — Mrs. Gray's Investment. — A Black-and-Tan Hen. — The Rule of Thirty. — To be Continued.

SINCE I have come into the country I find myself continually seeking reasonable excuses for not going into town every day. While I was engaged in planting my half-acre garden, I had no difficulty in the matter. I was obliged to give a day each to my peas, my beans, my corn, and my potatoes. I had decided to do all the work myself, and, therefore, it was really necessary for me to stay at home to accomplish it. To be sure, after working an hour or two of a morning, under the hot sun, I found it agreeable to my feelings to retire within the house and take a long nooning of five or six hours, relieving the tedium of the time with a book, an iced punch, a saucer of strawberries and cream, and a cigar. In this way I managed to make a good many working-holidays for myself. I saved, too, to some extent, my hands from being as blistered as they would have been had I worked steadily on the twelve hours' rule. As it was, I had my share of these little annoyances, and never, since the time I was a school-boy, and was regularly feruled by my tutor, have my hands presented as many blisters. But I persevered in my agricultural efforts, and, after a reasonable time, I had the satisfaction of seeing all the seeds I had planted — with the exception of the corn, which the hens, unknown to me, had scratched up — break through the soil, watered with the sweat of my brow, and send their green and tender shoots into the air. The corn I replanted, or, rather, I hired a gardener to do it; for, although my intentions were good in regard to doing all the work myself, after the first day I relinquished the greater part of the labor to an older hand than mine, and with very gratifying results, as my table, which is chiefly supplied with vegetables of my own raising, sufficiently attests.

I am quite certain that, even allowing for the wages I paid my gardener, I am obtaining my peas and string-beans, my beets, lettuce, and radishes for much less than I could purchase them in town, — besides having the advantage of getting them fresh from the garden. My corn is beginning to show its silken floss; my tomatoes are just coloring; my Lima beans are filling out famously; my cucumbers are ripening; my squashes are turning their yellow sides up to the sun; and my melons will be ready for eating ere the month goes out.

Then, too, in the matter of spring chickens, I am not badly off; and as for eggs, I get scores of them every day. It is very handy, my wife thinks, to have plenty of eggs in the house; and, aside from their availability in the matter of custards, puddings, cakes, etc., they are very convenient in concocting noggs and mulls. When, one rainy Saturday, not long since, I neglected to report at the granite building in Wall Street, and remained at home, ostensibly to do a little weeding, but really to recruit my exhausted system, — exhausted by a too close application to governmental work, — by making a lounging time of it, the savage literary friend, referred to in a former sketch, who came to see me, insinuatingly suggested that an egg-nogg would not be a bad thing to take. Thereupon my freshest-laid eggs came into use; the ancestral punch-bowl was brought out; a bottle of old Jamaica, which I would be willing to declare had lain in my cellar twenty years, if I had only lived here that time, or even half of it, was opened; a quart of pure milk, with the cream beginning to rise on the surface, was obtained; and, with a *quantum sufficit* of sugar and nutmeg, a drink worthy of being commemorated in verse by Tom Moore was concocted and quaffed, while conviviality and good-fellowship ruled the hour. Now, for the moral: You may make and drink egg-nogg in the city as often as you please, and you may regard it as very fine; but, until you make and drink it in the country, using fresh eggs and new milk in its composition, you can have no idea of its excellence. It is then a draught fit for the best of good fellows. It warms the cockles of your heart. It cheers, but does not — unless you drink too much of it, which, although sorely tempted, you will not do, being a reasonable human being — inebriate. It inclines you to be merry, and you are disposed, under its warming influence, to sing patriotic songs, and recall to mind all manner of pleasant scenes. Therefore does it seem to me that, among other reasons for going out of town, which I might but did not name, is that thereby I might the better obtain a bowl of egg-nogg.

The allusion made above to spring chickens reminds me of a little venture which my estimable wife made in the poultry line, when we first came to Woodbine Cottage. Aware of the fact that it is the proper thing to have hens in the country, and knowing, too, that hens are disposed to lay eggs, and convinced, moreover, that fresh eggs for breakfast are desirable, she gave the majority of the milkmaids who patronized us to understand that she would like to become the purchaser of a few hens. Of course, this desire of hers was noised about among the country folks for miles around, and, as the information spread from mouth to mouth, and from neighbor to neighbor, the number of fowls increased from the original half-dozen up to a hundred or more. When, therefore, the country folks began to ride up to the house, with crates and baskets filled with crowing cocks, cackling hens, and chirping chickens, it was as if Barnum were opening a new poultry show. The display was something quite magnificent, and, as it occurred on one of my stay-at-home days, I had the full benefit of it. Fortunately my wife, having secured from the first person who arrived the half-dozen fowls she desired, was not obliged to receive the remaining members of the procession individually as they drove up to the gateway. This part of the proceedings fell to me, and, if I may believe my wife, who kept watch of me through the window-blinds from within the library, I acquitted myself with great dignity and decision. To tell the truth, I was rather overworked on that occasion, and, after the first score of poultry-dealers had passed before me, and paraded their stock on the open veranda where I sat, I began to think the affair not so amusing as it struck me it would be when it commenced. I did n't mind the men so much as I did the women; for I found that, by offering the former mugs of ale, after declining to deal with them, I quite soothed their irritable feelings. Indeed the effect was much like pouring oil upon water; but with the women, who did n't take kindly to ale, it was more like casting oil upon fire. One, especially, flared up in fine style, and declared, with much shaking of chicken feathers in my face, that she had come ten miles, in the broiling sun, to sell me those fowls, and that it was n't treating her decently to refuse to buy them. That she would let her son — for she chanced to be a widow, a circumstance which I found was generally the case with my visitors — know of my meanness, and she guessed he 'd settle the matter with me, and let me see that, if I did come from the city, and put on airs because I was rich, — I forgave the woman her blissful ignorance of my pecuniary resources, — I was not going to ride over her and hers rough-shod.

Now, there are those fowls, she continued, three roosters and three hens, paired and mated from the egg. No Mormonism or any of that kind of foolery was allowed in her poulty-yard; and, if I did n't decide mighty quick to take 'em, she 'd get even with me before the day was over. But I was very decided, and refused to purchase them or parley with her any longer. She then offered them to me for half price, — she had asked five dollars a pair, — but still I declined; though I compromised the matter, by recommending her to visit my savage literary friend, just above me on the hill, who would buy them, I thought, provided he could get them at a bargain. I think he must have bought them, for the woman never came back to me; and, besides, I have noticed of late that his dog Jack, a wiry terrier of surpassing ugliness, has grown quite plump, as if he had been living on cocks and hens. Indeed, the feathers, both tail and pin, which ornament his shaggy coat, would serve to indicate this to be something more than a mere unfounded supposition.

The first arrival of poultry had been at six o'clock in the morning, and from that hour until past noon Union Avenue, in front of my house, was choked up with coming and departing wagon-trains. Every variety of the gallinaceous breed, from the ungainly Shanghai, all legs, to the pert little Bantam, without any legs of which to speak, was represented. I was greatly tempted, at one time, to buy a perfect fac-simile of the "old red" that whilom strutted and crowed at my Hillside home; also a noble English rooster, black as the ace of spades, graceful in his movements as Hamlet, and possessing a splendid scarlet comb, which waved like a red flag from a citadel. There were sundry game-cocks in the collection, and several times I was invited out into the road to see a fight going on between a couple of them; but I invariably declined, preferring to remain on my own veranda, and witness it from a safe distance. Besides, I did not know but that I might be asked to engage in combat with one or more of the disappointed poultrymen, and that was something I would rather not do. My barrel of Aster-ale, too, had given out, and I had been obliged to send down to Teuton Hall, in the village, for a keg of lager; but, somehow, the company outside the garden palings did n't take kindly to it, and failed to prove themselves good representatives of the Sanger-fest.

When, at last, they found that longer waiting was useless, and that there was no more ale, they began, one by one, to go home, and the screams and clucking of hens and the shrill crowings of the cocks grew fainter and fainter as they were carried back to their respective barnyards. By-and-by, all that was left of the poultry show were a few scattered feathers, and three or four diminutive chicks, which had escaped from thaldrom and hidden themselves under the currant-bushes, from whence they sent up feeble and unavailing "peeps."

I may as well here add that every one of the fowls that Mrs. Gray bought proved to be of the masculine gender, and in consequence I was obliged afterwards to visit Washington Market, and purchase such as lay eggs and are not given to crowing. I would rather have obtained them nearer home; but the country people round about all refused to sell me any. One of those which I bought, too, I lost before getting home. She was a little black-and-tan hen, with a couple of bright eyes, a knowing side-glance, a short bill, and clean legs, and the market-man swore awfully that she was a splendid layer and setter. Three eggs a day, he said, would not be a bit too many to expect from her, — though first along, being in a strange place, she might n't quite come up to that figure; but, if I only gave her time, and would feed her well on corn, and keep her pasture ground well supplied with pebbles and lime, she 'd do it.

It was no more than I expected to have him ask higher for that hen than for the others; but still, when he named ten dollars as her price, I hesitated somewhat as to purchasing her, but closed with him, however, after he demonstrated to me that she would not only pay for herself — even if she laid not more than one egg a day — with eggs at five cents apiece, in about a month, but yield a profit of five dollars to pay for her feed. I don't exactly understand now how he worked it out, but, at all events, he did it, and it was somehow in this way: — "Thirty days multiplied by five cents," he said, putting his head knowingly on one side, and doing a little legerdemain on his fingers, "makes fifteen dollars; deduct ten dollars as the price of the hen, and you have five dollars remaining with which to purchase her feed."

Even now it sounds correctly to me; but my eight-year-old boy ciphered it out somewhat differently. But, as I said above, I lost her bringing her home, and came exceedingly near to getting into a serious difficulty on her account, to say nothing of almost losing my own life. But, as the story is somewhat long, I will devote the next chapter to its relation.

CHAPTER IV.

The Shady Side of the Cars. — Muslin *vs.* Bombazine. — Kind Sir, She said. — An Apology. — My Grandmother. — Banting System. — Black-and-Tan. — On a Lark. — A Chase. — In the Tunnel. — Irritable Old Gentleman.

I LOST my black-and-tan hen bringing her home. And this was the way it came to pass. I had her, with the other fowls I bought, secured in a large wicker basket, and had brought them in safety from the market to the railroad, and placed them under the seat which I occupied in the car. It being a warm day, I hoped, because of the greater comfort it would yield me, to occupy it alone, and had consequently disposed beside me the various packages and newspapers which a dweller out of town is accustomed to carry with him whenever he goes home. I had buried myself, figuratively speaking, in the last number of the "Atlantic," and was so absorbed in its perusal that I failed to perceive the inquiring glances cast by the passengers, as they passed through the cars, at the unoccupied seat. I knew they would find plenty of seats in the rear cars, or on the sunny side of almost any one in the train. Consequently, I made up my mind not to make room for any one beside me, unless asked so to do. I might have had for a neighbor a nice young lady, as sweet as lavender, and wearing the coolest of muslin gowns, if I had chosen to offer one a seat; but I neglected all the pleasant opportunities which arose for so doing, and was just congratulating myself — for the cars were in motion — on having the entire seat to myself, when a fat old lady, with a bandbox and basket, a parasol and a palm-leaf fan, wearing the warmest of black bombazine dresses, and looking most distressingly red-hot and suffocated, made her appearance down the aisle, coming toward me. I lifted my eyes from the page before me, where I had been reading about the honey-makers till the murmur of bees filled my mind, the perfume of clover-tops my nostrils, and the flavor of honey my tongue, and looked about me. Every seat was filled, and I knew there was no help for me; my time had come. So, making a virtue of necessity, I moved, as the old lady got near, and offered her part of the seat. She took it with many thanks, regretting she was so large and fleshy, as she knew she should seriously incommode me.

"But Providence, kind sir," she said, "does not permit us to choose our mortal tabernacles of flesh, else I would have been a much smaller woman than I am, and you would have been spared the discomfort which is now likely to be yours."

I begged the old lady to make no apologies for her size, although the seat, I said, really might have been a trifle wider, thereby rendering it more comfortable for each of us, yet that she could be thankful I was not a large man. She said she was, and she had no doubt, either, but that I was myself.

I replied I was, on this occasion, but that, as a general rule, it was not applicable. I would prefer to be a little stouter and heavier than I am; still, as she justly remarked, "one cannot control these matters."

"For my part," I continued, "I like fleshy persons; they are almost invariably good-natured, kind-hearted, and jovial. I had a grandmother once — rest her soul in peace! she is dead and gone these many-a-year — who was much stouter even than you; and, though she was prone to regret her size, I would n't have had a single ounce of her flesh removed for anything. There was n't too much of that old lady for me to love, I assure you. Besides, I always had an idea that it was because my grandmother was so large that she used to cut me such great slices of pound-cake whenever I visited her. If she had been a thin, bean-poleish kind of a woman, the pieces of cake, I imagine, would have been of the same character."

The old lady at my side looked benignly upon me, and said that she believed I was right. She had an idea though, she said, of trying that new plan of reducing one's flesh, of which she 'd heard so much talk, — the what-do-you-call-it system.

"Oh, the Banting," I said.

"Yes," she replied, "that is it; though I should n't like to be obliged to give up bread. I don't believe, though, after all, that I shall adopt that — what-is-it system?"

"The Banting," I answered.

"Oh, yes, I 'll remember it now," she replied, — "Banting. I 've only to think of bantams, and that will remind me of it. Now, do you know," she continued, "that I 've imagined, ever since I 've been here, that I heard hens making a noise?"

"I think it very probable," I replied; "for, the fact is, I have a half-dozen of fowls in the basket under this seat. I 've a couple of bantams there, and a black-and-tan hen which is just the prettiest little fowl you ever saw."

"Now, do tell," she said; — "but what kind of a hen did you call it, — a black and what?"

"Black-and-tan," I answered.

"Well, now, really," she said, "I know a good deal about fowls, but I never heard before of one of that kind; and if you could let me see that hen I would regard it as a great favor."

Thereupon I managed, with considerable trouble, to get the cover of the basket opened, and take out the aforementioned black-and-tan. We were just approaching the Harlem Tunnel, and, before the old lady had an opportunity to examine her henship, we had passed into the darkness. Suddenly the hen, which had been lying perfectly quiet, struggled from my grasp, and before I could recover it, was flying through the car, striking with her wings the bonnets of the ladies, and knocking off the hats of the men. The commotion was fearful, — the women shrieked, the men swore, and the affrighted hen kept blindly flying about. None, however, knew what it was, but the general impression seemed to be that it was an invention of the Rebels — a kind of flying infernal machine — for the destruction of the inmates of the car.

When we reached daylight again the mystery was explained, and, with shouts of laughter from some and invectives from others, the owner of the unfortunate hen was called for, and, after many urgent requests, I at last rose, and sought to apologize for the annoyance I had unintentionally caused. The passengers generally accepted the apology, but one or two individuals said I ought to be prosecuted and made to pay roundly for the fright my hen had occasioned. All this while the black-and-tan was running about under the seats, poked at with canes and umbrellas, and finally took refuge, just as I joined in the pursuit, under the hoops of a sour-looking, tall, and bony maiden lady of an uncertain age, who sat in the adjoining seat to me, and who I noticed had turned a scornful look at me when I eulogized fat people. For a moment she screeched hysterically, and then fainted away; at the same time the hen gained the door of the car, which the conductor opened on his way to collect the tickets, and before I could grasp her had flown, screaming, off of the platform, and alighted in the charming village of Yorkville, where she now, doubtless, is experiencing the hospitality of that delightful suburban retreat.

In my efforts to catch her I came near to falling headlong from the cars, and, if the brakeman had not caught me, I should have followed after the hen. When I reëntered the car I was confronted by a lively old gentleman with a rubicund nose, and a gold-headed cane which he flourished energetically, who desired to know what the deuce I meant by insulting his sister.

I assured him that I had no intention of doing any such thing, and was exceedingly sorry that my little black-and-tan — mine, alas! no longer — had created such a serious disturbance.

The old gentleman, however, refused to listen to my explanations, until the old lady who had occupied the seat with me came to the rescue, and assured the would-be belligerent that it was entirely her fault that the fearful scene through which we had just passed had occurred. There was something about that old lady's voice of a soothing nature, or, it may be, something magical in her touch, when she laid her hand softly upon the arm of the excited old gentleman, that acted like an opiate upon his anger.

He yielded gracefully to her persuasions, and assured her that it gave him great pleasure to listen to her explanations, and that, moreover, he was convinced that his sister was a fool, and it was confounded nonsense for her to act as she did.

Meanwhile my old lady had, by the aid of salts, camphor, and other medicinal compounds, of which she appeared to have a large supply in her satchel, restored the thin lady to consciousness.

The excitement after a while subsided, and when I reached my stopping-place, I gave up my seat to the aforesaid old gentleman, who appeared delighted to take possession of it, and shook hands with me with great cordiality at parting.

Whether I shall ever duplicate that black-and-tan remains to be seen; but at present, my wife, who is of a saving turn of mind, objects seriously to my paying so high for any kind of a hen. The common hens, which lay one egg a day, she says, are good enough for our poultry-yard, and she trusts I will not spend any more money in buying new-fangled cocks and hens.

CHAPTER V.

A Brother of the Angle. — Country Scenery.— "American Angler's Book." Gentle Genio. — My Outfit. — A Fishing Party. — The Procession. — Prospect of Rain. — The Classic Bronx. — Many Flies. — Nary Trout. Mishaps. — It rains. — Going Home.

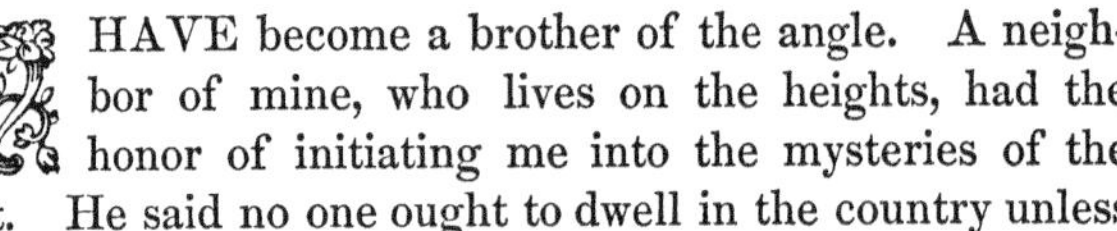

I HAVE become a brother of the angle. A neighbor of mine, who lives on the heights, had the honor of initiating me into the mysteries of the craft. He said no one ought to dwell in the country unless he were in the habit of going a-fishing. He quoted at length from old Izaak Walton to prove that one of the chief enjoyments of an out-of-town life consists in being able to go a-fishing. To live, too, near the sea, or a lake, or a running brook, was essential, he thought, to a proper appreciation of a country life. Thereby, one enjoyed better the special delights which the country affords, — the forest, with its leafy trees and shadowy nooks; the wide-spreading meadows, with their sunshine and buttercups; the breezy hill-tops; the quiet vales; the winding lanes, with raspberries and blackberries growing on either side; and, in short, all the charming sights and sounds that go to make up a country life.

After this conversation with my friend, I became inoculated with the desire to be an angler. So I took down, from its shelf in my library, the "American Angler's Book," and, in its perusal, lost all thought of the little task of thinning out my beets, which I had remained at home to accomplish.

Of course one cannot become an angler unless he possesses all the necessary tackle for the sport. Rods, landing-net, reels, lines, flies, baskets, high-topped boots, a slouched hat, and a pocket-flask are absolutely requisite in getting yourself up for a fisherman. When, after having spent much money and time, going from shop to shop with the "Gentle Genio," of the "Spirit," in obtaining these things, an express-wagon brought them home, my wife desired to know if I were going to open a fishing-shop. I told her no, but that I was going to shop for fish.

She trusted, she said, that I would have a good time of it when I went, but that she had not much hope of my success, for she had always understood that a true angler, like a true poet, must be born, not made.

Whereupon I told her that she knew nothing about it, and that, if she wished to have proven the falsity of her remark, she might accompany me on the morrow, and be a witness to my success.

This proposition seemed to please her very much; and, as I advised her to take the children and the nurse with her, and make a kind of picnic of it, — a gala day, as it were, to celebrate my inauguration as a fisherman, — she took kindly to the arrangement, and made a chicken-pie for the occasion, and added sundry sandwiches to the collation, and I filled my flask; and the next morning, though the heavens betokened rain, and my wife said she was afraid there would be a shower before night, we started.

"A cloudy sky, my dear," I said, "like that which is over us at this moment, is much more desirable than a clear one would be. Besides, you must allow that a warm sunny day would not be nearly so pleasant. The children would be hot and cross, the flies and mosquitoes would bite them, and their little faces would be sadly burnt."

"But, if it should rain, my dear?" she asked.

"Oh, never fear that," I answered; "I never knew it to rain when I went a-fishing, and I don't think it will begin to-day. Still, if it should sprinkle a little, the children can undress themselves and put their clothes under a stone while the shower lasts, and then, when it passes off, they can have them dry to put on again."

"That may be very nice for the little ones, my dear," my wife replied, "but what is to become of me in case of a shower? You can't expect me to follow their example."

"Well, no, perhaps not," I answered; "but then you have an umbrella, and can find protection, besides, under the trees; so that I don't think you need be greatly alarmed at the prospect of rain."

It was a pleasant thing to see our procession moving along the road, winding through the woods, to the Bronx. The neighbors came out of their houses to see us go by. Several of them prophesied that we would have a rainy day; but the larger portion of them wisely held their peace. First, as a pioneer, went the dog Jack, kept in place by my constantly throwing stones ahead for him to search for. Then came my eldest boy with a long fishing-pole and an umbrella. Behind him walked his two sisters, bearing between them a basket containing refreshments, and who, when they occasionally stopped to rest, abstracted therefrom the tempting peaches which lay within easy reach of their fingers. Then came the baby, reclining at ease in a four-wheeled carriage, propelled by the inevitable nurse, who always appears in our house simultaneously with the new infant. Her name is Kitty, and, though she is a good girl, and has had charge of several of my olive-plants, I don't think she will ever be called upon to take care of any more. Finally, bringing up the rear, with Mrs. Gray beside me, I walked, in a grave, sedate manner, as was becoming in the father of such a family and the husband of so dignified a woman as Mrs. G. She was not embarrassed with any luggage, if I except a gray shawl which she carried on her arm, and a palm-leaf fan which she held in her hand. As for myself, I was loaded down with many traps. My fishing-boots, the tops of which reached nearly to my shoulders, were extremely heavy, and when I put one foot down, it was exceedingly difficult to lift it off the ground again; each of those boots must weigh twenty pounds at least. Then I had my fish-basket, containing much tackle, and my private flask, slung across one shoulder, and a couple of poles over the other. Before we reached the banks of the stream we had added to our procession the popular simpleton of the village, together with his dog and two goats he was driving. I will say this of that poor fool, that he might have shown less wisdom than he did by joining our party. He left us, however, because he said it was going to rain, — and he knew enough to go into the house when it rained, never mind that some people said he did n't, — when we reached the classic Bronx, with its diversity of banks, here low and creeping up gently from the edge of the water, with an emerald sward; there higher, and fringed with the hazel, the dogwood, and climbing vines; and anon rising abrupt and rocky from twenty to thirty feet above the surface of the water, with dark pines and cedars stretching their huge branches far out toward the opposing shores. In some places the tide flows lazily and smoothly along, and the water-spider skims fearlessly across its glassy breast; at others, it goes tumbling and foaming over half-hidden rocks, and eddying around mossy trunks, and swirling swiftly into deep and silent pools. In these cloister-like spots, if anywhere amidst the stream, it is to be presumed that wily trout lurk; and into one of these, having first encamped my family on flat rocks and soft, green turf, I cast my maiden fly. It was a very fine-looking fellow, made up of gorgeously colored silks and feathers, and seemed to me to be of so attractive a character that no gay young trout would be able to resist making its acquaintance. But either the trout in that stream are old, staid fellows, who are not to be seduced by glitter and show, or else there are none there; for although I tried many flies of many kinds, and went from pool to pool, never a trout blessed my vision through the entire day, and only one fish attempted to take my fly; and he, from the voracity which he evinced, and the scientific way in which he snapped off the fly from the line, I am inclined to think was a pickerel.

Of course I met with many misadventures before the day was ended. I broke one rod; I entangled my line many times in the roots of trees and sunken rocks; I landed my wife's bonnet, which I took off of her head with a whirl of the rod, once, at least, in the centre of the stream; I caught my eldest boy just under the right ear with a hook that would fly off in a tangent, — an act which cost me a good draught from my private flask, poured on a handkerchief and applied to the wound to stop the bleeding; I slipped off of slimy rocks numerous times, and once, unfortunately, when I had the baby in my arms. I managed, however, to save the youthful scion of my house from a ducking, and only got a rebuke of a trying nature from my wife for my carelessness.

"Carelessness be hanged!" I replied, as I placed the baby unharmed in her arms; "it was n't that, but the slime on the rocks. You just try to walk across that point yourself, my dear, and if you don't measure your length in the water, I 'll agree to being called careless."

Mrs. Gray indignantly declined to comply with my request, and gave me to understand that it would be well for me to go and dry myself before I approached her again.

"I am dry," I replied; and I proved it by taking a long draught from my private flask.

To crown all, it began at noon to rain, commencing with a heavy shower, which wet us all thoroughly, including the little ones, who, owing to the number of tape-strings which got into hard knots, and would not be untied, failed to get off their garments in time to secure them from being wet through. We had just got the chicken-pie and sandwiches distributed in handsome style upon the table-rock, and were preparing to "fill our crops," as the children admonish the chickens to do, when the storm broke upon us. If the pie had been composed of young ducks, instead of chickens, it might have enjoyed it; for it was carried away in the freshet, and, the last I saw of it, was going with a rotary motion down the stream. The sandwiches, fortunately, were not carried away; and though they might be said to have been mustered out of the regular service, for the mustard was all washed out from between them, and they were soaked with rain and floated from the table, yet, after the storm had expended its fury, they were all recovered and made to do excellent service in allaying the hunger of the children.

After a while, when the storm had somewhat abated, and the rain came down only in a weak, unpleasant drizzle, we went stragglingly home. Dry clothes, hot tea, and a game of blind-man's-buff, restored the healthy tone of the family, and, at peace with all the world, we went to rest.

CHAPTER VI.

Fourth of July. — What the Parson said in his Sermon. — Its Sad Effect on the Minds of the Children. — I correct the Deplorable Impression. — Fireworks. — A Fishing Scheme. — A Visit to my Mother-in-law proposed. — It is unexpectedly prevented. — My Mother-in-law's Arrival Patriotic Noises. — Cold Punch. — In the Evening.

MY little ones are much excited over the prospect of soon having a Fourth of July to celebrate. They were a little in doubt, until I reassured them, whether we would have a Fourth of July this year. Since peace had been declared, and they had heard the Parson, in one of his sermons, say, as they related it to me, that all the swords were to be turned into pruning-hooks, the muskets into ploughshares, and the cannon into anchors, they could n't see how the soldiers were to be armed, so as to "turn out" on that day, nor how there could be any firing of guns. And you can't have a Fourth of July, you know, they said, unless you have pistols and guns, and such things, to load and fire off, and make a noise. "Well, I don't know about that," I said, "for after all the main thing on this day is to make a show, and also some noise. And with plenty of feathers, and flags, and shoulder-straps, and music, these matters can be accomplished. Besides," I added, "if there be no guns to consume powder, there will of course be more left with which to make fireworks. And if I remember rightly the experiences of past Fourths of July, considerable noise can be produced with crackers, double-headers, and torpedoes."

The idea of there being more fireworks in existence on the coming Fourth, fully reconciled my little ones to the loss of the swords and muskets; and, taking advantage of this acknowledgment on my part, they made me promise to lay in a larger supply than usual of fireworks.

But I told them we might all possibly go to their grandmother's to spend the day, and in that case they would have to be contented with a less number of fireworks, and a larger supply of cakes and peaches. The fact is that several of my artist friends had asked me to join them on a fishing excursion, to take place on that day, and I was desirous of going.

My wife, as I knew very well, however, would not consent to my being absent from home on this day, unless she could accompany me. Under usual circumstances this would have been impracticable, but in the present instance I thought it might be accomplished. To my satisfaction I found that the lake to which the party proposed going, was in the neighborhood where my wife's mother resided. I knew it would not do to let my wife know my plans, for she would then never consent to making her mother, as I hoped she would, a visit. So, a few mornings previous to the Fourth, just as I was on the point of departing for town, I suggested to my wife the propriety of taking with us the children and going to Coney Island on the coming national anniversary. Of course my crinoline half laughed at the idea.

"Then, my dear," I said, "perhaps we had better go to the city."

"Yes," she replied, "and have the children burnt to death with fire-crackers, and pistols, and all those kind of things. No, no," she continued; "I've seen all the Fourths of July in town that I wish to see. Did n't that blessed little boy singe off his eyebrows and eyelashes with gunpower last year, and come near in the evening to being carried off bodily into the air by a bundle of rockets, which he carelessly managed to light, while untying them? I tell you I am going to stay out here where there are no fireworks to be let off."

"Perhaps you don't know," I said, "that several of my artist friends have declared to me their intention of coming out here to spend the day, and are going to bring a large amount of fireworks with them?"

"Then," said my wife, quite excited, "you can have the benefit of their society, for I will take the children and go and visit my mother. How fortunate that I should have thought of it, and my dear mother, how glad she will be to see us!"

"But, my love," I interposed, "I do not think we had better go there."

"But I do," she answered.

And so the affair was settled.

I congratulated myself on the way to town, with the result of my diplomacy. During the day I told my friends that I would join them at the lake, for I doubted not I should be able to slip away from my mother-in-law's for a day's fishing.

But how vain are all human calculations. Man, indeed, proposes, but God disposes. At the very hour when my wife, my children, and myself, were arraying ourselves in travelling garments; when the carriage that was to bear us to the cars was approaching the door; and when my wife was giving the final directions to Kitty to keep the street-door locked, and on no account to admit into the house her cousins Mike, nor Pat, nor Tim, nor the rest of them, during our absence, up drove another carriage than the one we expected, and from it alighted — oh! unpropitious fate! — my wife's mother. She had come to pass the Fourth with us, — to witness the fireworks, and see the sights generally. Of course our trip was postponed. I suggested once or twice the propriety of my going to see that my mother-in-law's house was not set on fire by stray rockets, but my wife said it would be treating her mother disrespectfully should I leave home; so that I was fain to close my lips on the subject, and endeavor to have the old lady enjoy her visit as much as possible.

At last the Fourth came. My eldest boy, a lad of ten years, ushered it in by firing off a small cannon in his bed-room, which apartment adjoins the chamber occupied by his grandmother, — my esteemed wife's esteemed mother. The old lady was somewhat astonished by this, which was not at all decreased when Miss Em. let off a package of fire-crackers in the hall near her chamber door. At length, when she made her appearance in the breakfast-room, she was saluted with a shower of torpedoes, scattered by the hands of my seven-years'-old girl, and in shaking hands with the baby, managed to explode a pulling cracker which the latter had clutched in his chubby fist.

These little patriotic noises gave my esteemed mother-in-law a headache, so that instead of asking me to go to town with her, as she had hinted to my wife, the evening before, that she should, to view the military and the revellers, she was satisfied to remain at home, — much to my secret satisfaction, — where she found consolation in dipping into a bowl containing cold claret punch, which I had prepared for my own especial comfort. I do not know but that the day passed quite as pleasantly with me as if I had been up to my knees in water among lily-pads and rushes and slimy grasses, catching fish. My friends, of course, missed me more than I did them. I watched the children with their cannon and crackers, and thought of the days when I was as partial to these things as any of them. Whether my mother-in-law imbibed courage with the punch, or had become used to the din around her, towards evening she proposed going up to my savage literary friend's to see the fireworks, for I had told her that he had laid in a large supply. I said it was dangerous to go there. She was not afraid, she replied; and besides, was she not born in the days of '76? and was she not the daughter of a soldier who had fought in many of the battles of the Revolution, and as such should she not celebrate the day by beholding the fireworks?

"Certainly," I replied; and so forming a somewhat imposing procession, with the American flag waving, and bearing on my shoulder my assortment of rockets which I proposed to unite with those of my friend's, we marched thither.

Our combined efforts enabled us to get up an exhibition worthy of the occasion. It was, without doubt, the finest display of fireworks anywhere to be witnessed in the village. It comprised a large number of rockets, that left a train of sparks to mark their course, and which burst in mid-heaven, pouring a flood of diamonds, rubies, emeralds, and amethysts down upon the earth. Miniature volcanoes sent forth a shower of golden stars, and, at last, with a loud report, shot up into the sky hundreds of fiery serpents. Bengola lights emitted lurid flames, lighting up the entire neighborhood, and disclosing boys in the trees and lovers upon the sidewalks. Immense wheels, dazzling in their brilliancy and changing in their colors, like the kaleidoscope, now tinging the faces of the assembly with a sickly, yellow hue, anon casting a bluish glare, and finally spreading a roseate light over all, glared and whizzed like demons on a lark. Thus my neighbor and myself celebrated the evening of the Fourth. The children were greatly delighted, my wife was pleased, and my esteemed mother-in-law declared it was worth coming all the way from her home to see, and she hoped that none of us would ever go where fireworks are more brilliant and lasting than were these.

My esteemed wife's mother went home the next day.

CHAPTER VII.

An Arrival at Woodbine. — A Literary Young Lady; her Manuscript; her Opinion of Mr. Gray. — Pouting Red Lips. — Twilight and Moonlight. — Almost a Flirtation. — That 's why. — Saved. — My Neighbor's Fowls. — Corn *vs.* Tomatoes. — Amputating a Wing. — Dog Jack. — A Red Calf. A Connection. — The Result.

WE have had another arrival at Woodbine Cottage. No sooner did my mother-in-law leave us than her place in the family circle was filled by a young lady of literary proclivities. She came, one day, just as we were about sitting down to dinner, and brought with her a roll of manuscript and a good appetite. She wished me to read the former, while she assuaged the latter. I protested, but she insisted, and declared that it would not take me long to read it. I was really sorry to hear her say that, as I was quite charmed with her appearance, and had hoped that our interview might be protracted into the small hours of the night. However, I told her that, if it was as brief as she represented, I would prefer to eat my dinner first, and then there would be ample time for reading it afterward. She shook her head, but when my wife said that she could remain all night if necessary, she relented, and her countenance brightened materially. I may as well mention here that she was not an entire stranger either to me or to my wife, but I had made her acquaintance, a few years ago, when occupying an editorial chair. She used to write some pleasant little stories then, which were published in the columns of the "Home Journal," and won for her a reputation among its readers. She formed rather a high opinion, in those days, of my critical acumen, and used to favor me with her manuscripts for my opinion as to their literary merits. I tried to make my criticism as favorable as possible, though I may not always have been correct. Indeed, there were instances in which I passed judgment upon her stories without having read them; but, at such times, by skilful cross-questioning on her part, she generally managed to fix this disgraceful fact upon me, and then, with much seeming coolness of manner and pouting of red lips, which I would have liked to, but did not, kiss, she would gather up her manuscripts in silence, and go proudly away. She had very pretty ways, withal, and would glance at me, sometimes, in an inquiring fashion, out of her soft, brown eyes, which would have put my heart, if it had been a bachelor's, into a terrible flutter, and have tempted me to wish that she might always be coming to the office with manuscript for me to read.

She used to tell me that she intended to accomplish something very fine one of these days; and, as I saw the maiden had talent, I said much to encourage her, and gave her any quantity of good advice, which she may or may not have followed. I am inclined, however, to think that she did follow it. The manuscript which she brought with her to Woodbine Cottage turned out to be a good deal longer than I had any idea of, and, instead of my being able to peruse it that evening, I find myself, though a week has passed, still engaged upon it. My wife, however, fails to see the necessity of my spending so much time over it, especially since she herself was able to read it through in one afternoon.

"Ah! yes," I said, "but you did not read it critically, my dear, as I am doing. Every sentence has to be duly weighed and talked over, and that takes time, you know."

"Yes," she replied; "I have observed that you and Miss Floy spend a great deal of time over it, and it has sometimes occurred to me that you talk much irrelevant matter not connected with the subject of her manuscript. I don't see, either, what walking down to the Bronx in the twilight, and sitting on the veranda in the moonlight, with her, has to do with it. It is all very well for young unmarried critics to do thus; but for a staid father of a family, like yourself, who is getting bald, and whose beard is rather more than tinged with gray, it does not seem to me to be exactly the proper thing. It is not what I call legitimate criticism, but looks much more like a flirtation."

"Good heavens! my dear," I exclaimed; "I really believe you are correct. Why, the very thought nearly frightens me to death. It would be too bad if, at my age, and after the many years of happiness we have passed together, I should, at this late day, take to flirting with a literary young woman. Good gracious! it is terrible to contemplate. No more moonlight and Bronx for me, Miss Floy, if you please."

"Why not, I should like to know?" asked the young lady in question, who entered the library just as I had uttered these words.

"Why not?" I exclaimed; "because — because," I faltered, "the atmosphere is inclined to be damp at night, and I 'm afraid you may take cold and be ill, and I don't wish to have a sick literary young woman on my hands. That 's why!"

"Oh!" she said, in a tone, I thought, which implied a great deal more than she uttered.

I am very grateful to Mrs. Gray for calling my attention to the matter. If she had not, I might have gone on and on ever so far with Miss Floy, till I might have been tempted to take her hand and press it, and even have kissed her, which would have been very imprudent, not to say naughty, in me to do. Love-making is a very pretty pastime if you 're unmarried, and it fits very nicely into moonlight nights and twilight ramblings. But it won't do for a married man. He is almost certain of being caught at it, and besides, even if the wife did n't find it out, why, some one else would, and would reveal it to her, and then there would be a pretty time in the family. I don't mean to say that I have been making love to Miss Floy, or she to me; but it did seem to be tending toward it. To prevent anything, therefore, of that nature from actually taking place, I shall invite a young bachelor friend to stay at my house while Miss Floy and her manuscript remain with us.

I have had much trouble, lately, with my neighbor's fowls. They are continually getting into my garden and eating my tomatoes as fast as they ripen. My own fowls are shut up in the hennery, greatly, doubtless, to their wonder and disgust. The young roosters, I observe, are continually fighting each other, and it is no unusual thing for me, when I return home in the afternoon, to find one or two completely used-up chanticleers laid out on the floor of the hennery. I shut them up to save my tomatoes; but, as through shutting them up I am losing them, and at the same time losing my tomatoes by outside robbery, I don't think I shall make much by it. Even before they began murdering each other, my wife said she thought it would cost more to feed them with corn than the tomatoes they might eat would come to, and she thought the better way to keep them out of the garden would be to clip their wings, so that they could not fly over the garden fence. I tried it on one, but he bled so after I had finished, and seemed to suffer so much pain, that I declared I would n't do so cruel an act again for all the tomatoes in the world. He died that day,—bled to death, I think,—and his amputated wings kept flying around me, in my sleep, for two or three nights thereafter, reminding me, closely, of the cherubs carved on ancient tombstones,—all head and wings,—though wings alone were his allowance. Mrs. Gray persists in saying that I should have cut off only the feathered portion of his wings, and not subjected the bony and fleshy part to the shears. But I think, if it 's done at all, it 's best to make a clean sweep of it, and never leave the fowl a ghost of a chance ever to fly again. I am sure the aforementioned one never did, and I know, if I succeed in catching any of my neighbor's cocks and hens, they never will.

I came very near to catching one alive the other day, and, if I had, I would have made an example of him. As it was, my savage friend's dog, Jack, which I borrowed for the purpose, chased and caught the finest long-tailed, red-combed rooster which my neighbor owned; but, unfortunately, he killed him before I could get at him to cut his wings. That same dog, when, the following day, I set him on a dilapidated old hen, who was fattening herself on my biggest and ripest tomatoes, took it into his head to seize the red calf of the wild Irish girl, who attends to the pot and kettle branch of the housekeeping down in the kitchen, which she unwittingly and temptingly displayed before him. The result was a terrible outcry and commotion in the garden, the loss of the exile's services as a scrub, a suit brought against my savage literary friend for damages to her feelings and person, and the surgeon's bill, which I have agreed to pay.

CHAPTER VIII.

Our Policeman. — Our Silver and Jewels. — Police Duties. — How we were shocked. — A Night Alarm. — Burglars. — A Bat. — In the Basement. — Naked Feet. — Other Feet. — Miss Floy's Courage. — An Owl. — Cats. The First Shot. — The Result. — A Charge. — An Outside Attack. — Several Shots. — A Recognition. — Liberation. — Explanations. — The Toast.

WE have a policeman in our village. He is a very nice-looking fellow, and gets himself up in fine style. The regulation uniform of blue, ornamented with the representative brass buttons, fits him uncommonly well. When I first discovered him, a day or two after our arrival, just at nightfall, going by Woodbine Cottage, I called my wife's attention to him, and expatiated, at some length, upon the benefit which might arise from his proximity to our residence.

"If a burglar, my dear," I said, "should attempt, some dark night, to force his way into our dwelling, despite the bolts and bars with which our doors and windows are secured, to get at our silver and jewels," — here Mrs. Gray looked at the spoons on the table and the wedding-ring on her finger, — "it will be a satisfaction to know that such a bold and brave-looking policeman is about."

"Of course," said my wife; "and I suppose, too, that if wandering cows or pigs get into the garden in the night, he will be polite enough to drive them out."

"Oh, yes," I replied; "I believe that, in the rural districts, this is one of their prescribed duties."

The sight of that policeman certainly was a source of much comfort to both my wife and myself. We felt much more secure at night, believing him to be keeping faithful watch and guard about our humble cottage, than we should otherwise have felt. It was with a feeling of unusual satisfaction that I used to see that policeman, in the early dawn, while I was performing my morning ablutions, going homeward past our cottage. He never appeared weary, as one would expect a policeman who is up all night to be; but he strode along, in the dewy dawn, with the freshness of a morning-glory and the vigor of an elm. He looked as if he enjoyed the matin songs of the birds; but, most of all, it seemed to me as if he was getting up a good appetite, and would be thoroughly ready for his breakfast of ham and eggs when he got home.

Every one in Woodbine Cottage, from the eldest to the youngest, felt the safer for the proximity of that policeman. In starlight and moonlight nights, when the air was chilly and when it was warm, when it rained and when it was clear, when the winds blew and when they were whist, we all slept the more peacefully for his wakefulness; and, if a passing footstep disturbed our slumbers, we only roused up enough to say to one another, "It is, doubtless, our policeman on his round; let us shut our eyes again and go to sleep."

Possessed of this confidence in his watchfulness, it was, therefore, with a degree of disappointment which words cannot express that we learned that the policeman whom we had fondly imagined to be our policeman was not, and never had been, ours, but was enrolled in and belonged to the Metropolitan Police Department, and went nightly to his field of labor somewhere within the boundaries of New York island. It was a great shock to us when we ascertained this fact, and, until I got a brace of revolvers, we used to go to bed with much fear and trembling.

One night, after I had discovered that we did not own a policeman in our village, I was aroused from my slumbers by a singular noise, which proceeded from the basement, resembling very much that which might be produced by some one forcing the door at the head of the stairs. My wife, who is a very resolute woman, was the first to hear it, and called my attention to it by nudging me violently with her elbows in the region where my heart has its abiding-place, and whispering in an ominous tone the word thieves! As my sleep had been disturbed by dreams of robbers and garroters, I was fully prepared to learn that burglars were holding high-carnival down-stairs. A lamp was dimly burning in the upper hall, the light from which shone dimly through the open door into my room, casting weird shadows, which rose and fell in a mysterious manner, as the night wind blew fitfully upon it through the raised window-sash. Once I thought that the shadow of a man's head moved swiftly across the ceiling, and I instinctively listened to hear the sound of his footsteps in the passage-way. But nothing followed, only the shadow went back across the ceiling, and passed swiftly out of the chamber door.

"What the deuce do you suppose that is?" I asked, in a subdued tone. My wife replied that she did n't know, but that she had been watching it, and wondering, for several minutes, from what it proceeded. It would appear and disappear in a moment, and sometimes it was accompanied with a rustling noise, as if it had wings.

"Wings!" I exclaimed; "yes, yes, I see what it is now," as it whirled into and out of the room again at that moment; "it is a bat."

"A bat!" my wife screamed, forgetful of the robbers down below; "goodness, how you frighten me! They 're the bloodthirsty things that suck children's breaths, are they not?"

"Not that I have ever heard," I replied. "To cats, not bats, my dear, are ascribed such horrible proclivities."

"Hark!" she whispered, grasping my arm; "there is that noise again down-stairs, and — good gracious! — what is that?"

This last exclamation was called forth by a sound, as of

warning, uttered in a low semi-tone, which evidently proceeded from a confederate on watch outside, just beneath our window, and who, doubtless, had discovered that we were awake and alarmed.

"Hand the baby to me from his tender," my wife added, "and you go and see if it be really burglars who are disturbing our rest."

Slipping on my dressing-gown, and arming myself with a Colt's revolver, which I took from its case, which I keep in my dressing-table drawer, and taking the lamp in my unarmed hand, I proceeded resolutely to the head of the stairs leading down into the hall. Just as I reached it, my literary young lady, whose manuscript is still unfinished, aroused by our movements, softly opened the door of her room, and appeared before me in the most charming of night toilets, bordered with little frills, and edgings, and bits of lace, and asked what was the matter.

When I whispered the word "burglar," she turned very pale, but compressed her lips resolutely, and gave me to understand, by going back to her room and returning with my famous charter-oak cane in her hand, that she would accompany me.

There is a good deal of comfort experienced, when looking for burglars, in catching sight of a pair of bare, white little feet, as they come tripping down the stairway to join you in your dangerous explorations. To be sure, those feet do not, and never may, belong to you. Perhaps, for that very reason, they are the more interesting to you than they would otherwise be. You know all about the grace and beauty pertaining to your wife's feet, and have doubtless often seen them sink into the velvet rug at the side of your bed. You know the exact size of the gaiter-boot she wears, and have been commissioned, time and again, to bring home to her a new pair. Not always, to be sure, are you successful in fitting her with the first pair; but then it is no more than proper for a husband to run between his wife's feet and a shoemaker at least five or six times before he obtains the correct "fit." You have put her slippers on, and laced her gaiters for her many a time, and know all about the ins and outs of those blessed pedals; but the naked little feet of another woman you are presumed to know nothing about; and when, therefore, they come dancing behind you after midnight, helping to catch burglars, as Miss Floy's did with me, you can't very well avoid looking at and admiring them.

When we reached the door at the head of the stairs, I stopped to listen before drawing the bolt. All was silent, save the chirp of a cricket, which had a home in a crevice of the unused fireplace; but outside again arose the singular cry of the confederate burglar, in a long-drawn sepulchral note.

"Do you hear that?" I asked. "That is the burglar keeping watch outside."

"Nonsense," said Miss Floy; "that is an owl."

"An owl!" I exclaimed. "Well, then, I 'll bet there is no burglar inside."

And I courageously opened the door, and walked deliberately down the stairs. There was a fierce rush for a window; a rattle of tin pans; a discharge of one barrel of my pistol; screams of agony; a heavy fall; and one out of a half-dozen cats, which escaped through a broken pane of glass, fell upon the floor.

Then my wife above-stairs began to scream murder, putting her head out of the window, the better to let the neighbors hear her, and Miss Floy, who had remained at the head of the stairs with the lamp in her hand, as soon as the pistol was fired, hastened frightened away, letting the door, which had a spring-lock, only to be opened from the hall, close upon me, leaving me in darkness and surrounded by I did n't know how many wild and dying cats. From the violent way in which that feline monster travelled around the kitchen, I thought there must be at least three or four of them, and I expected every moment that one of them would attack my unprotected legs. Once, when he got into the flour-barrel, I thought I had him, and immediately fired my pistol into it; but the only result was a scattering of flour all over me, and a seeming multiplication of the number of cats. That old Tom appeared to be alive in nine places at one moment. Spirits could n't be more active; the servants' cups and saucers rolled off of the dresser; the handle of the coffee-mill whirled round; the tea-kettle fell from the range; the dripping-pan was tossed over the iron pot, which struck against the saucepan, and which in turn fell with a crash upon a lot of empty bottles. At last the stove-pipe gave way, under an impetuous charge, and, taking a flying leap over my shoulders, grimalkin lodged on the top step of the stairway, next to the door. Here was a dilemma. I knew the cat must be an exceedingly vicious one, for all the cats in our neighborhood are, and, under his present state of excitement, he would be likely to attack any one who might open the door above him or attempt to drive him away from below. I was much afraid that my wife or Miss Floy, one of whom would of course, I thought, come down to see what was detaining me, would open the door and admit the cat to the upper part of the house, and in passing he would undoubtedly attack whoever was standing there.

The outcry my wife made from the upper window had, I discovered, borne fruit, and I could hear, through the broken window, the voice of my savage literary friend, who, at the front of the house, was parleying with the inmates to get in. But they, thinking that he was one of the burglars, refused to let him in, and resolutely shut and barred the window. I tried to make him hear me; but, what with being at the rear of the house, and the noise the night breeze made as it rustled through the waving corn at the side of the house, my voice failed to reach his ears. I would have gotten out of the window, but it was screwed down; and, though cats could go through the broken pane, it would have been impossible for me to have passed after them. I did n't like to attack the cat crouched, ready for a spring, on the stairway, and I was afraid to fire at it again lest I might shoot some one through the door. I wondered, too, why neither my wife nor Miss Floy had come to my assistance, and only learned, after I succeeded in getting out of my cell, that both, after the appearance of the supposed outside burglar, had ingloriously fainted.

At last a happy idea struck me. I would fire another barrel of my pistol out of the window, and that would attract my savage literary friend to my side of the house. I no sooner thought of this than I acted upon it — bang went my pistol. Scarcely had the report subsided, when bang went a pistol outside, and, to my astonishment and fear, I heard the ball strike the wall close beside me.

"What the deuce do you mean by that?" I cried.

"Surrender, surrender, you bloody villain you, or I'll put another ball right through your heart!" was all the consolation I got from my savage literary friend outside. "I've got you fairly covered, you rascal, and you can't hit me, for I'm behind the big tree; but I'll send you to the other world directly if you don't throw your pistol right out of the window into the yard."

As I knew my friend was a determined chap, and cared no more for killing a fellow-creature — he'd been off to the wars with the old Sixty-ninth Regiment — than I would for killing a cat, I thought it, under the circumstances, wise to surrender. So, without another word, I threw the pistol through the window, and, as it happened to be cocked, which I had forgotten, it exploded with a report that not only astonished but alarmed me.

"Oh! you villain you!" exclaimed my savage literary friend, "but you came near killing me that time. It's only the tree saved me from being a dead man. But I'll fix you out now."

"For Heaven's sake, Jack!" I exclaimed, "don't fire again, and I'll surrender body and soul."

"What, what!" he exclaimed; "is that you, Barry? I thought it was some infernal burglar. What are you about down there? Why don't you go up-stairs?"

"For the very good reason," I answered, "that I cannot. The door is fastened, and I can't get it open. Come into the house and let me out."

"They won't let me in," he replied.

"They!" I exclaimed. "Who do you mean by 'they?' Surely there are n't any burglars in the house, after all, are there?"

"I don't know," he replied; "but your wife and Miss Floy refused to let me in. They took me, I believe, for a burglar. They were making a terrible outcry at one time, but they 've been remarkably quiet for the last five minutes. I'll try the front of the house again, and see what can be done."

Fortunately my wife had recovered her consciousness, and, when my friend called her by name, recognized his voice, and after a little explanation, came down-stairs and let him in. He immediately came to the kitchen-door to open it for me, and though the unfortunate cat was far gone toward that bourne where no caterwauls are heard, he yet retained sufficient life to utter a protest against my friend's stepping upon him, in the shape of several sharp claws inserted into his right leg.

The exclamation my friend made was not of a most Christian character, and I truly believe that, for a moment, he thought the burglars had really got him; but when he saw me, all covered with flour, — my face, hair, and dressing gown thick with it, — he forgot his pain, and laughed heartily at my appearance.

But all 's well that ends well, and though some of us were materially frightened by the events of the night, yet, after we had assembled together in the library, and had related our several experiences, and a bottle of California hock had been opened, and each had drank my friend's toast of "The Lord love ye," we once more retired, thankful that nothing really evil had happened to any one of us, to our peaceful rest, where we passed the remainder of the night undisturbed by burglars or the fear of them.

CHAPTER IX.

An Artists' Convention at Woodbine Cottage. — Salt Codfish. — A Miracle desired. — The Stark Blood. — Hampers. — Scarcity of Bedrooms. — The Remedy. — A Calumny; how I refuted it. — Mint-Juleps; where they were invented; a good Time to drink them. — Who my Friends were.

SEVERAL of my artist friends have been visiting Woodbine Cottage. They came out in a body one Saturday afternoon, and brought their rations with them. As they proposed to stay until the following Monday morning, they were wise in so doing; for, though Mrs. Gray had provided munificently for the family proper, yet she had not laid in a sufficient store of the good things of this life to have satisfied, in a hospitable manner, the additional appetites which gathered around our mahogany. Even before Mrs. B. G. knew that they were going to remain with us all night, she was in a state of the greatest excitement in regard to getting them a dinner.

"One cannot expect," she very justly remarked, "that ten hungry men — and I never knew any one to come from town who was not as hungry as a bear when he got here — will be satisfied with the simple salt codfish and potatoes which you, adhering to the fashion of your Nantucket ancestors, will persist in having for your Saturday's dinner. How often have I told you that Friday was fish-day, and not Saturday?"

"Why," I exclaimed, interrupting her, "I should say it would average about fifty-two times a year since our marriage, and that would make it" ——

"Never mind, Mr. Gray," she continued, "about figuring that up now. Pray talk sensibly for a moment."

"Certainly, my dear," I replied; "but what do you wish me to say?"

"I don't wish you to say anything, but I want you to do something. Show me how I can, with that one small codfish, provide your friends with a dinner."

"Let me think a moment," I said. After a pause, during which I gazed steadily into my wife's face, the expression on which was of the most hopeless character, I added: "If a miracle, my dear, could be wrought, similar to that which occurred early in the Christian era, when a multitude was fed with several small fishes, to say nothing of a few loaves of bread, we might hope to satisfy our visitors; but as we cannot expect an intervention of that kind in our favor, why, I think the best plan will be to tell our friends" ——

"*Your* friends, not mine, Mr. Gray," interrupted my wife; "if they were mine, they would have more consideration for me, and not have come here so unexpectedly."

"I think the best plan will be," I repeated, not heeding my wife's remark, "for me to tell them that we have been to dinner ever so long ago, and that, if they 're hungry, they had better go to the hotel and order dinner there."

"Never! Mr. Gray," my wife exclaimed, energetically, "as long as there is a chicken in the coop, a potato, an ear of corn, and a tomato growing in the garden, would I do so disgraceful a thing. I 'd get dinner for them if there were fifty instead of ten, and I knew I should die in doing it."

The old Stark blood, which, fortunately, was not spilled at the battle of Bennington, was stirred in her veins, and she appeared equal to the emergency.

Just at that moment, when I began to fear that my favorite cocks and hens might suffer decapitation, an express-wagon drove up to the door, and several hampers were lifted out of it and brought into the house. Their contents were speedily produced, and my wife had the agreeable satisfaction of knowing that, even if my friends should remain with us a week, the provisions would hold out until the end.

Although the question as to how my friends were to be fed was thus happily set at rest, it still remained a source of anxiety with me as to how they were to be disposed of when night came. I had, in reality, but one spare bedroom, and that was already occupied by my literary young lady. It would not be exactly the thing, I reasoned, to ask her to remove herself, with her extra hoops, frilled skirts, gaiter boots, and other interesting paraphernalia of a young woman's wardrobe, — which, in passing her room when the door was open, I had noticed displayed alluringly, but, I must confess, negligently, on the chairs and floor of the apartment, — to the nursery, that thereby a couple of artists might the better be accommodated. And even if she should, it would only put two of my friends to bed, and then, "What would become of the others?" would still remain an unanswered question. To be sure, the sofa in the library would hold one more, and the extension-table in the dining-room might be drawn out to its fullest length, fourteen feet, and on it four more, if they would be careful in turning over, might manage to get a wink of sleep. Thus seven would be disposed of, and chairs and the floor would have to be the couches of the remainder. I arranged this thus in my mind, but it was far from being satisfactory; and when, therefore, my savage literary friend offered to take five of them off my hands, I was extremely thankful, and was encouraged to tell Mrs. Gray that my friends were going to stay with us till Monday.

To my surprise, Mrs. G. said she was glad of it, for she knew the greater part of the provisions they had brought with them would spoil, if they did n't remain to eat it.

When I asked her where she intended to have them sleep, she said she had no intentions about it, but that they might sleep where they liked. There was room enough on the floor of the dining-room for twenty men; and she rather thought, judging from the number of demijohns and bottles they had brought with them, that the larger part of them would probably find the floor more convenient than any bed would be.

This was a calumny on the part of my wife which I refuted with much feeling; and, as she acknowledged to me afterward that she was in error, I have refrained from letting my friends know of this expression. The fact is that, though my artist friends, with few exceptions, can enjoy a social glass, not one of them ever allows himself to pass the bounds which prudence and good sense dictate as proper. The result is a general feeling of conviviality, an agreeable commingling of hearts, and an approach to a millennium state of happiness.

The first words which my life-long friend G. uttered on entering my humble domains, and which did honor alike to his nice sense of smell and his fine appreciation of the herbs of the earth, were, "I smell mint." The truth is that, if one herb grows better than another in my garden, it is mint; and, when I saw this imposing procession of artists marching two by two toward my house, I immediately plucked a handful of mint, which I bruised against the gate-posts which command the entrance to my possessions.

"For," I said to myself, "I will welcome them with sweet savors, and make their tarrying with me one of pleasantness and peace."

I defy any man, I don't care who he be, who grows mint in his grounds, to resist, in a summer's day, the delights of a mint-julep. It is the only drink which might have been made in Eden. There, in that pleasant garden where our first parents spent the only innocent portion of their lives, methinks the mint must have been a familiar plant. I can imagine how Adam and Eve, walking in blissful innocence across the dewy fields in the early morning, conversing of love, were arrested in their way by the delightful perfume which was exhaled by the humble plant upon which their virgin footsteps trod. Adam doubtless paused to pluck a few of the leaves, and, after regaling himself with their savor, passed them to Eve. She, woman-like, upon their return at evening to their home in that lovely bower which Milton so charmingly describes, probably sought to make "tea" of them. This was, however, to all intents and purposes, a failure. But Adam, who knew one or two more things than Eve, doubtless kept turning the matter over in his mind, while chewing the mint leaves in his mouth, and finally, perhaps on the very day he discovered the milk in the cocoa-nut, and which, on exposure to the sun, was fermented into a sort of wine, found that, by steeping the sprigs of the former in the juice of the latter, a new and first-class drink was thereby concocted, — a draught which was, as he doubtless remarked to Mrs. Adam, "a jewel to the lip." This phrase, in course of time, passing through the tongues of much posterity, was curtailed of its fair proportions, and became at last, in our day, a "julep."

Many worse things than juleps have come down to us from Adam, — sin and sorrow, and a whole Pandora's box of suffering.

When, therefore, G., the friend of my boyhood, said he smelt mint, and the grave, bald, and long-bearded W. reiterated his words, I did not wait for any one else to speak, and, by the time that the last of the procession had entered the gateway, a dozen goblets gleaming with ice, golden with whiskey, softened with sugar, and fragrant with mint, were awaiting them in the library.

It is a hot and dusty ride from the city to Woodbine Cottage, and, in travelling it, one is apt to get very thirsty; but a mint julep, if it be long enough, effectually cools the heated blood and moistens the dusty throat.

In addition to the two friends already mentioned, — the

first of whom is distinguished, in the world of art, for his golden sunsets and silvery coast-scenes, and the latter, by his mountain twilights and old-fashioned interiors, — I had the pleasure of welcoming him whose pictures of California scenery have the breadth and the grandeur of the mountains and the valleys they depict. There, too, was one who delights to represent upon his canvas those late autumns, when the naked limbs of trees stand out against the cold, gray sky, and the dry, brown leaves rustle under foot. And he was there who painted, with poetic feeling, a "Christmas Eve," wherein a troop of fairy spirits is ringing a merry peal on the brazen bell high up in the moonlighted belfry of an old stone church, on a cold, clear midnight. And the sculptor who brings out of the marble forms of beauty; and one who portrays your living self upon the canvas; and another who, in the guise of animals, shows up humanity and its foibles; and still another whose *genre* pictures of childhood and home-life are of the tenderest character; and, lastly, he who loves to represent the snow-clad mountains of Switzerland and our own northern land, were, by ties of friendship, brought together to Woodbine Cottage.

It would make too long a story were I to tell here how merrily the hours, while they were with me, went by. The songs that were sung, the tales that were told, and the puns that were perpetrated may never be recorded; but the delight of that time will ever remain fresh and green in my memory.

CHAPTER X.

"The Flag of Freedom." — Up a Tree. — An Echo. — An Artistic Event. J. B. Warwick, Esq. — The Great and Good. — A Corner-lot, and other Lots. — *Per Centum.* — A First-class Arrival. — My Artist Friends. — Twelve Hampers. — Three Dollars per Annum. — The Banquet. — Artist Appetites. — Usual Diet. — My Savage Literary Friend's Song. — The Genial Host. — "Let us love one another." — *Finale.*

IT had not been my intention to have written anything further than was set forth in the preceding sketch concerning the visit of my artist friends to Woodbine Cottage. But as the editor of the village newspaper, "The Flag of Freedom," has taken the liberty of chronicling in its veracious columns an account of the proceedings, I am induced, knowing that the circulation of the "Flag" is quite limited, and that comparatively few persons would be likely to see it, to transfer it to the pages of this volume. How the editor of the "Flag" became possessed of the information necessary to enable him to write the detailed report of the visit of my friends — especially the account of the dinner, at which he was not present — was a mystery to me, until I ascertained that his chief reporter, with a zeal which was more creditable to his enterprise as a journalist than to his self-respect as a man, occupied, during the progress of the feast, an uncomfortable position on a limb of an apple-tree in the orchard adjoining my garden, which not only commanded an uninterrupted view through the open window of my dining-room, but was within easy hearing-distance of the conversation which took place at the table. This circumstance will also account for certain mysterious sounds which, during the progress of the dinner, reached our ears, and which we ascribed to an echo. Many times during the evening, when a good story had been told, and after the appreciative laughter had run round the table, a subdued chuckle would be heard, which seemed so like a miniature edition of the Swiss mountain-artist's laugh, that we one and all decided it to be the echo of his cachinnation. I am now satisfied that it proceeded from the "Flag's" reportorial representative, who doubless enjoyed to a certain extent the festivities of the evening. However, it seems to me that our reporter could have found only about as much satisfaction in the entertainment as Shacabac did in the first part of the feast of the Barmacide, or as Sancho Panza did when the untasted dishes were placed before him.

The following is the account of the proceedings taken

FROM "THE FLAG OF FREEDOM."

AN ARTISTIC EVENT.

"Several times, within the memory of the oldest inhabitant, has our village been the sojourning place of distinguished people. The primeval occasion, according to J. B. Warwick, Esq., on which a first-class notable stopped for a night's rest in our delectable hamlet, was when the great and good George Washington, who enjoyed the *soubriquet* of 'The Father of his Country,' put up, shortly after the battle of White Plains, at the old Powell homestead, situated on the other side of the railroad track, and nearly opposite the corner-lot belonging to J. B. Warwick, Esq., which corner-lot, together with other lands owned by the same proprietor, and contiguous thereto, is, we understand from a perfectly reliable source, for sale. Any one desirous of purchasing a lot in this eligible locality, will do well to communicate with us on the subject. The little percentage which will go into our *porte-monnaie*, provided we dispose of one or more of these lots, although a small matter, will yet enable us to add materially to our stock of cigars and whiskey.

"This stoppage of 'the great and good,' as we said above, was the first event of the kind which occurred in the history of our village. Since then many notables have come and gone; but we cannot stay to enumerate all of the celebrated personages who have favored us in this respect. We have sometimes thought that many of the persons whose names are inscribed upon the roll of fame, owed to some extent their renown to the fact that they visited our village.

"In our present article, it is with pleasure that we record the visit to Woodbine Cottage of a half-score of the distinguished artists whose pictures at the National Academy of Design gave a weight and character to it which it would not otherwise have possessed. They came in a body, on the four o'clock train, last Saturday afternoon. It is to be regretted that the president of the village, and all others in authority, were not informed of the intended visit, else they would doubtless have been received in a manner befitting their distinguished character, and Luffy might have had at his hotel several bowls of punch prepared for the occasion. As it was, they got off of the cars in the most unpretentious manner, and immediately moved in two columns to Woodbine Cottage.

"The genial occupants of the cottage were as much taken by surprise as were the village authorities. They had received no warning of the intended honor, and were therefore unprepared to entertain them. The artists themselves, however, with a premonition and generosity which did honor alike to their heads and hearts, had provided for this emergency in a most munificent manner. Twelve hampers, containing edibles and drinkables of many kinds, we had the pleasure of observing on Whitny's express-wagon passing our office.

"If one of those hampers — we do not greatly care which, but would have preferred the one containing the 'Golden Wedding' champagne, the meat-pie, the cold duck and olives, and the peaches, pears, and melons — had been left at our residence just around the corner, it would have been a most satisfactory and agreeable circumstance to us, and we would have placed with much pleasure upon our newspaper subscription-book, as dead-heads, the names of all the artists so donating, who would thereby have received 'The Flag of Freedom' for one year. As they, however, omitted to perform this courteous act, we can only say that we would be happy to furnish them with the 'Flag' at the lowest subscription price, viz., three dollars per annum, — a deduction of fifty cents from the regular price, but which we invariably make to clergymen, artists, and literary men.

"The banquet to which these estimable and talented men sat down at Woodbine Cottage, on Saturday evening, was of the most gorgeous and tempting character. An immense game-pie, composed of ducks, woodcocks, quails, and grouse, ornamented the centre of the table. A jugged hare stood at one end, and a boned turkey at the other; while a boiled ham, a round of beef, broiled spring chickens, ducks stuffed with olives, boned sardines, and other appetizing relishes, were scattered at convenient distances. It was not our good fortune to be present at this festival; but when, from the elevated position we occupied, we heard the popping of champagne corks, and the various toasts and speeches uttered and responded to, and saw the good things of the feast disappear before the appetites of the artists, 'as leaves before a wild hurricane fly,' our mouth watered and our stomach craved that which it was not our privilege to enjoy.

"Until we saw those talented and estimable gentlemen dispose of what was before them, we had been possessed of the belief that they lived upon less sublunary fare than we every-day folks; sunrises and sunsets, moonlight and starlight, flowers and sea-foam, were a few of the dishes which we had heretofore given them credit for employing in their regular diet; but, after witnessing their capabilities with the knife and fork at Woodbine Cottage, we feel compelled to state that, as far as eating and drinking go, they will compare favorably with the performance, in that line, of the hungriest men we ever met.

"We cannot close our account of this interesting festival without referring to the happy manner in which Mr. G.'s savage literary friend sung a patriotic song of his own composing, which brought down the house, metaphorically speaking, and created a deep and abiding sensation in the breasts of the assembled guests. One of the artists, too, performed an Indian war-dance, which he learned during a short residence among a warlike tribe in the Rocky Mountains. The whoop which he gave semi-occasionally during its performance, and in which he was joined by the company, was of the most startling character. He also kindly offered to scalp any one who desired to have this little act performed. The bald-headed gentleman of foreign birth was the only one of the party who had the courage to offer to submit to the operation; but the Rocky Mountain man said it could n't be done on him, and begged some of the others to come forward. They all declined, however, but said that if they only wore wigs they would be happy to accommodate him.

"We must not neglect to speak of the genial and *sans-souci* manner in which Mr. Gray presided at the head of the table, — a manner which, in our humble opinion, could only be equalled by that in which the presidents of the 'St. Nicholas' and the 'Friendly Sons' societies may be presumed to preside on the occasion of their annual dinners. His parting toast of 'Let us love one another,' was given with a gusto and cheeriness which entitled the giver to be credited with desiring, with his whole heart, the entire fulfilment of the wish.

"We shall endeavor to give, in a future number of our widely-circulated weekly, a further account of the proceedings of the 'Artist Club' — for such we presume it is — while the members remained at Woodbine Cottage."

Thus ends the account of the dinner, as reported in "The Flag of Freedom."

CHAPTER XI.

My Melon-bed. — Temptation. — Outside the Palings. — Caught in the Act. — "Hi! hi!" — My Generosity. — Footprints. — Stolen Fruit. — "Black Matan." — Old Pokey. — Trouser Legs. — Gumbo. — A Dreadful Miss. — Providence. — "Kind Sir," she said. — Funerals. — Amen. An Ugly Dog. — Old Mother Hubbard. — Little Boys' Legs. — Horrible. A Dog-Fight. — Jack *vs.* Gumbo.

I HAVE been much "exercised" lately, in regard to securing my crop of melons. My cantaloupes do not appear to be equal to the temptation which, doubtless, assails them, for that they can elope nearly every night witnesseth; while my nutmegs disappear faster than ever their wooden namesakes of Connecticut did from a pedler's wagon; and my watermelons literally water the ground with their sweet juices, for many yards, in the direction of the village. I took a great deal of pains with my melon-bed, working early and late — that is, late in the morning and early in the evening for a brief period every day — in my shirt-sleeves, taking the starch out of many collars, and destroying the polish on my boots. I had to put the melon-seeds down several times, too, before they would come up. The first time they were planted too deep, — twelve inches is, I understand, rather deep for these seeds, — and, the next time, in such shallow ground that the motherly hens, in searching for early worms, came across the seeds in their scratching explorations around the garden, and unceremoniously put them into their own and their chicks' crops. Then, when the vines did appear, a lot of miserable little, brown-paper colored bugs walked into the garden and incontinently devoured them, root and branch. Owing to these drawbacks, it was comparatively late in the season before my melons began to come forward; but, after they once got started, they grew famously, and were the talk of the entire neighborhood. I am inclined to think that the reputation they acquired was not good for them, and proved their ruin. The glory of those melons, my wife told me, was being too widely noised about the village for their safety, and I now see the truth of her remark.

"Because you have a good thing in the melon line," said the far-sighted woman, "it is not necessary, as you are no gardener seeking employment, for you to bruit it abroad, thus placing temptation before, and offering a premium, as it were, for stealing, to little ragged boys, who would otherwise have gone through the summer living innocent lives. Mark my words, Mr. Gray; for just as certain as I stand here" — she was examining with me, at the time, the growing melons — "you will know little about the taste of these melons." As long, however, as the melons remained severely green, I gave little heed to her words; but when, as the fruit began to ripen, and I saw little ragged boys stop at the garden palings, and, looking through them, turn slowly away, whispering to each other, I asked myself if, after all, my wife might not be correct in her predictions. I felt certain of it when, one day, I saw a lad thrust a long pole, to which a fork was attached, through the palings, and stab one of my largest watermelons.

When I, cautiously approaching from the rear that misguided boy, gently seized him, asking him politely what he was doing, he, although somewhat surprised by my arrival, nevertheless replied that he was n't doing nothing. Speaking grammatically, under the rule that two negatives destroy one another, the boy told the truth; but he had no intention of so doing, and therefore I gave him no credit for not telling a falsehood. But when the lad added, with a grin that stretched his mouth from ear to ear, that he 'd heard tell of my melons, and kinder guessed he 'd like to try one, I could not resist telling him to take the melon he had seized and be off with himself before I changed my mind and set the dog on him. The celerity with which he gathered up that melon, and, with a victorious shout of "hi! hi!!" made off down the road, near the corner of which, lying in wait for him, lurked several of his companions, was a sight to be enjoyed by any one who did not own, as I do, a melon patch.

Whether my generosity was appreciated by those little rascals, and they felt that my kindness should be treated with due consideration, I cannot tell; but, at all events, several days elapsed without my discovering any little boys looking over my garden palings. Small lads, however, cannot be forever resisting temptation, and, therefore, I was not surprised one morning, when I went into the garden to take my before-breakfast walk, to see the impressions of small feet on the soft mould of the melon-bed, and to find that several of the finest ones had disappeared.

Melons, under most circumstances, when fully ripe, are agreeable eating; and, as stolen fruit is said to be the sweetest, I have little doubt that my melons tasted uncommonly well, that moonlight night, to the villains who surreptitiously helped themselves to them. Still I have bought a dog to assist me in keeping possession of my melons; for, although I have no objection to little boys eating melons at night, I have myself a predilection for them at breakfast and after dinner.

The dog I have purchased has a fine reputation for catching fruit-stealers. Indeed, the old lady of whom I bought him — the same, in fact, whose acquaintance I made in the cars, and to whose curiosity I was indebted for the loss of my black-and-tan hen — gave me to understand that, from early puppyhood, his chief diet had been the legs of little boys. The number of trousers he had torn in getting at those legs, she said, had kept the principal tailor of her village in business all the year round, and she verily believed he would have starved to death many a time if it had n't been for that dog.

"What he will do, kind sir, when he learns," she said, "that I 've sold my 'black matan' out and out, I don't know; but I should n't wonder a bit if he 'd move right off to your village."

"Oh, that would n't answer at all," I said; "we 've a good tailor there already, and I should prefer to throw what business I could, through the dog, into his hands, than to have a perfect stranger reap the benefit of it, and I shall recommend all the little boys, whose trousers' legs the dog tears, to go to Cronin for repairs, in preference to any new man."

"Perhaps you are right," the old lady replied; "but you must n't forget that our tailor and my dog have worked together a good many years, and naturally may be presumed to be attached to each other, — especially when you take into consideration the fact that, in the winter season, when little boys' legs are not quite so available as they are in summer time, old Mr. Pokey always keeps a lot of bones on a plate ready against my 'black matan' coming along past his house."

"Certainly," I replied, "and I 've no doubt but that our Mr. Cronin will do the same. But, allow me to ask, by what name did you call the dog just now?"

"Oh!" she answered, "the dog's name is Gumbo; but I generally speak of him as my black matan."

"Black what?" I asked.

"Why, black matan," she replied, — "same as you called your hen, you know, — on account of his color."

"Ah, yes, I see now," I responded; "but, really, I don't think he belongs to that breed of dogs. It strikes me that he is a mongrel, and might, with truthfulness, be termed a 'yaller cur.'"

The old lady deprecated any such appellation, and half refused to sell him to me unless I would let him remain a "black matan." When at last, however, I had paid the money for him, and was going away, she was more than ever inclined to break the bargain; for, as she very justly remarked, "the poor boys will miss him dreadfully, and I 'm much afraid that Mr. Pokey will never forgive me for selling him. But Providence, kind sir," she continued, after a pause, during which she wiped her eyes with the corner of her black bombazine apron, which must have been pretty rough on her eyelids, "does not always permit us to have our own ways in this wicked world; but sometimes, I must confess, controls our actions in a most incomprehensible manner. I don't think, kind sir, that I ever should have married, but for an overruling Providence, my poor husband, — now dead these twenty-five years come the sixth of October next, — and it was a very rainy day when he died, and gloomy enough; but fortunately we had a fine day for the funeral, and, though cold, it was clear, and there were a great many persons present. Did you ever have a funeral, kind sir?" she asked.

I said I never had, and I hoped it would be many years before that sad event, so far as I was personally concerned, took place.

"I mean, kind sir," she said, "a funeral in your own family. Of course, I know that you have not been funeraled yet."

I assured the old lady that Providence had dealt very tenderly with me and mine, and that the heavy folds of the pall had never swayed in sunlight or starlight within my dwelling, and I trusted that it would be a long time before such sorrow were mine.

Thereupon the old lady said, very pathetically, "Amen;" and then I bade her farewell, and went home.

"What, in the world of wonder, Mr. Gray," asked my wife, as I entered the house, have you brought home such a looking dog as that for? Why, it is uglier than your savage literary friend's."

"Well, my dear, what if it be?" I replied. "The dog is a good dog for the purpose I desire, and I don't think you ought to object to him because he is n't quite an Apollo in appearance. He knows a trick or two, and can balance himself on his tail in a surprising manner, and stand on his head with his tail in the air equal to the famous dog which old Mother Hubbard possessed. Besides, he 's great on rats, and cats, and little boys' legs."

"Great on little boys' legs!" exclaimed my wife, in astonishment, putting up both hands; "why, what do you mean?"

"Mean!" I replied; "why, that I don't mean to lose any more melons. Do you think that I intend to be robbed of my melons without getting something back in return?"

"And what do you expect to get back?" she asked.

"Oh, pieces of trousers," I answered, "and, perhaps, pieces of legs."

"Horrible!" she cried; "how can you speak so cruelly?"

"Cruelly, is it?" I asked; "wait a moment. There, do you see that little rascal yonder?" pointing through the open window to a crouching figure that was creeping, in the twilight, along a line of currant-bushes, leading to the melon-bed; "look, now, Gumbo! legs!"

The dog went through the open window like a shot, and the next moment there was a terrific fight going on between my savage literary friend's dog Jack, which I had mistaken for a robber of melons, sneaking along toward them, and my own Gumbo. Before those dogs could be separated they had smashed all the glasses in one of my forcing-beds, knocked down the frames upholding my tomatoes, destroyed my wife's choicest carnations and dahlias, and caused me to break the handles of two hoes and a pitchfork. The conflict lasted fully twenty minutes, and the injuries which both dogs suffered can never be repaired. Jack had his tail bitten off quite short, and the ears of Gumbo were chewed into ribbons. If dogs could use crutches, these two belligerents would each be halting around upon two pairs apiece; but, as it is, they are compelled to lie quietly curled up in separate corners in the barn, eying each other vindictively, until their many wounds are healed.

In the mean while the naughty boys of the village run rampant, at night, through the melon-beds of my friend and myself, and, in the daytime, fearfully excite the two dogs by throwing stones at the hospital wherein they are confined.

CHAPTER XII.

Goat *vs.* Cow Milk. — My Old Lady. — How to secure a Goat. — Mr. Pokey again. — Gumbo. — Buts. — Going a-Goating. — Taking possession of the Goat. — The Start Homeward. — Down in the Dust. — A Round Turn.—A Turnip-field. — Here and There. — A Happy Thought. Not Quick enough. — Losses. — A Rope. — Caught. — Home at last.

I HAVE bought a goat. Next to owning a cow, a goat, especially if there be a youthful scion of your house who delights in fresh milk, is a desirable investment. Cows, beside being much more expensive, require greater care, and are more troublesome to keep than goats. Goat's milk, too, is richer and more nourishing than that of cows. At least the old lady — the same one of whom I procured the "black matan" dog — so assured me when she sold me the goat which now eats off my turnip-tops. She further said that I would not require a barn in which to keep it, as I would if I were to get a cow.

"All you need do, kind sir," she said, "will be to put a box in one corner of your garden, and throw a little hay into it, and then you have your goatery ready for its occupant. And as for feed, why, a smart goat will feed itself, and this goat is one of that kind. Where she can't find grazing there ain't none, kind sir, worth speaking of."

Even during the short time I have owned that goat I have discovered that she can more than feed herself. Such slight guardians to cabbage and carrot fields as fences and stone walls, offer no impediment to the entrance of my goat. Simply tying two of her legs together is of little use in preventing her from making any field, to which she may take a fancy, her foraging-ground.

The only way to prevent her from poaching on my neighbors is by tying all four of her legs together, and then tethering her to a stake driven into the ground. Even then, unless the knots are securely tied, she will slip the rope, and make off for the nearest garden fence. On these occasions I find that the dog Gumbo, who has nearly recovered from his wounds, is of great assistance in bringing back the runaway; indeed, the old lady, when she sold me the goat, more than hinted that she was obliged to part with her for the reason that she no longer had the "black matan" to keep watch over her.

I may as well here record the fact that, when the tailor, old Mr. Pokey, — who mainly depended upon Gumbo's efforts in the trouser-tearing line for, so to speak, his bread and butter, — learned that he had been sold and emigrated from the village, he gnashed his teeth fearfully, and, sharpening his longest shears, vowed terrible vengeance against the old lady for parting with him. He so frightened her that she drove over to see me one day, and tried to buy him back; but when she saw the frightful condition in which he was, arising from his fight with Jack, she declined to risk the purchase, and left him to die, as she said, on my hands. It has since come to my ears that old Pokey failed in business the week afterwards. During this interview with my old lady I discovered the old lady had a goat for sale, and, on my making an offer for it, which was promptly accepted, I became the owner.

Now it is one thing, as I found, to buy a goat, and quite another to get it home. When, therefore, one breezy afternoon I said to Mrs. Gray that I thought it would be a good plan for me to take our eldest boy and walk over to the Corners for the goat I bought, and drive her home, she replied that she thought it would be, and added, moreover, in a slightly sarcastic tone, "that she hoped I'd have a nice time of it, but" —

"But me no buts, my dear," I interrupted; "we will leave that," I said, laughingly, "to the goat."

"We will leave it to the goat," she answered, "as you will probably find."

I paid no attention, however, to her remarks, and, calling my little boy to accompany me, walked off toward the Corners. It is only about three miles distant, and the road is a pleasant one, winding for the greater part of the way through woods of hickory, chestnut, and butternuts. At times the path leads along the banks of the river Bronx, and the rippling of the water over its rocky bed falls in pleasing murmurs upon the ear. "Autumn," I said to myself, as I walked along, "is the best season of the year to dwell in the country, for then it is in its glory. The air is pure and invigorating, and the temperature cool and delightful. Nature allures her lovers to follow winding streams, to clamber rocky mountains, to wander through shadowy forests, where the leaves strew the ground and rustle beneath their steps, and from her outspreading arms drops down upon them the harvests of the year. Already the harvest is being gathered. The reapers are busy in the fields. I hear the whetting of the scythes and the creaking of the loaded wains as they bear the golden sheaves to the granaries. The apples — red, russet, and yellow — are ripening in the orchards. The corn is turning into gold, and the pumpkins, seen through the green stalks of the maize, which still wave triumphantly through many fields, lie basking in the sunshine. The grapes are growing purple on their vines, and all the products of the earth, having produced each after its kind, are waiting to be garnered. At this season it is a luxury to be out-of-doors; and whether it be early in the morning while the dew still jewels the grass, at noontide when the sun shines warmly, or at twilight when the stars begin to glimmer, the open fields, the mazy orchards, and the silent woods possess charms for the thoughtful and observant mind. Nature is wonderfully suggestive at this season, and many are the lessons she teaches to humanity." I must have spoken a part of this aloud, for my little boy asked, "Where are the apples and the grapes?" He did not see them. However, he took much pleasure in picking up the early fallen nuts scattered under the trees, and in gathering bunches of autumnal flowers which bordered the roadside. When we reached the old lady's, he exchanged these yellow, purple, and scarlet flowers for a huge slice of pound-cake and a glass of new milk. After fortifying myself with something more substantial, I prepared to return home. The goat, which is a large white one, with curving horns and a brisk little bit of a tail, was brought out, and a rope about six feet long being tied to her horns, I, taking the other end of it, set off for Woodbine Cottage. The old lady cast an old shoe after us for good luck; but, as it struck the goat, it was the cause of frightening her, and made her start on a run. As this action was totally unexpected to me, the rope was drawn out of my hands, and to regain it required unusual activity on my part, and a nice little race ensued, which attracted the attention of the lookers-on, and resulted, after a five minutes' run, in victory to my side. The goat, on finding herself hauled up, with an alacrity which was surprising, turned and made a rush at me, butting me with her head and taking me off my feet in a twinkling, and going herself over my prostrate body in a way which spoke well for her agility. Before the rope tightened in my hands I was on my feet, and brought her up again with a round turn. This time, however, when the goat made a dash at me I was prepared, and by stepping quickly aside I let her go by without encountering any harm. This seemed somewhat to astonish her ladyship, and apparently had a good effect; for on the instant she became perfectly docile, and moved along for five minutes in a quiet and orderly manner.

While I was congratulating myself, however, upon her good behavior, and counting in my mind the number of quarts of milk our babe would have per day, the goat made a dash for a field of turnips we were passing, and with a sudden spring, which jerked the rope out of my hand, went over the fence like a flash.

I walked quietly to the fence and looked over it. The goat was standing a few feet distant, gently cropping the tender shoots of the turnips as if she enjoyed them. I remained for several minutes calmly watching her, and once in a while she would raise her head, shake it defiantly at me, whisk her stump of a tail derisively, and utter a little bleat, which seemed plainly to say, "Catch me if you can."

I seated my little boy on the top rail of the fence, and then got over into the field, and, as if I were myself seeking for tender turnip-tops, cautiously approached my lady, who would let me get within a few paces of her, when with a spring she would carry herself far out of my reach. This little manœuvre was performed several times, until I began to lose the small stock of patience of which I was possessed, and to ask myself how it was going to end. I tried to drive her into a corner of the fence, but she was too knowing for that, and on such occasions would make a long run, and only stand still when she reached the opposite side of the field.

At last a happy thought occurred to me. I pulled a turnip and held its white root temptingly before her. She looked at it a moment, sniffed at it, and began to curvet and prance upon her hind legs in a most graceful and pretty manner, and at the same time, too, approaching nearer and nearer, but never for a moment getting close enough for me to catch her. She evidently desired the turnip, but was rather suspicious of me. Finally, I decided to let my little boy try his powers of persuasion; and calling him to me, put a turnip into his hands and directed him to try to get the goat to take it, while I would seize upon the rope. The ruse would have been successful but for one circumstance, — I was not quite quick enough.

The moment the goat saw the little boy holding the turnip out to her, she rushed for it, knocked the lad down, seized it, and was off before I could grasp the rope which trailed behind her.

I have lost a good many things in this life by not being quick enough. I have lost sweethearts, money, the cars, the boats, and numerous dinners; but I don't remember that the losing of any one of them ever made me so angry as did the loss of that rope. I know there have been men who would gladly have missed a rope; but for these persons I never had any sympathy. Such men have an antipathy to rope-walks, and would go a mile out of their way rather than walk through one. They cannot hear, either, the word noose without experiencing a peculiar tickling about the throat. But, thank Heaven, I am no such individual. Therefore it was, when I picked up my little boy, who was more frightened than hurt, from the midst of the growing turnips, that I spoke of the goat to myself in no Christian terms, and promised her a good beating when I should get hold of the rope again.

One can't, though, if he applies himself diligently to securing it, be forever losing the end of a rope. Nor is man to be foiled by a goat. He must win in the long run; and though it was a long run in this instance, and wilted my collar, and will probably result in bringing something else besides chickens home to roost in the future, yet on the third trial with the tempting turnip, my little boy, protected by a breastwork of rail-fence from the goat's attack, and the latter being out-generalled and coaxed into a corner, I obtained possession of the coveted rope, and consequently of the vivacious goat.

To get that goat out of the turnip-field and into the road again, was the work of but a few minutes; and for the next mile she travelled along at something more than a two-forty gait. Perhaps the bunch of flexible branches — birch and elm — which I carried in one hand, and applied without remorse to her flank and rear, had something to do with the celerity of her movement.

At the end of that mile we had a little set-to. The goat put her forefeet firmly down in the green sod, and refused to advance another inch. Beating her did no good, but seemed rather to confirm her in a desire which she apparently had of staying where she was all night. Fortunately, though, my little boy, who had been left far in the rear by our swiftness of movement, came up, still bearing a coveted turnip in his hand, and with it managed to coax the goat into a forward movement. That movement never stopped until we reached Woodbine Cottage, and I had housed my goat in the goatery, which the old lady had suggested as an appropriate abiding-place.

What trouble that goat has given me since she came into my possession I have hinted at in the beginning of this sketch; but the half is not yet told. The babe, though, is flourishing like a green bay-tree under his new diet, and growing stout and hearty.

CHAPTER XIII.

A lost Goat. — Red Cabbages; their Cultivation. — A Challenge; its Acceptance. — Milking-time. — My savage Literary Friend. — A horrible Suggestion; its Non-fulfilment. — The Pound; its Uses; its neglected State. — In and Out. — Remorse. — Self-inflicted Punishment. — Two Days and a Night. — Plans for liberating the Goat. — A Fool's Proposition; its remarkable Success. — The Goat at Home again.

MY goat has been in the pound. It happened in this way: One night she got into my savage literary friend's plantation, and ate up all his red cabbages. If there were one thing more than another which my friend experienced satisfaction in seeing grow, it was his red cabbages. When he set out these plants, a couple of months ago, he expatiated at length to me on the superiority, over all others, of red cabbages for the purpose of pickling. During the dry weather he watered the plants morning and night. He poked a good deal about their roots, loosening the earth, and supplying them to a certain extent with guano. When they began to "head up" he was much delighted, and used to take his friends who called on him out into the garden to see them. I must say they grew famously, and promised to become the prize red cabbages of the county. It happened one day that he incautiously spoke to me before the goat — who was being milked at the time — of the wonderful progress those cabbages were making in their growth. I noticed that the goat pricked up her ears at the word red cabbage, as if she understood what was being said, and I observed to my friend he had better look out for his cabbage patch, as my goat would probably pay it a visit. He laughed derisively, and said that I gave too much credit to my goat for understanding; besides, his fences were goat-proof, and he defied any goat to scale them.

Thereupon the goat shook her horns defiantly, wagged her brief tail, and kicked over the milk-pail. This was at dewy eve; the next morning my friend's red cabbages were gone, and the footprints in the garden mould showed that my goat was the offender. There was much other food for my goat in that garden besides those cabbages: there were white cabbages, and corn, and beets, and carrots, and all the appetizing viands in which goats delight; but she had been challenged, as it were, to attack those cabbages, and she did it. A dozen heads of red cabbages seem to me more than a meal for one goat; but she was equal to the emergency, and, though the eating of them must have occupied her the whole night, she succeeded in stowing them all away before sunrise.

When milking-time came that morning, the goat was not to be found. Search was made for her throughout the length and breadth of the neighborhood, without success. My youngest began to experience the pangs of hunger, and cried aloud in the bitterness of his grief. But it was of no avail; the goat was not forthcoming, and the boy was in danger of starvation. Before this result, however, came to pass, it fortunately occurred to Mrs. G. that cow's milk could be given to him with a view of satisfying his desires until the goat came home. As he took kindly to it, I don't think he knew the difference.

Just after breakfast, my savage literary friend made his appearance, with a countenance expressive more of sorrow than of anger, and told us of the loss he had suffered. He would like, he said, if I had no objection, to take a view of that goat, and see how she looked. He did n't wish her any especial harm, but still it would be a satisfaction to him if those twelve red cabbages should disagree with her. He would like, too, to see how she managed to carry them about. When I told him that she could not be found, he seemed to be quite pleased, and chuckled with much satisfaction. He would not be surprised, he said, if she had burst herself. Such fatalities did sometimes happen, and he had read of an ox that was killed that way through getting into a clover-field.

This idea was so horrible that it quite shocked us, and the baby, as if he understood it, cried most lustily. Deeming that this might be the case, I went up to my friend's plantation to see if the remains of my goat could be found. On my way there I pictured to myself the fearful scene which would await my sight. I seemed to see a pair of horns lying loosely, with a wreath of red cabbage around them; the short and familiar tail, with more red cabbage about it; four little hoofs embalmed in more red cabbage; besides much hair, mixed with much red cabbage, scattered all about the grounds. But no such sight appalled me. I only saw the standing stalks of the cabbages, a few scattered leaves, and the marks of cloven feet in the earth. All that day and the following the search for the goat was prosecuted unavailingly, and it was not until nearly night of the second day that my eldest boy brought the news that our goat was in the pound.

The pound is essentially a village institution, and is to vagrant animals what the jail is to vagrant men. As I had endeavored, when I first came to Woodbine Cottage, to get a cow, which had greatly annoyed me, placed in the pound, without accomplishing it, and had learned, much to my disapprobation, that, although the village could boast of a pound, there yet was no pound-master, and consequently the pound was never used, I was on this occasion quite surprised, therefore, to learn that my goat was a prisoner. Nor was my surprise in any degree lessened when, on going to the pound, I discovered the secure character of the place. A high board-fence surrounded the enclosure, and an equally high gate, padlocked and nailed up, should, but did not, give entrance to it. It was evident to me that that gate had not been opened for years. The oldest inhabitant could scarcely recall the time, and the question as to how the goat got into the pound must ever remain unsolved. The probability is, however, that immediately after partaking of my friend's red cabbages, she was attacked with qualms of conscience; and, knowing that she deserved to be put into the pound for her wickedness, voluntarily went thither, and, scaling the fence, became a penitent and remorse-eaten goat. In the early dawn, with the morning-star only as a witness, must she have accomplished this feat, which, in the annals of the village, has never been rivalled.

For two days and a night that poor goat had patiently suffered, and, we trust, atoned for her naughtiness. Goat nature, no more than human nature, however, can reconcile itself to too prolonged a punishment, especially where it is self-inflicted; and when, therefore, the close of the second day drew nigh, and food within the enclosure grew scarce, it is no more than might have been expected that the goat should desire a change of scene. Although she was able to get in, it is very evident that she was not able to get out, or else she would have accomplished it. She could only call for assistance; and, as her bleat is a peculiar one, it was early recognized by a passer-by, who informed my little boy of the lost goat's whereabouts.

Quite a crowd was gathered about the pound when I arrived there, and the question as to how the goat got in had not only been duly discussed, but the next important question as to how she could be got out was under consideration. The key of the padlock was lost, and to open the gate was impossible. Through the various knot-holes and crevices in the fence the goat could be seen marching disconsolately around the pound, seeking vainly for a point of egress. She had worn a dusty little pathway for herself, close beside the fence, and, as she kept following it, would stop ever and anon, like the novelist's solitary horseman, to look about her.

Several methods were discussed for getting her out. One being to throw a rope over the fence, and allow her to twist her horns into it, and then she could be drawn out. Before any mode was decided upon, however, the fool of the village came along, and suggested the plan of knocking a board off of the fence, and thus letting the goat out. This was immediately adopted by the assemblage, and with such unanimity of procedure that no less than twenty boards were knocked off in a brief time, and an opening sufficiently large to have driven an elephant through was effected, though the goat, with that swiftness and strength which is inherent to her, made a rush when the first board flew, and knocking down and going over the luckless wight who had so kindly opened the way for her, made a straight line for Woodbine Cottage, which she reached in safety, much to the delight of the little ones assembled there to welcome her.

CHAPTER XIV.

Reminiscent. — "A Vanished Love." — Wedding-bells. — "To my Wife." Blackberrying. — An Explorer. — Mountain Streams and Rocky Pools. School-days.

IT is something — not much, perhaps, but still something — to sit alone for an hour or more in the early morning within the shade of an old apple-tree, such as grows in the orchard adjoining Woodbine Cottage, and hear the breeze murmuring through the leaves above your head, and watch the idle play of the shadows on the turf at your feet. A feeling of unutterable peace is engendered in your breast, and a dreamy indolence takes possession of your mind. You dream dreams and see visions. You recall the past with soft regret and look with hopeful eyes into the future. If you have passed the meridian of life, the past with its changes will be sufficient to occupy your thoughts without the necessity of seeking to peer into the future. Your dead and buried loves of long ago will, very properly, at such moments, ask for a place in your memory. You will be apt to recall the time when to some vanished Madge or Kate you made love on the mountain-tops, or at the sea-shore, or down in the valley, and wrote such verses as these: —

A VANISHED LOVE.

He loved her, and his eyes revealed
The passion that his tongue concealed:
He lived a sweet and charmèd life,
And dreamed she was his darling wife.

With him 't was spring the whole year through;
For him alone the violets grew,

And blossomed in the sylvan shade,
That he might crown his rustic maid.

Alas! his dreaming came to naught;
His love with grief and tears was fraught;
And she — the blessèd one! — is dead,
And violets bloom above her head.

If you are blessed with a wife, though, the present is probably the all-in-all to you. You feel that your lines have indeed fallen in pleasant places, and you are contented with the position in which it hath pleased Heaven to place you. If your memory glides back into the past at all, it is only to recall the days of your courtship, when time moved on jewelled wings, and brought at last the hour when the merry music of your wedding-bells filled your ears. Since then, with her beside you, the years have rolled calmly and silently along, so that you scarcely noted their passage, or perceived the marks which age was leaving on your brow and scattering in threads of silver amidst her hair. Most grateful should you be if this be the case, and the present with its joys and blessings prove wealthier than the vanished past.

Feeling thus, it will not be strange if, as I did, you indite some lines to your wife, on her approaching birthday, similar to these: —

My darling wife, once more I bring
  A birthday tribute unto thee;
Once more, with words of praise, I sing
  Of all that thou hast been to me,
Since first, whilst standing at thy side,
  That day of all the year most blest,
I held thy hand in mine, my bride,
  And clasped thee closely to my breast.

Since that sweet time we two have walked
  Together down the sloping years,
And gayly laughed, and gayly talked,
  Despite life's growing cares and fears;

When petty troubles filled my heart,
  And shadows hovered round my way,
Thy smile could make them all depart,
  And change December into May.

I know full well that thorns have sprung
  Within the path I 've led thee through ;
That thy fond bosom has been wrung
  By acts I now would fain undo ;
But underneath the foolish deed,
  And careless words oft breathed by me,
Thy gentle spirit still couldst read
  The story of my love for thee.

Though thou hast passed life's matin hours,
  And reached the summer's golden time,
Know that the season's later flowers
  Are rich as those of April's prime ;
That thou to me art still as fair
  As on the day I called thee wife ;
And that thy presence, like a prayer,
  Forever sanctifies my life.

Since I came to Woodbine Cottage I have resumed many of my boyhood's amusements ; and, every few days, recently, I have gone with my little ones to gather blackberries on the neighboring hill-sides. They grow about here in great abundance, and are large and of a fine flavor. I feel as if I were living my childhood over again. The same thickly clustered bushes, into which I used in by-gone days, on the banks of the Hudson, to scramble, scratching my hands and tearing my clothes in my efforts to get at the luscious berries, which strove to hide themselves under the protecting leaves, seem to grow here, and to hold as many berries, and be guarded by as many thorns. But what are a few scratches and rents, to say nothing of stained fingers, in comparison with the pleasure one derives from contemplating his heaped basket of ripe fruit! The obtaining of it was an enjoyment superior even to that which will be found in partaking of it. Then, too, consider the fun which the little ones have had! What marvellous sport it was for them to clamber up the steep rocks, and climb over the high rail-fences! How venturous, and at the same time delightful, it was for them to wander out of your sight for a while, and nearly out of the hearing of your voice, while they explored, in a spirit worthy of a Christopher Columbus, the course of the mountain stream which came tumbling over rocks from no one knows where, and going, foaming and singing, no one knows whither, forming deep pools where wonderful fish — trout, perchance — might be dwelling, and making miniature Niagaras, beautiful to look at and perilous to cross, as it dashed over rocky precipices! Ah! we grown folks are apt to forget that we were once young, and found pleasure in blackberrying and wandering in the woods; but after a little while spent in the country, if we are surrounded by children, the remembrance returns to us, and inclination often leads us to renew with them the delights of our school-days.

CHAPTER XV.

Three Good Things, — A Wood-fire, a Barrel of Ale, and a Package of New Books. — A Reminiscence of Hillside. — The Ills of the Flesh. — Cosmetics. — The Blazing Fire. — A Back-log. — My Cherry-tree. — A Load of Wood at Half-price. — The Package of Books. — A Mug of Ale. — Our Club. — In the Library. — The President. — The Members. Magazines. — Books.

THREE good things have come recently to Woodbine Cottage,—a wood fire, a barrel of October ale, and a package of new books. Heaven sent the first, the brewers the second, and my publishers the third. When I say that Heaven sent the wood-fire, I mean that Heaven caused the tree to grow from which it was made, and inserted into the early autumn the cool night which induced me to build it. How my friends, the great Albany brewers, however, knew that I was going to have a wood-fire blazing on my hearth, and, therefore, the very day I lighted it, sent me a barrel of Aster ale, of which to quaff foaming mugs sitting before it; or how my publishers, making up into a package the books which had for several weeks past been arriving from various publishers who were kind enough to send them to me, had foreseen the pleasure I would take in examining them, with my wife and little ones seated around me, before that blazing fire, I cannot tell; but so it was, and if a man ever enjoyed the first fire of autumn, it would not have been necessary to have gone out of my cottage that night to have found him.

These late October nights, full-mooned and frosty, are delightful to know, especially if you make their acquaintance from your library window. I do not so much enjoy being out among them, and I confess that I more fully delight in the daytime, when I can walk in the sunshine, and, sheltered from the wind, creep along through the autumnal woods, which have put on their robes of purple and gold, and orange and scarlet. The nuts are ripe, the chestnuts have opened their prickly burrs, and the walnuts unclosed their hard shucks. The apples are being gathered into the cellars; the rosy Spitzenberg, the purple Seek-no-farther, the yellow Pippin, the Greening, and all the newer varieties, are forsaking the orchards for the homes of man. We are getting along towards Thanksgiving Day, and already the savor of pumpkin and mince pies is wafted to us. Oysters, too, are in their prime. I drank my first hot whiskey punch of the season, too, to-day, and now have just tapped a barrel of October ale, — that ale of which a modern rhymer thus sings: —

"October's brewage, pure and creamy,
  Fragrant of hops and malt new made,
To childhood's hours, so sweet and dreamy,
  Fraught more with sunshine than with shade, —
Carried us back to when we rambled
  With pretty Madge o'er hill and dale,
While trusty Watch before us gambolled,
  Long ere we knew the taste of ale.

"The scent of blossoming hops was wafted
  From fields where vines innumerous grew,
And 'midst its perfume there was grafted
  A savor which the barley knew.
Those climbing vines, those fields of barley,
  Heard then full many a pleasant tale,
While for her kisses we did parley,
  Recalled to mind now o'er our ale.

"Those halcyon days long since have vanished,
  For Madge, dear Madge, is now but dust;
Her form on earth for aye is banished,
  Her spirit mingles with the just.
But while remembrance bids us weep her,
  Our love through life will never fail,

> For in our heart of hearts we 'll keep her,
> And drink her memory with our ale."

I had not known the delights of a wood-fire before since I left Hillside, nearly ten years ago; and when I got the fire fully under way, and saw the bright flames rushing up the chimney, the shadows dancing on the ceiling, the light gleaming on the polished andirons, the children nestling on the thick rug at my feet, roasting chestnuts and watching the smoke-wreaths, I half thought that those early days of married life had come back, and I was in the old house again where I had passed so many joyous honeymoons. The sight, though, of several more chubby little faces and pairs of naked feet than I had known in the olden time showed me that years had passed since then; and though I will not say that Time has dared to lay a finger on my wife, yet I will confess that he has not passed me by unrecognized. There are deeper wrinkles on my brow, more gray hairs in my whiskers, and the bald spot on the crown of my head, which could then have been covered with a dime, could not now be hidden with a silver dollar. One cannot expect, though, to be a boy forever; and though he may, to a certain extent, retain his youthful feelings and lightness of step, sly wrinkles will creep around his eyes, and sober moments come to confront him. The very sight of his children, as they play around, perpetually reminds him that his days of childhood have departed, and that henceforth his steps will glide into shadowy paths, and the ills which flesh is heir to will crowd upon him, and sight and hearing will grow feebler, the strong voice yield to weakness, and the vigorous walk become tottering and uncertain. "In short, my dear," I continued, — for I had been uttering something like the above to Mrs. Gray, — "the silver cord will be loosed and the golden bowl be broken." I spoke in such a melancholy tone that it quite moved my wife, who said, in a cheerful voice, "Don't, my dear, let it grieve you that you are not so young as you once were. Look at me; see how well I bear up under my years and the increased cares which these little ones entail upon me."

"It is all very well," I said, somewhat maliciously, I confess, "for you ladies, who employ all kinds of cosmetics, and *rouges*, and powders, and hair-dyes, to keep up your youthful appearance; but we men, who do not care to resort to such artificial aids, must grow old in spite of ourselves, though you remain, apparently, as blooming and fair as ever."

Now, if there be one thing more than another which Mrs. G. prides herself upon, it is in the non-employment of these toilet articles; and as she knew that I was aware she never used them, she contented herself by answering me simply with a rebukeful look.

The fire blazed on the hearth magnificently; the smoke rolled in clouds up the chimney; the wood sputtered and snapped as if it were alive, — which, indeed, a portion of it was, — and, from the great back-log the sap oozed out in as lively a manner as did the foam from around the faucet entering my barrel of ale. I was quite struck with the appearance of that back-log, and it suddenly occurred to me to ask my wife where it came from.

"Ah," she replied, "I have been waiting to have you ask me about it, for there is a history connected with it."

"A history!" I echoed.

"Yes," she replied; "you remember the story of the boy George Washington and the cherry-tree?"

"Of course I do," I answered. "It was rather impressed upon me, when a child, because I was once naughty enough to tell an untruth. But what has that got to do, I should like to know, with our back-log?"

"Well, there is a similarity between the two," she replied.

"You don't mean to say," I exclaimed, "that our little boy has been cutting down our cherry-tree?"

"I do," she replied, "and that back-log is the result. It took him, though, all day to chop it down, and he had to call to his assistance one or two elder boys; but he persevered, and though he blistered his hands fearfully, and tore his jacket in an unmendable manner, he finally got the tree down."

Now, if there was one tree in that garden which I prized above another, it was that cherry-tree. Not that I had obtained from it much fruit, — for what, between the children and the birds, very few of its cherries graced my table, — but because it was a large and handsomely formed tree, and was an ornament to my grounds. I was quite provoked, therefore, when I learned that my small boy had cut it down, and was disposed to punish him for so doing. But when his mother told me that he had come to her in the morning, and asked if she would like a load of wood, at about half the cost which the woodmen charged, and promised to obtain it for her before night; and she had made a bargain with him to that effect, and he had innocently gone to work and laid low the pride of my fruit-trees, and was inclined to glory in his success, I was disposed to forgive him the injury he had unwittingly inflicted.

When, taking him on my knee, I told him of the error he had committed, and gave him much good and fatherly advice in regard to future cherry-trees, his under-lip quivered, and his eyes were dimmed with tears, as he promised me "never any more" to cut down a cherry-tree.

This little affair being happily settled, we took kindly to the wood-fire, and, as it blazed up more brightly than ever, and threw its heat out further into the room, we grew warmer and more comfortable; and, my little boy lugging out the package of books from behind the door, we placed it upon the table, and proceeded to investigate its contents. Before doing so, however, I proposed to my wife that now, since cool weather had set in, and the evenings were getting long, that we institute a sort of club, of a semi-literary, semi-gossiping character, to which the children, and whoever of our friends might chance to drop in upon us, should be admitted, and take part in the proceedings.

"Good gracious, Mr. Gray!" exclaimed my wife; "what an idea! It 's preposterous! I never heard of such a thing in my life. The thought of you and I forming a semi what-do-you-call-it-kind of a club, is really too ridiculous."

"Why is it ridiculous?" I asked.

"Oh! because it is," Mrs. G. answered.

"Well, if you can advance no better reason than that, Mrs. Gray," I replied, slightly excited, "you will never convince me of its ridiculousness. If you don't choose to join me, my dear, you need not; but in that case I shall go to town and apply to the 'Century' to be admitted as a member, and shall thenceforth pass my evenings at the club-house."

"But suppose the 'Century' don't think you worthy of membership, and reject you, what will you do then?"

"In that event, Mrs. Gray, I shall join a 'Free and Easy' that holds its meetings at Luffy's tavern here in the village."

"Rather than have you do that, my love, I will unite with you in forming a club at home, of which you shall be president and I secretary."

The little ones agreeing to this, I proceeded to inaugurate, by electing myself president of the same, the club, to which I gave the name of

IN THE LIBRARY.

"This club," I said, speaking officially, and seating myself in the large mahogany arm-chair, which had come over long before the *May-Flower* reached these shores, "is, I trust, destined to become a great institution in Woodbine Cottage. Matters pertaining to pleasure and instruction will have consideration at its meetings. Many important subjects will be discussed; books and pictures will be treated of, and, perhaps, occasionally a story will be told."

Here the children clapped their hands approvingly, and the eldest boy exclaimed, "Hear! hear!" I also took the opportunity, which the occasion presented, to swallow a mug of ale, and, after wiping the foam from my beard, proceeded to open the package before me.

The magazine, "Our Young Folks," which I drew forth first, caused Miss Em. to clap her hands with glee, and to exclaim, "Now I shall be able to learn whether my workings out of the charades and enigmas are correct." The next was a copy of the "Atlantic," which my wife claimed as her own. Then came "Harper's," which my eldest, who is partial to the pictures and the editor's drawer, took possession of. The next treasure was a package of bound books.

"My dear," I said as I put these volumes carefully aside, "I think I will take charge of these, and during the coming winter it shall be my pleasure to read them aloud to you. Of one of these volumes, the 'Edinburgh Review' — high authority, my dear — says: 'It exhibits a brilliancy of poetic diction and a power of melody of a very high order.'"

"Why, when, my dear," asked Mrs. Gray, "did you read this in the Review? And what a memory you must have! Why, I 'm certain if I had read it only yesterday I should not have remembered it even till now!"

"Oh, well, you women," I replied, placing my glasses on my nose, and looking wisely at her from above them, "can't be expected to have such memories as we men possess. Why, bless you, my love!" I continued, looking boldly at her now through the glasses, "I remember everything I read. I never forget a sentence."

"I wish, my dear," my wife made answer, as she heaved

a little sigh, "that you would not forget to perform, as you do, many little requests which I make of you in regard to household matters. If you have a good memory for some things, why not for everything? If you can remember what is said about a book which you have never seen, why cannot you remember to stop at the shoemaker's, as I so often request you to do when in the city, and get the children some shoes?"

"Yes, papa, do!" exclaimed Em.

And "Yes, papa, do!" echoed her three successors.

"Well, my children," I said, "your poor papa will endeavor to remember it; but you must be aware that he cannot remember everything, though your dear mamma thinks he can; and that, moreover, it is very important that he should remember everything the 'Edinburgh Review' says about books."

"Poor papa, indeed," said mamma.

And "Poor papa," echoed each of the children.

"My dear," I said, reprovingly, "I shall be obliged to close this meeting of the club unless better order can be kept. The children cannot be allowed" — and here I looked very sternly at them, which made Em. tremble — "to create such a disturbance with impunity. Yes, my dear, the meeting stands adjourned."

CHAPTER XVI.

My Literary Young Lady; her Manuscript; her New Play.—Night-Work.—Lady Macbeth.—A Critic on a Lounge.—An Interruption.—Outside Callers.—A Sad Case.—A Rude Fellow.—Rev. Mr. Stricklebat.—My Revolver.—An Explanation desired.—Crazy People.—A Haunted House.—The Revelation.—A Play-woman.—The Dominie's Sermons.—Missions to perform.—Sundry Gifts.—Dispersing the Rabble.—A Glass of Old Port.—Peace.

Y literary young lady promises to be as much of a fixture at Woodbine Cottage as my old soldier was at Hillside. She dropped in upon us just at dinner-time one evening several months ago, to spend an hour or two, and has been with us ever since. I am happy in being able to state that it is not owing to my not having read and given my opinion as to the character of her manuscript that she remains with us, for I accomplished that task many weeks since. When I gave up my twilight walks to the Bronx, and my moonlight conversations on the veranda with her, I found that I had more time to devote to the perusal of her manuscript. In fact, in less than a week after these peregrinations and *conversaziones* ceased I had finished my allotted work. I am afraid, though, that the favorable opinion which I passed upon Miss Floy's production incited her to make a fresh incursion into the field of literature. Indeed, I know it was so; for the very next day she came to the dinner-table with exceedingly inky fingers and a badly arranged waterfall, besides being minus a collar and with boots unlaced, and, asking me to excuse her untidiness,—she termed it, however, appearance,—said that the praise I had bestowed upon her recent production had induced her to commence

writing a play — a drama in five acts — which she intended to complete before she left Woodbine Cottage, and which, when finished, she desired to submit to my judgment.

Now I have not, I know, a great deal to do; but still, after devoting fifteen hours a day to prescribed duties, I have not much time, taking out sleeping hours, to give to extra labor. I told Miss Floy as much, and added that, unless there was some "let up" on my present duties, I did not know when I would be able to read her play.

She replied that she had considered all that, and, if my wife had no objection, she thought a good plan would be to come once a week, after the little ones had gone to bed, to the library, and read aloud to me what she had written during the preceding days.

"But what if I should fall asleep?" I asked.

"Oh, then," she replied, "I will stop reading. Besides," she added, "by this means Mrs. Gray will also have the pleasure of hearing my play."

"Which privilege, I presume," I said, rather maliciously, "she may never otherwise have."

"Oh, yes, she will," said Miss Floy, quickly, "but not, perhaps, until it is acted at the theatre; and that, you know, may not be for some time to come."

"That is true," I answered; "but still, do you think that my wife will care to listen to your play?"

"Oh," said the incorrigible young woman; "I know she 'll like dearly to hear it."

"Well," I said, "if she has no objections, I don't know that I have; only be careful not to make your readings over an hour long."

She promised to observe this rule, and then retired triumphantly to her apartment.

I saw nothing more of that young lady for three days. She took her meals quite irregularly, and, I understood, was *en deshabille* all the time. She evidently had a severe attack of drama on the brain, and was actively engaged in working it off. I could hear her, though, from time to time, when I was in the house, reciting aloud passages of her composition ; and once, when there was a terrible commotion in her room, and it sounded as if every article of furniture therein was being indiscriminately broken to pieces, I knew that a climax had been reached, and probably the first act was finished. And I was right; for late that very evening I was aroused from my after-dinner nap by a tap on the library door, and as I opened my eyes Miss Floy, looking very much like Lady Macbeth, glided into the room, clad in a long white gown, ruffled around the throat and down the front in a double row, between which little pearl buttons were studded. Her hair hung in slightly disordered masses around her face, which was exceedingly pale, while a touch of *rouge* on each cheek rather added to the pallor, which was assisted by a dark line drawn under her eyes. She bore in one hand a lighted candle, and in the other a roll of manuscript.

I confess I was somewhat startled at her appearance; having the sanctity of my library invaded at that late hour — it was close on midnight— by what looked like a female apparition, rather overpowered me; but I was, fortunately, equal to the emergency, and instantly recognizing who it was, and, further, knowing that my hour had come, I prepared myself, resignedly, by elevating my head on the sofa and turning a little more on my right side, to listen to the first act of Miss Floy's drama.

After all, it is not an unpleasant thing to hear an agreeable young damsel, with a musical voice, and clad in an attractive costume, read aloud a play possessing more than ordinary merit. Perhaps, too, the fact that Mrs. Gray was beside me, hemming a dainty bit of ruffling, added to my contentment.

As it was a warm night, the window near which Miss Floy sat was open, the blinds only partially closed, and through them the moonlight fell in softened radiance upon her face, lighting up and giving a more than usual intellectual cast to her features. The reading of the play proceeded very successfully, and without interruption, until near the close of the second act, where the villain of the play is about to commit a deadly assault upon the heroine, a young, lovely, virtuous, and unprotected orphan girl, when Miss Floy and myself were startled by a violent hammering at the front-door, accompanied with a loud demand for instant admittance.

Who it was or what it all meant I could not imagine; and although I had from time to time, in the pauses of Miss Floy's reading, heard a suppressed murmur of voices, as if some persons were talking just in front of the house, I had paid no attention to it, and therefore this sudden attack upon my door took me by surprise. My wife and children were quickly alarmed, and the latter, being much frightened, set up a series of cries, which, combined with the shouts outside, "served," as the newspaper reporters say, "to make night hideous."

The noise below continuing with unabated vigor, Mrs. Gray urged me to hasten my movements and go down to the door and see what the trouble was.

When, therefore, I opened the door, I demanded, in no mild tone, to know what was meant by disturbing me and mine at this hour of the night. The persons outside seemed rather surprised at my questions, and a burly fellow whom I did not know, but whom I understood afterward was the bully politician of the village, seized me by the arm and said, "Murder was what was meant, and they would like to see the young woman as I was a-murdering."

I shook off the grasp of the rude fellow, and turning to my nearest neighbor, the Rev. Mr. Stricklebat, asked him to oblige me with an explanation of the strange proceedings in which he was taking so active a part. The old gentleman shook his head, and turning to one of his parishioners, another neighbor, said: "Well, well, this coolness on his part is more than I expected to witness! I think we had better proceed to search the house."

Ever since I learned that we possessed no policeman in our village, I have kept a loaded revolver in my dressing-table drawer; and, as I had taken the precaution to bring it with me down-stairs when I came, I was prepared to prevent any such proceeding on their part. So, when I produced the pistol, and assured them that my house could not be searched, they not only gave up the point, but evinced a decided disposition to retreat. Of the half-dozen individuals present, only the Rev. Mr. Stricklebat showed any courage, and when the others fell back, leaving him standing tall and gaunt before me, I said that if he would like to come into the house he could do so; and as there was evidently an egregious blunder of some kind committed by some one, I would be pleased to have him enlighten me in regard to it.

When he entered, closing and locking the front-door, I ushered him into the library. He seemed suspicious of the pistol until I laid it on the table, when he brightened up and said that it did really seem as if a mistake had been made, and, as it had probably originated with him, it was proper that he should endeavor to explain. "But who," he asked, wiping his bald head with his handkerchief, "was uttering those terrible threats which had so alarmed him?"

"What threats?" I asked. "I have heard none."

"None!" he exclaimed. "Then we outside were all crazy, or else the house is haunted. Do you mean to say that you were asleep when we came to the door, and that you heard no fearful imprecations?"

"Well," I answered, "I was not asleep, that is very certain; but, as for — say no more!" I cried; "I understand it all now!"

And I sat back in my chair and laughed heartily. This proceeding on my part seemed to frighten the old parson more than the display of the pistol had; for he evidently thought I had gone mad. And it was not until Mrs. Gray and Miss Floy, who, reassured by my laughter, had appeared, that I could find breath to explain to the old man the error into which he had fallen.

Then I asked Miss Floy to bring to me her manuscript, and requested her to read aloud several passages, before the old dominie could understand how it was that he had been deceived into supposing he heard two distinct persons, and one of these apparently a man. When he did realize it, however, and heard Miss Floy declaim at one moment in a most masculine voice, and the next in her own silvery tones, he was greatly impressed, and asked me, the next day, if she was a "stage-woman."

When I told him that she was not, but that she was engaged in writing the play, — the recital of some portions of which had so disturbed him, — he said that he had always preached against plays and play-actors, play-writers and play-goers; but he began to have his doubts whether, after all, he was in the right. He had been led, since the occurrence of last night, to think seriously upon the idea whether, after all, a certain mission is not given to everybody in life to perform. "To one is given, as in my own case," he continued, "the gift of writing and preaching sermons; to another, as in her case, the gift of writing and performing plays. Now, it still further occurs to me that, if I was given the gift of a play-writer, and, as is apparent in her case, accompanied with the gift of a play-actor, I should accept that as my mission on earth, and would live, as far as possible, in accordance with it. I don't think I myself shall ever go to see a play enacted; but I shall never again preach against them, or those who go to witness them."

When the old parson became assured that there was no murder being committed in my dwelling, he went out to the rabble gathered at the door, and, explaining the matter to them, advised them to go quietly home, which advice, with much laughter, they followed. Then he returned to the house and told me that he had been engaged, at the late hour of midnight, in writing his next Sunday's sermon, when he was verily surprised to hear, rising on the silent air, what was apparently the voices of two persons engaged in an angry dispute. Several expressions of a threatening character attracted his attention and decided him in going to learn from whence they proceeded. Aware that mine was a Christian household, he could not at first credit his ears when he found that these high words proceeded from my library. He was led to suspect that a fearful deed was about to be committed, and, on rousing a neighbor or two, and stopping a couple of passers-by, who heard with him the frightful imprecations, the party decided to invade, *vi et armis*, my dwelling. With what result the reader is already acquainted.

The old dominie seemed, before he left us, to fully enjoy the blunder he had made, and, as I was fearful that the exposure to the night air which he had undergone might be detrimental to his health, I opened a bottle of crusty old port, which had cobwebbed for years in sundry cellars, and the companions of which were only accustomed to being opened on birthdays and christenings. I think if the old parson finished his sermon that night, it possessed more than usual excellence; for, when he departed, he gave us all his blessing, and we, during the remainder of the night, slept in peace.

CHAPTER XVII.

An Autumnal Storm. — At Home. — Boots. — Balmorals and Polish. — In a Shoe. — Small Feet. — St. Crispin. — The Tapping of a Little Foot. "Why the Shoe Pinches." — New Principle. — The Poetry of Slippers. Cinderella's Glass Slipper. — A Plain Moral. — The Ancients on Shoes. Asleep.

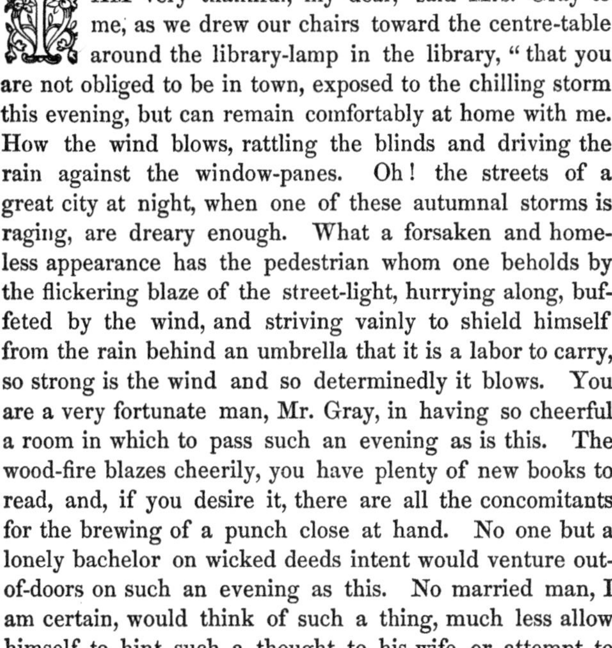

I AM very thankful, my dear," said Mrs. Gray to me, as we drew our chairs toward the centre-table around the library-lamp in the library, "that you are not obliged to be in town, exposed to the chilling storm this evening, but can remain comfortably at home with me. How the wind blows, rattling the blinds and driving the rain against the window-panes. Oh! the streets of a great city at night, when one of these autumnal storms is raging, are dreary enough. What a forsaken and homeless appearance has the pedestrian whom one beholds by the flickering blaze of the street-light, hurrying along, buffeted by the wind, and striving vainly to shield himself from the rain behind an umbrella that it is a labor to carry, so strong is the wind and so determinedly it blows. You are a very fortunate man, Mr. Gray, in having so cheerful a room in which to pass such an evening as is this. The wood-fire blazes cheerily, you have plenty of new books to read, and, if you desire it, there are all the concomitants for the brewing of a punch close at hand. No one but a lonely bachelor on wicked deeds intent would venture out-of-doors on such an evening as this. No married man, I am certain, would think of such a thing, much less allow himself to hint such a thought to his wife, or attempt to execute it. It would be preposterous, my love, — would it not?"

"It would be so, Mrs. Gray," I answered somewhat quickly; "but I do not really understand the object of your remarks, my dear, for I assure you *I* have no intention of venturing abroad to-night. If you think, because I told the servant, when I first came home, to get my thick boots and apply some oil-paste blacking to them, that I purpose going out, you are much mistaken. I shall probably require the boots to-morrow morning, but not before. Besides, this evening I propose devoting to our club, and as there is little prospect of visitors, suppose we begin immediately."

"Well, what shall we talk about?"

"Why, if it boots nothing to you, my dear," I replied, "let the subject be boots."

"Boots! Mr. Gray," exclaimed my wife in surprise; "what kind of boots?"

"All kinds," I replied; "from the famous seven-league ones of the times when giants were abroad, to the Balmorals and Polish boots worn by the ladies at the present day."

"The subject does not, I confess," said Mrs. Gray, "seem to me especially interesting; but you may perhaps be able to state facts sufficiently interesting to keep the little ones, who appear to be wide enough awake at this moment, from falling asleep. I know you to be fearfully correct in your statement of facts, and have often wondered that you would condescend to build castles in the air, or read fairy tales, as you sometimes do."

"Or 'Mother Goose's Melodies,' I suppose," I suggested: "you remember, of course, the nursery rhyme about the old woman who lived in a shoe, and whose progeny was so numerous she did n't know what to do?"

"Yes," she answered.

"Well, that old woman is one of my facts, or, rather, she represents a fact. The story, if interpreted, would read something as follows: The old woman is plainly nothing more or less than the foot itself; the children are the five toes; the shoe was a fashionable one, doubtless, made so small as to cramp the foot until it wished its five toes were out of the way. But, what to do to get them out of the way was the puzzle of its life; so to settle the matter it put on a white stocking and a black, and then put its toes to bed in the end of the shoe, where, owing to the limited space they occupied, they suffered terrible punishment, which was renewed every day as long as the shoe lasted."

"The shoe then should have been made on a larger last," was Mrs. Gray's bad pun.

"You are correct, amiable woman," I replied; "or else the plan now in vogue in Paris, of amputating one or more of the toes to allow for the narrowness of the shoe, should have been adopted. The fact is, my dear, we are remarkably partial to small feet, and will suffer almost any inconvenience and not a little torture, rather than wear boots or shoes of a proper shape. Nature has been unkind enough to give us feet the shape of which is not in accordance with our ideas of true beauty; therefore we seek, by aid of the followers of St. Crispin, to bring their form up to the ideal standard we have marked out for ourselves."

"This, then, is the reason why the shoe pinches, I suppose?"

"Certainly, my love," I answered; "and it is that you may avoid such an infliction in future that I have sought for and found a sole that will unquestionably supersede all others, and be the means of restoring the form of the foot to its primeval shape. The remedy consists simply in making the sole of the boot correspond exactly to the shape of the natural foot; and when this is once adopted, we shall hear no more complaints of feet diseases."

"It is all very well for you, Mr. Gray, whose feet are by no means small, to speak thus; but do you think the ladies will consent to put such an ungracefully shaped shoe as this would be on their pretty feet? Could you find a bootmaker in the land who would make one? Would any fashionable *bottier* of Broadway, think you, deign to place a shoe of that pattern in his show-window beside the tiny Cinderella slippers, the dainty dove-colored gaiters, the bridelike white satin shoes, or the strong, thick-soled, and healthful Polish boots, that lace high up and support the ankle better than any other? No; I'll answer No a hundred times."

Mrs. Gray's excitement was curious to witness, and as she rose and stood before me, her little foot — incased in a toilet-slipper, ornamented with an exquisite rosette—tapped significantly upon the carpet, as if to assert the right of dainty feet to wear any shaped shoes they could get into, provided Fashion stamped them with its sign-manual.

"Besides, Mr. Gray," she continued, "what do you know about the proper shape of a shoe? How long since you devoted yourself to investigating the subject? Ah! my St. Crispin, I fear you know very little in regard to it."

"To confess the truth," I said, taking my place upon the rug before the fire, "my knowledge is limited to a little work, entitled, 'Why the Shoe Pinches,' recently written by a learned German Professor of Anatomy in the University of Zurich. The first thing, the Professor says, to be considered is the great toe."

Mrs. Gray dropped her eyes as if ignoring that useful member of the pedal family; nevertheless I continued, growing more oratorical as I proceeded, as follows: —

"This toe does most of our walking for us. A line drawn from the point of this toe to the middle of its root would, he says, if continued, pass to the middle of the heel, but, as boots and shoes are made, the tendency is to twist the toe out of this line. Therefore he claims that the shoe should be made to suit the natural position of the great toe as well as the little toe (which has hitherto had a disproportionate share of the attention of mankind). Boots, if made on principle, ought to be so shaped that when a pair are side by side, with the heels in contact, the inner lines of the front part of the soles should also be in contact along the whole edge to the end of the great toes, so that if the toes are to be pointed this must be done by taking away from the outside alone. Now, then," I continued, dropping the Professor, "I must allow that this style of boot would, until we became accustomed to it, seem very inelegant, and give all who wore them the appearance of turning in their toes; but the comfort thereby gained would outweigh, in my opinion, appearances which, after all, only possess a fictitious value."

"Well," my wife replied, "all I can say, Mr. Gray, is, that if you can get the fashionable bootmakers of the city to introduce Balmoral boots, or any other kind adapted for ladies' wear, made on this scientific model, why, I will promise to adopt them, but with this understanding, that you will first make your appearance in boots similarly constructed."

"Certainly, my dear," I replied; "it is but right that the stronger sex should take the lead in an innovation of this kind; so you need not be surprised if some day I appear wearing this new style of boot."

"Remember, Mr. Gray," she said, "that, for my part, I am perfectly satisfied with the present fashion, and would not willingly exchange the shape of my stout Balmorals, my cloth gaiters, or my kid slippers, to that for which you have been pleading. Every age and nation has its peculiar fashion of coverings for the feet, and I have never seen or read of any which I thought better adapted for the people of to-day and of this country than those now made and worn. Tell me, if you can, of any superior, or indeed equal, to the present make."

Thereupon Mrs. Gray subsided into an easy-chair, thrust one of her slippered feet beyond the hem of her dress, and apparently studied, with the air of a *connoisseur*, the brilliant rosette, with its gold buckle, that crowned the instep.

"There is a deal of poetry," I mused aloud, "embalmed in a lady's slipper; there is romance in a pair of gaiters, and love has before this lurked in a satin shoe. It was an ancient custom, more honored in the breach than in the observance, to cast an old shoe after a departing bride and groom to bring them luck. Immense good fortune befell one Cinderella because she chanced to have a small foot, and attended a ball wearing glass slippers. I have not heard that a single gentlewoman who was at the ball given to the Prince of Wales, when he was in this country, possessed the wit to follow Cinderella's example. Had one done so, she would, doubtless, at this moment be the bride of the prince. The moral is plain: if you wish to marry a prince, dance in glass slippers at balls given in his honor. There will doubtless be another prince here before long, and the young ladies will do well to enclose the above moral in the casket of memory."

I turned my eyes toward Mrs. Gray for an approving smile. Alas! the dear woman was asleep; it was evident to me that she cared nothing about princes, and the thought consoled me.

"Mrs. Gray," I said, and I stirred the contents of a goblet, which somehow happened to be before me, and from which a lemony-whiskey-sugary incense arose, with a spoon, causing the glass to jingle, and thereby arousing my estimable spouse, who immediately sat erect and looked at me inquiringly, as if she were not certain of what I had been talking. "Mrs. Gray," I continued, apparently not noticing that she had been asleep, and dissimulating so cleverly she actually was convinced, if she thought of it all, that she had been awake every moment, — "Mrs. Gray," I repeated for the third time.

"Well, I hear you," she interrupted; "that is the fifth time you've uttered my name. Children, listen to your father. Proceed."

Dear woman, she evidently had been dreaming, or

else the contents of her goblet had been too much for her.

"Mrs. Gray," I uttered again.

"Why, dear me!" she cried, "what is the matter? Go on."

"Mrs. Gray," I added, impressively, for the fifth time.

"Well!" she said, regarding me attentively.

"You alluded a moment since," I said, — although in reality it was fifteen minutes, but I did not wish her to think I knew she had been asleep, — "to the different styles of coverings for the feet that, in various ages of the world and among various nations, have been in vogue."

"Good gracious!" she interrupted; "I said that in the early part of the evening."

I paid no attention to her remark, and proceeded.

"The ancient Egyptians, as we learn from their paintings and sculpture, wore a sort of skate of basket-work. The Assyrians, who were addicted to clambering over rocky mountains, protected their feet in stout, thick-soled buskins. The Persians were partial to slippers. The Greek women wore sandals, but the men liked nothing better than to go barefoot; consequently the Romans, who had boots and shoes for all classes of society, kicked them out of their possessions, and became the actual leaders of the world. The Greeks, however, may be said to have carried their shoes on their legs, as they wore a kind of skin-protector; hence the epithet of 'the well-greaved Greeks.' The Emperor Caligula performed a neat feat when he adopted for his own use the little spiked shoe, with its thick sole, until then worn only by the common soldier. The Lacedemonians revelled in red shoes. A Roman citizen usually wore black shoes on simple occasions, and purple ones were worn by coxcombs on occasion of balls being given to princes and such ilk. The ladies of Rome delighted in white and red shoes. The chief magistrates, also, on days of ceremony, appeared in red shoes. The noble classes had silver crescents on their shoes, which served as buckles. In the ninth and tenth centuries the greatest princes of Europe wore wooden shoes, or the upper part of leather and the sole of wood. In the reign of William Rufus, a great beau, one Robert, surnamed Ramshorn, introduced a curious shoe, with long, sharp points, stuffed with tow, and twisted like a ram's horn. In Richard the Second's reign the points of these shoes were of such a length that they were tied to the knees with gold and silver chains. In Chaucer's time the upper part of these shoes were cut in imitation of church windows, and worn by many unholy persons. In 1463 the Parliament of England prohibited the use of shoes or boots with peaks exceeding two inches in length, under severe penalties; but the sentence of excommunication was necessary before the points went down to two inches. King John had exquisite taste in boots, as we read that he ordered a pair for his royal spouse 'to be embroidered with circles.' Henry the Third was a bit of a dandy in his *chaussure*, for he had his boots powdered with lioncels. Henry the Seventh, and his bluff son and successor, wore shoes so broad that they obtained the name of 'ducks' bills.' In Elizabeth's time we first hear of shoes being made right and left. This fashion, however, went out, and was not revived until the beginning of the present century. During the past fifty years we have not materially advanced in comfortable and satisfactory shoes. I expect, however, that, with the help of the Zurich professor, the people will put their feet only into such boots as are natural in shape, and, consequently, worn with ease and propriety."

I may have talked on in this fashion for an hour longer, though I cannot tell, for I had been reading up the subject from encyclopædias and other books, on purpose to surprise Mrs. Gray with my knowledge concerning boots and shoes; but, thinking I had spoken sufficiently, I turned to her and asked: —

"And now, my dear, what do you think of my observations?"

Mrs. Gray was again asleep. The children, too, were locked in slumber. I looked at my watch, and found it to be twelve o'clock.

"My dear," I said, touching her gently on the shoulder, "the meeting of the club for this evening is dissolved."

Mrs. Gray, after waking, said, "Very well." And the little ones when aroused naturally commenced to cry.

CHAPTER XVIII.

Milking. — A Difficult Process. — Exodus of Servants. —A Sweet Disposition. — Down in the Dust. — Flanderian Oaths. — Defiant Goat. — Over the Palings. — Good Exercise. — Billy-boy.— Black-matan.— Gingerbread and a Rope. —Victory.—A Right and a Wrong Side.—Cream.

 HAVE learned to milk my goat. Now, if there be one thing more than another which a man who lives in the country and keeps a cow or a goat ought to know, it is how to milk. Not that I would advise him to follow up the practice every day, for it is to be presumed that he will have a servant, who will, as a rule, attend to this business; but it sometimes happens that servants leave you without warning, or go to "wakes" or weddings, and don't make their appearance at milking-time, as they promised to; and then, unless you are yourself capable of milking, you might as well be without the lacteal-yielding animal; besides, the poor creature will suffer if she be neglected.

Therefore it was, — after having been placed in such a quandary, through reason of my two servants leaving house affairs to take care of themselves, by going off one Sunday afternoon and failing to come back until the following day, whereby my family suffered much inconvenience, dinner being delayed to an unreasonable hour at night, and the goat going without being milked until much beyond her usual time, — therefore it was, I say, that I decided to learn the art of milking.

I essayed to milk our goat on the occasion to which I have just referred, but utterly failed of accomplishing my object. The process looked to me, when I had watched a person milking, so perfectly simple, that I supposed it would require no more skill than it would to pump a pail of water. In the first place, the goat would n't stand still, but kept moving about in a most unnecessary manner; swaying first to one side and then to the other; then backing with great rapidity and skill, and anon making a forward movement, accompanied with a kick of her hind-legs which invariably sent the pail flying behind her, and, until I became a little posted in the movement and prepared myself for it, leaving me sprawling on the turf. Every time, though, that I got hold of her udders, I worked and tugged at them with such zeal that I thought either the milk must flow or they would come off. But, though I squeezed and twisted them in every imaginable fashion, not a drop of milk rewarded my exertions. I tried to coax her by singing, —

> "Nanny goat, nanny goat, give down your milk," —

a little poem slightly altered from one addressed to "cushy-cow," in "Mother Goose's Melodies;" but all to no purpose. She was apparently as coy about disposing of her milk as if she were only a kid of tender age, instead of being the matronly old goat she was.

Now, I have a very sweet disposition, to which Mrs. Gray, if she were asked, would testify; but there is a limit even to my sweetness; and when that goat had bothered me for about an hour, and I had become heated by chasing her around the garden, and got my garments soiled by falling in the dust, I made up my mind that any further mild proceedings on my part, in connection with that animal, would be entirely thrown away, and that rigorous measures ought to be adopted if I expected to accomplish anything in the milking-line.

So I swore a terrible Flanderian oath, and, shaking my fist at the animal, gave her to understand that her fun was played out, and that I did n't intend to stand any more of her confounded nonsense.

That the goat understood every word I uttered, I am convinced; for she stood still, listening quietly to what I had to say, until I had finished, when she put her head down between her fore-legs, shaking it defiantly and wagging her brief tail in a most provoking manner. She allowed me, moreover, to get almost to her without stirring; and then, with a bound and a wickedly sounding bleat, she dashed past me, went over the garden palings, and scampered down the road.

It may be a pleasure as well as good exercise for an amiable man, of a quiet Sunday evening, to chase a goat along a dusty highway, but, as my amiability had departed, I came to the conclusion that I would see the goat drowned first, before I would follow her, notwithstanding that my wife urged me to do so, and the baby, when he saw his expectant supper go flying in the way it did over the fence, set up a most pitiful cry, and refused to be comforted. Still, I felt that something must be done, but was in a quandary as to what course to pursue. So I bethought me of the black-matan Gumbo, and, whistling him out of his cloisters in the barn, where he still leads the life of an invalid, I started him in pursuit of the goat. He moved off at first briskly, and with an angry yelp, on three legs, but gave out before he reached the goat, who stood defiantly awaiting him in the middle of the road, and returned limping and with drooping tail to the grateful precincts of his hospital quarters, from which neither threats nor coaxings could again induce him to come forth.

Just then the fool of the village, who seems to possess more good sense than some persons who are not called fools, came along, and when he saw the goat far down the road, where she had halted to curvet and prance like a gay war-horse, and perceived me standing at the gate looking at her, he began to chuckle, and, in a peculiar drawling fashion, with a treble voice, he said: "Guess your goat 's run away ag'in, squire. Why don't you catch it, squire?"

And then he chuckled. "You 'd better go to the pound ag'in in the mornin', squire, an' see if it 's there."

"Hang the goat!" I exclaimed.

"What'er for, squire?" he asked.

"Because," I replied, "she is more trouble than she is worth."

"Guess you donno much about goats, squire; do yer?"

"No," I said; "and I don't want to, either. Look here, Billy-boy, if you 'll catch and bring that goat home to me, I 'll give you a quarter."

"Don't want yer quarter, squire," he replied; "want a hunk o' gingerbread an' a rope."

Billy was promptly supplied with a piece of gingerbread and a rope, and immediately set off to capture the goat. He went shambling along down the road, talking witlessly to himself, until he passed the goat, which had watched him until he had gone by with suspicion, when, seemingly reassured that he intended no attack on her liberty, she commenced curveting and dancing upon her hind-legs as before. When the fool had gone a few yards past her, he sat down upon a stone at the road-side, and began to eat his gingerbread and chuckle to himself. The goat, attracted by his manners, gradually drew toward him, prancing and snuffing about him until she was nearly within his reach, when he tossed her a piece of gingerbread, which she seized and swallowed. Then he tossed her another bit, and, at last, she went close to him and nibbled it from his open palm. Thereupon he slipped the rope over her horns, and, drawing it into a knot, led her, feeding her with a bit of cake, and chuckling loudly as he walked along, triumphantly back to Woodbine Cottage.

Then it was that, under the instruction of the village fool, I took my first lesson in milking. I learned, to commence with, that there was a right as well as a wrong side to a goat, and that no goat which has any respect for herself will permit you to milk her from the wrong side.

Though, why one side is not as good as another I cannot understand; but I suppose education is at the bottom of it. Then the poor fool showed me how to draw, in a proper manner, the milk from the willing goat; and, after a few unsuccessful attempts, I at last succeeded in obtaining about a pint of pure milk. From that day onward I have, at sundry times, followed up this employment with encouraging results, and I am inclined to believe that the cream which rises on the milk which I obtain is thicker and richer than that drawn by ordinary individuals.

CHAPTER XIX.

Goodly Company. — Not dressed. — Lamb and Wine. — Elia. — Bridget. Charley Lamb's Failings; his Works. — "La Veuve Clicquot." — "Golden Wedding." — Native Wines. — The Banks of the Ohio. — My Friend's Verses. — "The Wine King." — Longworth.

"WE will have a goodly company around us this evening, my dear," I said to Mrs. Gray, as we drew our chairs toward the centre-table; "a brave company of wise men and beautiful women, whose like we do not often entertain."

"Why, gracious! Mr. Gray," exclaimed my wife, involuntarily smoothing her dress with one hand and arranging her curls with the other, "what do you mean? If you have invited any distinguished persons to be present at our club this evening, I shall never forgive you. Look at me." And the interesting woman rose and promenaded to and fro. "Am I dressed to receive company?"

"You certainly appear to be dressed sufficiently well for the wife of a quiet man like myself," I replied, "albeit your gown is not of *moiré antique*, trimmed with costly lace, nor bestud with diamonds; but for all that it is of fine material, and, in my eyes, shows exquisite taste in the wearer."

"You are a flatterer, my dear; but, tell me, who do you expect here?"

"None other than those now present," I replied, bowing gravely to the right and left.

Mrs. Gray gazed around her in astonishment.

"My dear," she asked, "are you well this evening? There is no one present but you and I, so far as I can perceive."

IN THE LIBRARY. J. F. Weir.

"You are mistaken, my love," I answered; "for there is Shakspeare looking down upon us from the wall, and Milton, Burns, and Byron standing in the corners of the room. And there before you, in that costly work, appear the lovely features of many of the women of the South. Besides, here, at my elbow, is Lamb, embalmed in beautiful type and on tinted paper, forming a volume which it would have gladdened his heart to have beheld. Did you know, my dear, that 'Elia' was one of the few English writers of the present century whom I should have been glad to have met?"

"I did not; but I can easily understand, knowing your tastes, that such is the case. But why do you like Lamb?"

"For many reasons. Not only is his character a most lovable one, but his writings are filled with tender thoughts, quaintly yet naturally expressed. His humor is never low; his wit, while sharp, is without malice; his sentiment, though pathetic, is never mawkish in character; and his show of learning does not degenerate into pedantry. Gentle in his manners to a degree that would be pronounced effeminate in any other whose life, like his, was not passed as the nurse and comforter of his sister Bridget Elia, he winds himself into our hearts, and never fails of there finding a welcome. What a lesson does the story of his life teach! his sacrifice of self in behalf of his sister; his yielding for her sake his young love; his patience, his cheerfulness, his pure, childlike disposition, and his unwavering regard for all his friends, — these things teach us a lesson which, if we be true men and women, will prove that Charles Lamb did not live his life in vain."

"You speak feelingly, my love. But had he no unpleasing traits? Was he perfect?"

"Alas! my dear," I replied, "we are none of us perfect. Perhaps it is better for us that we are imperfect, — else we had no need of a Saviour. Charles Lamb had his failings; because he was weak at times we are enabled, perhaps, the better to understand and appreciate him. There could exist no sympathy between us, if it were not that he possessed mortal weaknesses. My dear, let us think of Lamb only as 'the gentle-hearted Elia.' Have you read his entire works?"

"I believe so," she answered; "I am sure of it, if they be comprised in his 'Essays of Elia,' his 'Rosamund Gray,' his tragedy of 'John Woodvil,' his farce of 'Mr. H——,' and sundry poems."

"And you have never read his letters and final memorials, edited by Sergeant Talfourd?" I asked.

"Never," she replied.

"Then, my dear, allow me to say," I continued, "that you do not yet know the loveliness of his life. You will find in these four volumes," I added, after a pause, placing my hand on the books, "the complete works of the dear and quaint old writer, Charles Lamb. And now, my love, with your permission, we will drink to his memory in a glass of wine."

"Certainly, Mr. Gray; what kind do you desire? Will you have 'La Veuve Clicquot,' or the 'Golden Wedding?'"

"Oh, we will take the 'Clicquot' first, and, while the bead is on, I will sing you a song of mine, and then we will have the 'Golden Wedding;' for, though this be a new brand, its name will serve to remind us of the fifty years of unceasing, watchful love and care given by Charley Lamb to his sister Mary."

And then I sung the following song in praise of "La Veuve Clicquot": —

> I love the wine
> Pressed from the vine
> That in la belle France grows;
> It sparkles bright,
> With rosy light,
> And is la veuve Clicquot's.
> The widow Clicquot!
> Fill high — drain low:
> Vive la veuve Clicquot!

Let poets sing
Of maids and spring,
And western wine that flows;
Autumn for me,
And widows free,
With wine of veuve Clicquot's!
The widow Clicquot!
Fill high — drain low:
Vive la veuve Clicquot!

While lovers kiss,
And dream of bliss,
And speak in whispers low,
My sweetest dreams
Shall be of Rheims,
And of la veuve Clicquot.
The widow Clicquot!
Fill high — drain low:
Vive la veuve Clicquot!

The wine I praise
Embalms my days,
And strength and joy bestows;
It warms my heart,
Bids grief depart,
And is la veuve Clicquot's.
The widow Clicquot!
Fill high — drain low:
Vive la veuve Clicquot!

No other wine
Is half so fine, —
No vines that vineyard shows
Such grapes can bear,
Whose vintage rare
Will equal veuve Clicquot's.
The widow Clicquot!
Fill high — drain low:
Vive la veuve Clicquot!

Then, when I drain
This rich champagne
From goblet that o'erflows, —

Or guest, or host, —
One health I 'll toast,
'T is hers — la veuve Clicquot's, —
The widow Clicquot!
Fill high — drain low:
Vive la veuve Clicquot!

"Are you aware, my dear," I asked, as Mrs. Gray, having changed the wine and glasses before me, resumed her chair, "that there is a prospect of our having, in a few years, a superior red wine of native manufacture equal to Burgundy?"

Mrs. Gray, not being aware of it, shook her head to signify as much.

"Now, red wine," I continued, "is much needed," — Mrs. Gray this time nodded assent, — "and, in this connection, a friend of mine, who lives out West among the vineyards that line the banks of the Ohio, has ventured a verse or two on the subject. I have not the poem before me, but, as near as I can recollect, he sings: —

'Our Bacchus-god is pale as yet, —
A wreath of lilies crowns his head,
Where not a single rose is set,
Nor gleams his flag with bars of red.'

Again," I added: —

"'The wine that 's white is like the light
Through crystal air of morning shed;
But all of evening's soft delight,
And warmth, and love, are in the red.'

And, once more, in view of the successful consummation," I continued: —

"'Lo! when the sun, at evening's close,
Encouched on ruby clouds shall sink,
And to his soft and sweet repose
The merry millions fill and drink;

"'No lifted cup in all the West
But shall reflect with deepened hue
The rosy smile wherewith he blest
Their revels when he bade adieu.'"

"Beautiful, my dear, very beautiful," exclaimed Mrs. Gray, as I finished. "Let us toast their author." And we did so.

"And now, Mrs. Gray," I said, "I will sing to you some other verses of my own, — not so good as the lines I just repeated; but, as they are mine, you will, I trust, not criticize them too severely." Thereupon I assumed my favorite place upon the rug before the fire, and in a not unmusical voice, I hope, entranced Mrs. Gray with the following, entitled —

THE WINE-KING.

I SING in a goodly measure
The rhyme of the twining vine,
That yields its autumn treasure
Of pure and sparkling wine;

Of the luscious grape that blushes
Where western waters glide;
Of the rosy flood that gushes
From presses deep and wide;

And the king who caused to flourish,
To blossom and to bear,
The vine whose grapes shall nourish,
Whose wine shall conquer care.

Then with clusters white and yellow,
Purple, and black, and red,
God-Bacchus, the jolly fellow,
Should crown the wine-king's head.

For there is no wine surpasses
This of the golden West;
'T is the wine to toast the lasses,
And cheer the welcome guest.

Then give to the wine-king glory,
Shout songs of praise and mirth,
Nor ever forget his story,
But *long* recall his *worth*.

"There, Mrs. Gray," I exclaimed, rubbing my hands together in a congratulatory manner, as I concluded the song, "what do you think of that?"

"I think, my dear," she replied, "you will never be a great singer, nor a great poet."

"Mrs. Gray," I said, very decidedly, "the meeting of the club is adjourned."

WATCHING THE ECLIPSE. J. G. BROWN.

CHAPTER XX.

An Early Eclipse. — Smoked Glass. — At Breakfast.— What my little Ones and Myself talk about. — Great Travellers. — Ballooning. — Re-dressing. Smut and Purity. — Little Cherubs. — All Day. — An Observatory. — A Telescope. — Miss Floy complains; her Indignation. — Sights through a Tin Telescope.— " So high." —Spots on the Fingers and on the Heart. — Miss Floy correct.

WE had an eclipse in our village the other day. It commenced, I think, about sunrise, for the children, I observed, were engaged in smoking, over a candle, a bit of glass, at that early hour of the morning, and immediately thereafter proceeded to injure their eyes by looking sunward through it. They must have been very industrious, for I noticed, when they came to the breakfast-table, a half-hour afterward, that each one's nose had a smutty spot on the end of it; that his fingers were blackened and his clean clothes soiled. Thereupon I made up my mind that eclipses before breakfast were nuisances. I was more than ever convinced of this when my wife ordered the nurse to take the little ones from the table and re-wash and re-dress them. But there was no redress for the annoyance which this proceeding caused me. The carrying away of those children destroyed the pleasant bearing of the breakfast-table; for as I had already filled their several plates with food, it did not seem to me exactly the thing to remove them from the table on account of a smutty finger or two, and before they had partaken of it. Besides, I missed the prattles of the little ones, who, at breakfast, usually give me the programme of the coming day's proceedings, as far as they are individually concerned, and which is sometimes of the most wonderful description. They are much given to going on long journeys, and will obtain my mature advice as to the best and most expeditious manner of going to the far-off places which they propose to visit while I am gone to the city. They have travelled a good deal, recently, in the balloon, which they had heard me speak of as being moored near the Central Park, and in which I had nearly been seduced into making an ascension by my literary young lady, who held out remarkable temptations as inducements for me to go up with her some fine afternoon. I made up my mind, however, that railroading on the Harlem route was as much in the way of venturousness as I cared at present about undertaking; and, so I quietly replied to Miss Floy, when she importuned me to accompany her, "Sufficient for the day is the evil thereof." But my little ones took the risks, and many a time — as they gayly informed me at the breakfast-table they were about to accomplish as soon as I had taken my departure — undertook long journeys to Jerusalem, and Bagdad, and Mesopotamia, and Hong Kong, and other places of renown, in that balloon. And then, when I came home at evening, they would give me an animated account of their visit.

On the present occasion, however, I was obliged to go to town without being informed where my little ones intended spending the day; for, although they retired from the table in good order and without any special outbreak, yet, when they reached the nursery, I judged, from the tumult that ensued, that war had been declared between them and the nursery maid, and it would be some time before they found their way back to the breakfast-table. And I was correct; for, although I lingered at the table so long that I was in danger of losing my usual train, not a glimpse of my little ones did I again obtain.

Now, if I had my own way, — which, indeed, I seldom do,— I should have kept those children at the table. What matters a speck or two of black on the outside of the body, so long as the spirit within is white and unsullied? Why take exceptions to garments a little soiled, when we know that the wearers would assume the spotless robes of angels were they to pass from earth to heaven?

I said something like this to Mrs. Gray, as the children disappeared from the breakfast-room; but she, being a trifle over-nice and somewhat particular, replied that what I had said sounded very pretty, but that, for her part, she liked to see the children tidy and clean when they came to the table; and as for their being angelic, and prepared to assume the robes of which I spoke, she hoped it was so; but that, judging from the uproar they were then making, it seemed to her more probable that they were preparing themselves to put on robes just the opposite of those which angels wear.

As this was the most severe language I had ever heard my wife utter, I declared myself to be quite shocked, and, as my train was about due, said I would not remain any longer at a table where such sweet cherubs as were our boys and girls were wanting. Then, hoping that Heaven would give her a more amiable disposition before I came back, I took my leave and departed.

I think the eclipse must have lasted, in the vicinity of Woodbine Cottage, all day; for when I came home, late in the afternoon, I found the children very much more begrimed with lampblack than they were at the breakfast-table, still engaged in looking at the sun. My eldest boy had erected an observatory in the garden, and had a telescope in active operation. He had made a good many pins, he informed me, by letting his brothers and sisters look through it, at five pins a sight.

For the benefit of little boys who might like to know how to manufacture telescopes, I will state that it was constructed mainly of a tin trumpet or horn and a piece of smoked glass. He had made an unsuccessful attempt in the telescope line, I was informed by his mother, with the glass chimney belonging to our evening lamp, but failed, because he accidentally broke it. Miss Floy, too, complained that in his scientific operations he had purloined her eye-glasses, and, in smoking them, had heedlessly allowed the flame of the candle to play upon their tortoise-shell rims, which had thereby been greatly damaged. Wherefore she prayed that he might be punished. I said he should be, and that she might inflict it.

"You may read aloud to him," I said, "a scene from your new play; but if you don't regard that as a sufficient punishment, why, you can read to him two. And that, I am certain, will be enough to deter him from ever again robbing you of your glasses."

Thereupon Miss Floy became quite indignant, and gave me to understand that she regarded me as a mean man. She added, moreover, that my children, owing to my indulgence, were going to ruin, and that I was not fitted to be a father. Solomon, she continued, knew a thing or two about the management of children, which, if I were wise, I would adopt. She despaired, though, of ever hearing me speak or seeing me do other than acts of foolishness.

Which sentence I pronounced ungrammatical, and said that it was in keeping, however, with much of the language to be found in the various acts of her play.

This provoked her past all bearing, and she retired to her own apartment in great vexation of spirit, where she had a good crying-spell, which calmed her, and enabled her to come down to dinner in the most charming of gowns, and as merry and cheery as a robin.

I do not suppose that anybody ever saw half such strange things at an eclipse as my little ones did. By the aid of the tin telescope the man in the moon was brought home, as it were, to their very doors; and as for spots on the sun, they saw them so distinctly that they could almost have put their fingers upon them. The littlest chap, who has n't cut his teeth yet, and lives almost exclusively on milk-punch and such like beverages, gave me to understand, in his way, that he saw rather more than double, and counted several moons and suns as big as his head and "so high."

After all, I think I was mistaken in saying that an eclipse before breakfast is a nuisance. I did n't know, when I said it, that it was going to last all day, and be such a source of pleasure to the little folks. I even begin to wish now that there could be an eclipse every day, though I suppose, in that case, the children would not be as much delighted with it as they now are, and that smoked glass and tin telescopes would soon be at a discount.

"Well, well," I said to my wife, after the little ones had told me all they could about the eclipse, and how much they had enjoyed it, "who would n't be a child again, and find pleasure in eclipses and smoked glass!"

"But they do get themselves terribly smutty," said my wife.

"True; but it will easily wash off," I replied. "Now, I saw men down in Wall Street and thereabouts, this forenoon, who would n't have taken a smoked glass in their hands, for fear of soiling their fingers, for a great deal; and yet, I tell you, those same men had blacker spots upon their hearts — and which can never be rubbed off — than they could have got upon their fingers if they had handled all the smoked glass which has been used to-day."

"Well, what of it?" asked Miss Floy.

"What of it?" I echoed; "why, really, nothing, except that I 'd rather be like one of these little ones than one of those bad men."

"Which desire, however laudable," said Miss Floy, maliciously, "can never come to pass; the longer you go among those 'bad men' the more like them, and the less like these little ones, will you become."

And I think Miss Floy, for once, is correct.

CHAPTER XXI.

Family Shopping. — Obliging your Neighbors. — "Something." — An Elderly Female. — An Innocent Orphan. — A Monster. — "Shame! Shame!" — A Blue-eyed Young Woman. — Who 'll hold the Baby? — All Aboard. — Tilly Slowboy. — An empty Seat.— My Friend Opposite. "Banbury Cross." — A Surprise. — My Fat Old Lady. — A resident Mother-in-law. — Smithers.

NO one lives in the country and goes to town every day, but comes home, semi-occasionally, laden with bundles. He is expected to do a great deal of family shopping, and there is little unprocurable in the country which he is not, at least, asked to procure in the city. Some persons are always to be seen carrying baskets which are empty in the morning and full at night. A black-leather carpet-bag, however, is preferable, as it conveys the impression to the uninitiated that you are travelling. To be sure, there are many articles you are called upon to obtain in town which you cannot get into a carpet-bag, or even a basket, for that matter, and which you are obliged to carry in your arms. For instance, I was asked, a short time since, by a neighbor — one who is perpetually tormenting me to do this and obtain that for him in town — to bring out for his wife something which would be delivered to me at the *dépôt*, so that I would have little trouble in the matter except to take charge of it on the cars, and that he would be at the station when the train arrived, to relieve me of it there. This proceeding was so much more considerate than was usual on his part that I promised, unreservedly, to oblige him; nor did I even inquire what the "something" was which he desired me to bring to him.

He said further that an elderly female, dressed in black, whom I would find in the ladies' sitting-room, would hand it to me, and he hoped I would experience little trouble with it.

When, therefore, I went, in the afternoon, to the *dépôt*, and into the ladies' sitting-room, I had no difficulty in discovering several elderly females, but none of them had the bundle or package I was seeking for. I looked at each of them successively, and was on the point of turning away empty-handed, when the elderliest of the said elderlies, dressed in the rustiest of black bombazines, rose from the corner in which she was sitting, and, calling me by name, asked if I had promised to take charge of a baby for Mr. Smithers. As Smithers was the name of my neighbor, and as this was evidently the elderly female of whom he spoke, I felt satisfied that the "something" I had promised to take charge of was the infant she carried in her arms.

With that quickness, however, which is characteristic of the Grays, I immediately denied the soft impeachment, but confessed that I did promise to take out a bundle for said Smithers. Then it was that the elderly female displayed her eloquence and diplomatic powers.

"Is it possible," she exclaimed, in the most tragic of tones and manners, "that any one who pretends to be a man, and is a father, would refuse to take charge, for little more than half an hour, of a young and innocent orphan babe, a girl at that, just recovering from a severe attack of measles, especially when he had promised a good Christian man, whose wife intends to adopt as her own this sweet child, that he would do so without fail? Such conduct, I say, is atrocious, and I, for one, would only believe savages capable of such an act. None but a monster would be so cruel-hearted."

I endeavored to explain to the spectators assembled in the sitting-room that when I promised to take something to my neighbor I had no idea that it was to be a live baby, and that, if I had known it, I should, as I now did, most certainly have declined obliging him. It was bad enough, I said, to travel with one's own baby, even when you have a nurse to attend to it; but when a strange baby is cast into your arms, it was simply abominable. Besides, I had a bundle of my own to carry, which, as they could perceive, was not inconsiderable in size, and which really required all my attention.

Thereupon the half-dozen elderly females in black, and the younger females in colors, therein assembled, cried, "Shame! shame!" and my particularly elderly party exclaimed, striking an attitude, and holding the infant aloft as if she were going to dash it down upon the floor, unless I would consent to take it, "Cruelty, thy name is man."

"Oh, as to that," I said, "I won't deny it; but I 'll be hanged if I 'll consent to carry that infant out to Fordham." And I resolutely buttoned my coat up about the throat, and turned toward the door.

Straightway the females surrounded me, and both young and old, in their sweetest and softest spoken words, began entreating me to reconsider my decision, and take that innocent little babe to its expectant friends. One blue-eyed maid said she would help me take care of it, and, as she spoke, she smiled on me in a most captivating manner.

Now, if there 's one thing more than another which I cannot resist, it is a pair of blue eyes; and when is added to this a smile which would set a bachelor crazy, I feel very much as if it were all up with me, and my only resource is an honorable capitulation. I do not think, however, that, in the present case, I should have given in had I not, through some hocus-pocus operation of the elderly female, found myself in actual possession of the baby, without knowing how the change from her arms to mine had been effected, and only, indeed, recognized the fact as incontrovertible when I saw the aforesaid female disappearing from my sight in the distance.

I am not a man who thinks it undignified or who is ashamed to carry a bundle or a basket; but, I confess, I did feel a trifle shy about entering the cars with that baby in my arms. I tried to get the blue-eyed young woman to carry her; but she excused herself by saying that she was not strong enough to do so. Just then, when I had fully decided to make a virtue of necessity, I spied my savage literary friend, to whom I called, and, stating the strange position in which I was placed, requested him to hold the infant for me a moment while I bought my ticket.

To my infinite regret he politely but firmly refused to do so, and said he would buy a ticket for me. I afterward tried to have several of my acquaintances take that baby, but they invariably refused, to a man, and it was not until the conductor shouted "All aboard!" that I mustered sufficient courage to enable me to enter the cars with that orphan in my arms.

Of course, the seats in the forward cars were all occupied, and I was obliged to pass through the entire train, until I reached the last car, before I could obtain a seat. I did not, I must acknowledge, attract as much attention, during my promenade, as I had anticipated. Not more than a dozen persons gave any heed to me or my charge. Indeed, I managed the matter so adroitly that I passed through the first car without attracting a single observation. I purposely carried the babe head downward, so that she looked like a bundle of dry goods. I think this inversion of the child produced a slight strangulation, which prevented her from crying aloud for a few minutes, but from which she recovered when I was about half way through the second car, and from there on, until the last car was reached, she made the most insufferable noise of which a child is capable. Perhaps I rather added to the intensity of this outcry by allowing, *à la* Tilly Slowboy, that infant's head to come in contact with the corners of sundry seats and the sides of several doorways as I went along. The louder the child cried the more nervous I became, and by the time I had found a vacant seat, I was completely exhausted, and felt exceedingly like sending my neighbor Smithers and his wife, the elderly female in black, the managers of the orphan asylum, and the poor little brat herself, to that place where the chief employment is presumed to be the gnashing of teeth.

Of course, the blue-eyed young woman deserted me long before I reached my car, a nice young man having offered her a place at his side when we passed through the first car. So I found myself at last, with a big bundle and a baby, unsupported by a friend, in one of the new style of rail-cars, the seats of which, like those of the city horse-cars, are opposite each other, and extend on each side its entire length. To be sure, my savage literary friend sat nearly opposite to me; but he was apparently absorbed in reading the "Evening Post," and paid no attention to the signs I made for him to come across to me. I could see, though, that he was watching me from over the top of the paper, and every once in a while would hide his head behind it, while he indulged in a provoking laugh. Perhaps he was laughing at something he was reading; but as the editorial page, which was before him, seldom contains a humorous article, I was induced to believe that he was laughing at me; though why he should have done so I can't imagine. He could n't have seen anything comical about me. And if he, or any one else, thinks it 's funny to take care of a strange babe, who will persist in crying, in a railroad car, I can only say he will find out his mistake when he tries it. There are a good many annoyances connected with "tending baby," even under the most propitious circumstances; but these are greatly aggravated when you find yourself placed in the condition I was.

I will do the baby the credit of saying that, after I had restored her to a proper position, and so long as I kept her undergoing a severe treatment of jolting by riding her on my knee to Banbury Cross, she refrained from crying; but the moment I stopped, she would recommence with increased vigor. When the conductor came to collect the tickets, I tried to get him to take the babe while I searched my pockets for it. But he plumply refused, saying that he was hired by the railroad company to run trains and not to hold babies, and that he 'd be shot — or something worse — if he 'd take her. Then I tried my neighbors on each side of me; but each said he did n't see it. So I placed the baby, who immediately began to scream, on the floor at my feet, and in doing so I somehow managed to loosen the string which bound the bundle that lay on my lap, and the contents of which — it contained, I may as well state, three hoop-skirts, which I had purchased for Mrs. Gray, Miss Floy, and my eldest girl — thereupon spread themselves out, in a sudden and surprising manner, in the very face of the unaccommodating conductor, reminding him, doubtless, of the curious little boxes from which, when the covers are loosened, grinning skeletons jump forth. The astonishment of that conductor was only equalled by my own dismay. The spring he made backward was of the acrobatic kind, and the exclamation he uttered savored more of profanity than religion. The peal of laughter that ran around that car, too, was not calculated to soothe my already disturbed feelings, while the yells of the baby and the invectives of the conductor were about equally mingled.

I am a mild man, and can endure a great deal of vexation without being disturbed in my temper; but there is a limit to my patience, and then I am inclined to be a trifle wicked. The time had arrived when I was prepared to make a dash at somebody; but, fortunately, at that moment, my good angel, in the shape of the fat old lady of black-matan memory, made her appearance on the field of action, and taking the babe, who instantly became quiet under her touch, said she would take care of her until I arrived at Fordham. This was such a relief to me that I instantly grew amiable, and gave the conductor to understand that I looked on the whole thing as a good joke, which, if he was n't disposed to accept, he might leave alone. So he said, "All right," and went on his way rejoicing.

Then I essayed to fold up the skirts in the compact form in which they were when I received them from the maker; but although I tried with many crinks and twists of the arms, I utterly failed to bring them under subjection. I made up my mind, therefore, that there was a knack about doing these things which could only be attained by experience, and required the same skill to perform as goes to make up a first-class prestidigitator. I snapped three or four of the steel springs in my endeavors to accomplish my purpose, and, after all, was obliged to give it up unsuccessful. In fact, my parcel, when I did get it together, looked much like the upper half of an inflated balloon, and bore no resemblance to the compact little package it was when I entered the car.

I had no more trouble with the infant, thanks to my old lady, until I reached the end of my journey, where, of course, Mr. Smithers was not present to receive my charge. The consequence was that I was obliged to carry that babe home to the bosom of my own family, much to the surprise of Mrs. Gray and my own vexation.

The reception with which a man meets when he carries home a strange babe is not apt to be of the most flattering description. He is viewed with a suspicious eye; he is obliged to answer a good many questions, and his replies are not always regarded as perfectly reliable. This pertains more especially to his reception if he be blessed with a resident mother-in-law. But as I was not thus blessed, I will do Mrs. Gray the justice to state that she received my account of the manner in which I received the babe with great consideration; and when Mr. Smithers came for the child, which he soon did, she gave him to understand that he need never expect me to perform any similar service for him or Mrs. Smithers, as I was not to be subjected to so great an annoyance. And I, for my own part, told him that when I did another errand of any kind for him in town, he would be likely to know it.

And all that Smithers said in reply was, "Jest so."

CHAPTER XXII.

Indian Summer. — A Sunday Morning. — An Impromptu. — Sunlight and Shadow. — Mrs. Gray's Ignorance. — My Vanity. — Indian Summer in Town and out of Town. — City Folks and Country Folks. — In the Woods, on 'Change, and up and down Broadway. — Miserable Dinners.

WE are enjoying our Indian Summer just now at Woodbine Cottage. It is of the most cheering description. Never, within the memory of that most respectable of mortals the oldest inhabitant, has more delightful weather been known. A week ago the small boys of the village were skating on the ice in a field just below my cottage, and now the weather is mild enough for the same boys to pick, in the same lot, if they would grow there, ripe strawberries. Words fail to render a just idea of its lovely character. Balmy as June, it yet possesses the freshness and invigorating qualities of October. It falls across the skirts of the departing year like a gleam of sunshine in a shady place. No wonder the poets have loved to sing the praises of the Indian Summer, or the Indians themselves regarded it as Nature's thanksgiving time. Verily, it is the amen of the year, — an outwardly expressed sign from mother earth that her part, in the proper carrying out of the obligations of the various seasons to mankind, has been faithfully performed, and that the seeds sown in her bosom have germinated and grown to maturity, and been gathered into the garners. The harvests throughout the land have been plentiful. All the fruits of the earth have repaid the husbandman many fold for his labor, and it seems proper that Time should pause in his course a little while, and let Nature sing *Jubilate* in this touching and beautiful manner.

I uttered these words, or some very similar in character, to Mrs. Gray, as we were preparing for church one Sunday morning.

"I declare, my dear," she said, "you are really growing to be quite poetical in your language."

"Oh! that 's nothing," I replied. "Now listen. This, I think, for an impromptu, is not bad:—

Fair morn, that ushers in the day,
  When heaven and earth are most in tune,
Thou art the Sabbath of the year,—
  A perfect day in perfect June.

No cloud shall o'er thy sky appear,
  Nor wind disturb thy quiet rest;
But Peace, dovelike, shall o'er thee brood,
  And every hour be counted blest.

"And did you," asked the delighted woman, "write those lines?"

"Certainly," I replied.

"And what prompted you, my dear," she asked, "to write that 'impromptu,' as you termed it?"

"I was prompted thereto," I answered, "by a picture, entitled 'Sunday Morning,' painted by Durand, and which, I believe, has been engraved and published. But I have done something better than that, my dear, in the way of verses descriptive of a picture."

"And, pray, what are they?" my wife asked.

"Why, my lines on Bierstadt's 'Sunlight and Shadow.' Did you never see them?" I asked.

Mrs. Gray having given me to understand that she never had,—though I am quite certain she had; but she likes, I find, occasionally, to minister to my vanity,—I thereupon read to her the following lines, entitled—

SUNLIGHT AND SHADOW.

The sunlight on the pavement falls,
And on the old tree's rugged trunk,
And up the church's ancient walls
It creeps, like prayer from holy monk.

Through waving boughs it softly floats
In glowing showers of radiant light,
And all the air with golden motes
Is warm and tremulous and bright.

The shadows, made by flickering leaves,
Dance daintily upon the earth,
And over all the silence weaves
A peace which seems of heavenly birth.

The old crone seated at the gate,
Bowed down with sin and years and woe,
Is typical of that estate
Where only shadows come and go.

But far within the sacred pile,
And clad in robes both rich and gay,
Kneels one whose heart is free from guile,
Who walks in sunshine every day.

The church, on which the ivy clings,
O'ergrown with lichen and with mould,
To many a heart the memory brings
Of bells which chimed — of bells which tolled

And these bells marked the lights and shades,
The joys and sorrows of our lives,
Which came alike to youths and maids,
To husbands and to wives.

But while on earth we still may stay,
And live the lives which God hath given,
Though shadows lie across our way,
The sunlight will be found in heaven.

When I finished, my wife declared that she had never

heard prettier verses, and she thought that it was entirely owing to the Indian Summer and our living out of town that I was enabled to write them.

"Yes," I said, "it is not improbable. At all events the city is not the place wherein to enjoy the Indian Summer. It is necessary to be in the country to fully appreciate it. There, 'Where twinkles in the smoky light the waters of the rill,' and when, as you ramble along, 'The sound of dropping nuts is heard, though all the air is still,' is the proper place to be at this loveliest season of the year. Many must content themselves, however, with the town at this period, and deem it fortunate if at such time they can break loose from the cares of life, and wander for a brief hour or two in the Central Park. Not that I ever performed this latter feat when a denizen of the city, for, to tell the truth, I am not partial to long walks; but then it sounds very nicely thus to write about it. Oh! yes, Indian Summer in town is, I assure you, my dear, quite different from the same season in the country. And it is kept by country folk and city folk very differently. The former get up in the morning, and, after saying their prayers, look forth upon the broad fields and the thick woods, all wrapped in the smoky haze peculiar to the season, and knowing that their year's work is almost ended, and their crops gathered into the barns, experience a comfortable glow about the heart, and devote the day to visiting among their neighbors, with whom they talk about the harvest, and drink sweet cider and eat apples. The old women sit in the sun, and knit and gossip among themselves; while the young ones, with their lovers, hide themselves in warm and cosey nooks and listen to tales of love. In the city men go about their business as usual, and the bulls and bears on 'Change growl at and hug each other as if it was n't Indian Summer; and though some individuals when they meet pronounce it to be charming weather, almost too warm for overcoats, and not a bad day for mint-juleps or sherry-cobblers, the majority of them don't care a button about it. Those dear creatures, the ladies, however, really seem to enjoy it. They fill Broadway from morning until night. They go up and down its sidewalks like an army with banners, and make severe raids on milliners', dressmakers', and dry-goods' shopkeepers. They wear light silks and carry sunshades, and leave off their furs, and take colds, and ices at Maillard's, and do an infinite deal of unnecessary shopping; and this is about the way that country folk and city folk keep the Indian Summer."

My eloquence so astounded Mrs. Gray, that she remained for several minutes utterly incapable of saying a word, but at last, taking up our collection of prayer-books, and marshalling the children in a kind of military order, she stated that she was ready for church.

As we walked towards the sacred edifice it occurred to me that possibly my wife, who had, in our days of city life, been slightly up and down Broadway, might have taken exceptions to the last portion of my remarks. Though I saw no good reason for this, and consoled myself by thinking that we were all miserable sinners.

CHAPTER XXIII.

A Birthday. — Apples and Oranges. — Several little Ones. — A Learned Dissertation. — "All About It." — Daniel Due. — An Honest Man. — Dyeing. — A few Rhymes. — Due's Death. — The Club adjourned.

Y dear," I said to Mrs. Gray, as I lighted the evening lamp in the library, "if you will permit me to ring the bell for the maid to come and take the children, we will have a meeting alone by ourselves of our club this evening."

"Certainly, if you desire it," she replied; "but I half-promised them they might sit up this evening, and have some apples and walnuts; you know it is Mary's birthday."

"No! I was not aware of it," I answered. "But if this be the case, the little ones may, assuredly, be permitted to remain up later than usual, and have their apples and nuts, and join in the proceedings of the club. Let me see," I added, thoughtfully; "perhaps, after all, I did not forget that this was an eventful day, and provided for it accordingly. Young Lemon-peel," I continued, addressing my little boy, "suppose you go and examine my overcoat pockets, and if you find anything in them, bring it to me."

The roguish ambassador departed upon his mission, his eyes twinkling like stars, and his boots making a terrible clatter on the floor of the hall. During his absence, "Little Mary," I said, "tell me how old you are."

The little one, looking up into my face, answered:

"I 'm eight years old to-day, papa, and I think I ought to have a present."

"You are a very old girl for your age," I continued; "don't you think so, mamma?"

That estimable person only shook her head, as if to say that, so far as she was concerned, she wished she were a trifle older. I seated little Mary on my knee, and gave her to understand that as soon as the ten-years-old chap in the boots came back, the present she wished for would be forthcoming. As he entered the room, "the baby" left me to go and meet him. He had a small package of candies in one hand, and his other hand and pockets were filled with oranges, while a great doll was in his arms. Em., the eldest of the flock, who had been sitting at her mother's feet, reading aloud, at sight of the oranges, dropped her book and sprang to assist her brother in bringing these treasures to me. Between the trio's efforts, the oranges were dropped and went rolling about the floor. Then ensued a scramble for them, and as *pater familias* joined in, he succeeded in obtaining the lion's share.

"How very dignified you appear, Mr. Gray," exclaimed my wife, "prone on the floor. Suppose visitors should come in!"

"Well, what then?" I asked, recovering, however, my erect position.

"Nothing," she replied.

"Oh!" I answered.

It was, perhaps, well that this episode ended thus quickly and quietly, for little Mary was anxious to see her doll, and the other children were eager to put their teeth into the oranges, and, though the latter proved to be sour, they were none the less enjoyed.

"Oranges, my dear," I remarked, while the children were enjoying their collation, "are essentially a tropical fruit."

"Indeed!" interrupted Mrs. Gray; "I always thought they grew in the Arctic regions."

"The orange-tree, (*Citrus aurantium*,)" I continued,

giving no heed to Mrs. Gray's remark, "is to be found in profusion in nearly all of the warm climates of Europe, Northern Africa, and many parts of Asia and America. This orange" — taking one into my hand — "came, probably, from one of the Southern States, — Alabama, perhaps, where our good friends, the authors of 'Souvenirs of Travel' and 'Beulah,' reside."

Mrs. Gray thereupon regarded the said orange with great interest, as if she thought it might possibly speak a word or two regarding these lady friends.

"The islands of the Azores are famed for producing a fine variety. Did you ever see an orange orchard?" I asked.

Mrs. Gray never had.

"Nor have I," I continued; "but some time or other we will take a trip southward and look upon the orange-trees, and taste their fruit in its excellence."

"You have seen the orange-tree, I suppose," said Mrs. Gray, "growing in greenhouses?"

I had.

"So have I," exclaimed Em., who had, with the others, been standing open-eyed and open-mouthed around us. "I've seen them: their leaves are green and glossy, and their flowers white and pretty; their perfume is very sweet, too, and sometimes it almost makes me faint away. Grandma's tree used often to have flowers, and green oranges, and pale yellow ones, and those of a deep orange shade, all at the same time. I used to think it was a very nice sight, and I wondered why peaches and apples, and other fruits of the North, did n't grow so. Why don't they, papa?"

And, with this question for me to answer, Miss Em. seized another orange, and stood before me sucking its juice, while awaiting my reply.

Not being able to answer the question, however, I said:

"My little girl, I gave to you, a short time since, a book

called 'All About It; or, The History and Mystery of Common Things.' Now, I think if you will get that book to-morrow, probably you will be able to find in it the reason."

She promised to do so, and then, as it was nine o'clock, and "the baby" exhibited unmistakable symptoms of sleepiness, my wife rung the bell for the maid, who bore the little folks away to their cribs and couches.

After they had gone, Mrs. Gray and myself turned over the pages of many books, both large and small, including the "All About It" book, without learning from any of them the reason why the orange and lemon bear flowers and fruit at the same time, and peaches and apples do not.

"My dear," at last I said, "we will not puzzle our brains any more about it."

"But I am dying to know, my dear," she exclaimed.

"That, somehow, reminds me," I answered, "of Daniel Due, a very honest man whom I once knew, and who, meeting with an accident one day, shortly afterward took to dyeing."

"Did it kill him, Mr. Gray?" she asked.

"What," I rejoined, — "the 'accident,' or the 'one day,' or the 'dyeing?'"

"Pshaw!" she replied; "did he die, Mr. Gray?"

"No, thank fortune!" I answered; "he never dyed Mr. Gray."

"Gracious!" she ejaculated, "what a foolish man you are. Did he die himself, my dear?"

"Often, my love, often," I answered, — "at least, so far as his hands and arms were concerned."

"Then only his hands and arms died?" she said.

"Oh, yes, other things, too," I replied.

"His legs, perhaps?" suggested Mrs. Gray, ironically.

"Well, I am not sure about them," I answered, "but I think it probable."

"Mr. Gray," said my wife, sitting up in her chair like a judge, "did you see this man Due die?"

"Several times, my love," I answered; "and he dyed very well."

"Died very well, did he? he must have been hung, then," she added, savagely; "for when people die in their beds they usually are very ill."

"But he is n't dead yet," I said.

Mrs. Gray was dumb with astonishment.

"Listen," I continued, "while I relate the story of, and explain the mystery regarding —

"HONEST DANIEL DUE."

He was a very honest man,
None honester, though saint or sinner;
His name was Daniel Due, but Dan
We called him, when 't was time for dinner.
He worked on shares my father's farm
For thirty years, nor pay demanded,
Until he broke his favorite arm, —
His left one, — for he was left-handed.

And then he said he must retire
From active life, so took to dyeing;
But first my father paid his hire,
Which long had been on interest lying.
Six thousand dollars, I believe,
And something more, his wages came to;
At first this sum he 'd not receive,
And no receipt would sign his name to.

'T were deuced hard, he said, if he
Must do a thing that *seemed* like stealing;
He did n't see how it could be;
'T were very much like double-dealing;
It did n't have an honest look, —
Six thousand dollars was a "stunner;"
He guessed 't would buy up Sandy Hook,
And every ship and every gunner.

'T was long before he would give in,
And take the money that was due him;

At last my father raised a din,
  And vowed most fervently he 'd sue him.
The money he should have — 't was his,
  And he for years had worked to win it;
Cried Dan, "Now, squire, your dander 's riz,
  And this here Dan is goin' to shin it.

"I never have been sued," he said,
  "And I've been, boy and man together,
Just thirty years a-breaking bread,
  Through summer and through winter weather;
And honest bread it was and good,
  And you know, squire, the one as made it,
The very pink of womanhood,
  Though she 's your wife, — now I have said it."

And then he stood and scratched his head,
  And opened wide his eyes in wonder;
At last he cried, "Just shoot me dead,
  If I hain't got a plan — by thunder!
We 'll compromise the matter, squire;
  I 'll take six hundred — you, what 's over;
Then I 'll have just my honest hire,
  And on it I can live in clover."

A happy man was Daniel Due;
  He thought he 'd put it mighty clever,
But father knew a trick or two,
  And said, "Dan, you 'll our friendship sever,
Unless you 'll take your money now;
  Another "nay" from you, and never
Will I recognize you by bow
  Or word from this time on forever."

So Dan, more frightened far than hurt,
  Took up the gold, and went to dyeing,
And now he wears a colored shirt,
  And goes about the village crying,
From door to door, that he will dye
  On such a day, if Heaven be willing;
He 'll do it too, before your eye,
  And for the sum of one small shilling.

When Dan comes near my father's place,
  I tell you there is some confusion,

Danger is written on each face,
  For Daniel has one strange delusion,
And thinks he only can repay
  My father for his honest action,
By taking all our clothes away,
  To dye them to his satisfaction.

No matter what the garments be,
  If Dan but gets them they are "his'n;"
And when those clothes again you see,
  You think that Joseph's coat has risen.
The shirts are often dyed pea-green,
  The pantaloons are red or golden;
And silken robes, of wondrous sheen,
  To every color are beholden.

But Dan will live — and he will dye
  As long as dyeing holds in fashion, --
An honest man who scorns a lie,
  And never gets into a passion.
And when, at last, he comes to die,
  Attended by a good physician,
His soul will float across the sky,
  And into heaven's bright elysian.

"Oh!" exclaimed Mrs. Gray, as I concluded my recital, "I understand it clearly now — the dyeing and all that."

"And now, my dear," I remarked, "this concludes another meeting of our club around the evening lamp, and a very pleasant evening it has been. And now, with your permission, my love, we will adjourn *sine die!*"

"You have my permission, Mr. Gray." And straightway we adjourned.

10

CHAPTER XXIV.

An Old-fashioned Thanksgiving Day. — A Fast Day; how to keep it. — A Thanksgiving-Dinner. — Roasted Pig. — A Serious Misfortune. — Bierstadt, the Artist; his unnatural Inclinations; why he paints Fine Pictures. — Ice-water *vs.* Wine. — After-dinner Verses. — Arrival of Midnight and Miss Floy."

"SHALL I ever live," I asked Mrs. Gray, as we drew our chairs up before the blazing wood-fire, the other night, "to see an old-fashioned Thanksgiving Day, — such an one as I knew in my grandmother's time, when, having eaten just as much as I could of chicken-pie and turkey, with lots of vegetables, and heard my respected grandfather repeat, as he always did on such occasions, by way of a grace between the meat and the pudding, these quaint lines: —

> A turkey boiled is a turkey spoiled;
> A turkey roast is a turkey lost;
> But for a turkey brazed the Lord be praised.'

I still had room enough in my slender corporation for many magnificent slices of mince, pumpkin, and apple-pie, saucers of real calves'-feet jelly, — none of your gelatine innovations, — apples, raisins, and walnuts, all washed down with a glass of generous old port wine, given to me, at my last gasping extremity, by my over-indulgent grandparents? — I ask, shall I ever see such a day again?"

Mrs. Gray replied that she thought I never would.

"Not but that I am thankful enough in my heart," I continued, not heeding her interruption, "and sometimes go to church on these occasions, and eat a good enough dinner; but the spirit of the thing is gone. I cannot get up the proper degree of enthusiasm or appetite. Somehow, Thanksgiving Day seems a little *passè;* and I relish a fast day, which does not come quite as often, much more."

Thereupon Mrs. Gray said that she did not believe it.

"This clothing myself in sackcloth," I went on, paying no attention to my wife's remark, "and casting ashes upon my head, is a novelty for me, and wonderfully pleasing to the children, who 'admire' to see me do it. Then, as to the matter of fasting! it is a very good thing; and though I get wonderfully hungry at about my usual dinner-time, I manage to stick it out for an hour or two longer, when telling you, my dear, that I will go out and take a walk to carry off the edge of my appetite, I incontinently make a straight line for the nearest restaurant, where I indulge in an expensive course of oysters, raw, fried, stewed, and roasted, and frequent mugs of Aster ale. I discovered, too, one day, that notwithstanding my precepts and example in the house, when I went out to take my walk, you had a habit of sending to the same restaurant I frequented for a hundred oysters for yourself and children, though I never could discover any signs, when I returned home, of you or they having partaken of such fast-day alleviators."

Hereupon Mrs. Gray emphatically denied that she had ever condescended to adopt so miserable a piece of deception; but that she was not surprised to learn that I had been guilty of such deceit.

"What I wish to speak of," I continued, making no reply to my wife's last remark, "is Thanksgiving Day, and especially the thanksgiving-dinner, which should, after the first requisite in any dinner, namely, quality, recommend itself to those seated around the mahogany by its quantity. There should be enough and to spare of everything, and everybody on this occasion should eat as much, and perhaps — the children especially — a little more, than they want. In addition to the oysters, soup, fish, turkey, chicken-pie, vegetables innumerable, and pastry and dessert unlimitable, there should unquestionably be a roasted pig, — one which would have delighted even Charley Lamb, — a young, succulent, and crisply-cooked morsel, innocent of the sty, and stuffed with sweet smelling and savory herbs. Do you remember, my dear," I asked, "last Thanksgiving Day," and how we kept it at Mansfield Place?"

Mrs. Gray said that she did.

"But you do not remember," I continued, "because you never knew it, of the serious disappointment I met with on that day."

My wife looked up inquiringly.

"I had been drinking a bottle of choice wine," I said, "with a ruby-nosed friend who duly appreciated it, but who unfortunately had an engagement, as he expressed it, 'with an early dinner,' — I don't think he cared a dime for the giver of it, — and was obliged to leave without giving me an opportunity to open another bottle."

"Which I am very glad to learn," interrupted Mrs. Gray.

"But for which I was sorry," I replied. "So, while I sat mourning over my sad fate, — that of having no one for whom to open my second bottle, — I heard the door-bell ring, and exclaimed, 'Heaven fortunately has sent another mouth to moisten with wine. I will be thankful this day.' But when I saw who it was, my cup was dashed, unfilled, to the ground. For Bierstadt, who travelled overland to San Francisco, dwelt a week or two among the Mormons, clambered up the Rocky Mountains, slept — what to ordinary mortals would have been rheumatic slumbers — on the bleak sides of Mount Shasta, wandered foot-sore and weary through the Yo-Semite Valley, and lived years in Dusseldorf, among tuns of lager-beer and clouds of tobacco-smoke, scarcely knows the taste of liquor, and has never smoked a pipe in his life. The moment, therefore, I heard his pleasant voice, I knew that I would have to close my little wine-shop, and betake myself to that beverage which was found in Eden before Eve pressed cider from the apple. The first thing the man asked for, as I knew he would, was ice-water. Ice-water on Thanksgiving Day! the coldest day, too, of the season; and when, from my windows, I could see in the open lot, opposite the house, the boys skating on a little pond that winters there. Heaven forgive the man, I say, his unnatural inclinations. I tried to persuade him, in my smoothest tones, to forego, on this occasion, his favorite beverage, and quaff with me the amber-tinted wine. He said that would sound very well in poetry, and that wine was a nice thing to look at, and sip occasionally at a wedding; but for a steady drink he thought water preferable. Thereupon, I had the bottle, tall and graceful in form, and the delicately thin glasses, removed, and a double-walled ice-pitcher, with the figure of a polar bear on its top, filled with ice-water, and a stout goblet accompanying it, inhospitably placed before my guest. He drank copious libations, and declared it better than the wine of any vintage. Perhaps, after all, my dear, he is correct. I doubt if the grand pictures, full of power and broad effect, — of snow-clad mountains, deep and fertile valleys, bounding torrents and water-falls, broad lakes and flowing rivers, primeval forests, and rocks, such as that which the sacred writer had in his mind when he said, 'The shadow of a great rock in a weary land,' — which Bierstadt now turns yearly from his easel, could be painted by him if he clouded his clear brain with even the choicest vintages the world has known. The ice-water proved so great a temptation, that he dined with us for the sake of obtaining another glass of it."

"And was the refusal of our artist friend," asked my wife, "to partake of wine with you, the 'serious disappointment' on that day to which you refer?"

"Yes," I answered; "but I never bore him any ill-will on that account."

"Well, that was kind in you, I confess," said my wife, in a slightly ironical tone.

"I think it was," I replied; "but never mind. Did n't we have roasted pig that day for dinner, my dear?"

"No," she answered; "it was on the Thanksgiving Day of the previous year. Don't you remember that you wrote a poem in praise of roasted pig, which you recited at the table, where several artists and other friends were present?"

"Oh, yes," I replied; and my wife expressing a desire to hear again the lines in question, I turned to my writing-desk, and taking from one of its pigeon-holes a few sheets of paper, read aloud to her the following —

AFTER-DINNER VERSES.

THE curtain rises with unusual grace,
And shows a dining-room in Mansfield Place.
The hour — past seven, as any one may see,
Who 'll look upon the clock, and not at me.
The persons present — need my tongue reveal
The names of those my Muse would fain conceal?
Yes, did I hear? then be it so, my friend,
I 'll introduce them all before I end.
But, in the first place, I 've a tale to tell
About a pig whose tail curled very well, —
A tender suckling, guiltless of all sties,
His mother's pride, the darling of her eyes;
The loudest squeaker 'mong her little ones,
The Benjamin of all her many sons,
Torn from his mother's lactage-giving breast,
Where, not two moons ago, he first found rest,
By rude hands he was hurried to the slaughter,
And murdered just to please the butcher's daughter.
Stuck in the throat — his end, indeed, was bitter,
But 't was the end of all his mother's litter;
That sort of death, prefaced by no disease,
Runs through her family with perfect ease.
This little pig, as every one must know,
Was country-bred, — the butcher told me so, —
And butchers, as a class, all speak the truth,
Unless they learned to lie in early youth.
My confidence in him is clearly shown,

By buying sausages of him alone.
I 'm thankful though, the question does not lie
Between the bloody butcher-man and I;
Another chap, a youth of eighteen years,
With a white apron and uncommon ears,
Warts on his fingers, grease upon his hair,
And with a rowdy, semi-Bowery air,
Told me the fellow who had sold the pig
Unto the butcher was a perfect prig,
And, knowing him to be more knave than clown,
Believed the pig was stol'n from "Nestledown."
Alas! that such a sweet, young pig should die!
His bones lie here; his shadow none can spy;
His cheerful squeal, dried up and put away,
Will serve, perhaps, another pig some day.
What of his flesh? The larger part doth rest
In peace and safety under Gifford's vest.
The cracklings — soft! a lady 's in the case, —
She 's had her share, I read it in her face;
Of dressing, stuffing, call it what you will,
The long-haired Beard-ed man has had his fill.
Then Wheeler round, and none of you will fail
To see the wretch who robbed me of the tail, —
That lovely caudal, curled, and crisp, and red,
Once full of life, but now extremely dead.
His little ears, — of dainty pink within, —
Which never listened to a word of sin,
Were just the bits to give the gentle maid
Who on my left sits tastefully arrayed.
And of the ribs — those covering the heart —
This maiden's mother had a matron's part.
Then there 's the gravy — who but marked with pain,
The many times I asked for some in vain?
Who heard not all the pleading words I spake,
Imploring gravy for my stomach's sake?
Composed — the gravy, not the thing which aches
When unripe fruit, or cucumbers, one takes —
With dexterous skill and culinary care,
Of liver, heart, and other tidbits rare,
Next to the brain, — which he who got required, —
The sauce is by most epicures desired.
Ought any wife among you give a guest
That which she knew her husband liked the best?
Wedlock forbid! Then why keep back from me

Those spoonfuls which mine gave to McEntee.
Who got the feet, and who the head did gain,
Are questions which my muse will ask in vain;
That wreck, that skeleton of youthful pork,
Torn, cut, and mangled by the knife and fork,
Alone remains to claim a pitying tear,
From the old cook, who 'll drown her grief in beer.
Nipped in the bud, — plucked off like unripe fruit, —
Torn from the earth ere' he had learned to root,
The little pig no more his squeak shall raise,
Nor scamper after straws in wild amaze;
No more shall kink his lovely tail in air,
Nor think his bristles very pretty hair;
Cock his bright eyes up at the noonday sun,
Prick up his ears and nimbly frisk and run.
No more partake, his hunger ne'er appeased,
Of various meals just when and how he pleased,
But having, haply, given up the ghost,
Part of his flesh was Coffin-ed by your host;
The rest, partaken with no sense of fear,
May prove to you a nightmare *souvenir*,
Unless you follow this advice of mine,
To drink the pig's repose in sparkling wine.

And so, occupied with many pleasant reminiscences of by-gone Thanksgiving times, did my wife and I, before the blazing hearth, sit and chat until midnight and Miss Floy — who had been scribbling in her own room — came in together.

CHAPTER XXV.

Edwin Booth as Hamlet. — In the Library. — A Smoky Scent and a Lemony Perfume. — Chartreuse. — A Thimbleful. — Jolly Monks. — "The Lover's Appeal." — The Game of Billiards. — Berger. — His Marvellous Feats. — Another Player, Pierre Carme.

WE had been to town to see Edwin Booth in "Hamlet," and, returning by a late train, did not reach Woodbine Cottage until long after midnight, yet neither Mrs. Gray nor myself were disposed to sleep. We sat in the library, before the grate, the dying embers in which I was stirring into something like life with the poker; while Mrs. Gray was turning over the pages of "Shakspeare." A small copper kettle, on the smouldering coals, seemed to be singing its very life away, and losing itself behind a cloud of steam that issued from its nozzle. A smoky scent and a lemony perfume filled the apartment. A storm was brewing without, but something better was brewing within. I was thinking of the wassail-bowls of olden times, of the flagons of Flemish beer, of the nectar of Jove, of the sack that Falstaff quaffed, of the Lachryma Christi which princes drank, of the thimbleful of Doppel Kümmel I tasted on board of the Russian flag-ship last season, and of that precious *liqueur* Chartreuse, of which even I have often sipped.

"It is certainly very excellent," I uttered.

"Excellent!" echoed Mrs. Gray; "he is wonderful."

"I don't know its superior," I said.

"Its!" exclaimed Mrs. Gray; "he, you mean;" and she glanced suspiciously at the contents of my glass.

"No, my dear,' I responded; "I prefer the neuter to the masculine gender in this case."

"You are wrong, so far as grammar is concerned, Mr. Gray," she replied; "but if you will indulge in these obnoxious punches I ought not to expect anything more grammatical from you. I shall, no doubt, be addressed, by-and-by, as 'it,' or by some term quite as inappropriate."

"Mrs. Gray," I exclaimed, "you astonish me; of what or whom, pray, were you speaking?"

"Why, Mr. Booth's personation of *Hamlet*, of course."

"Oh!" I said, "I thought it was of something else."

"What 'something else'?" she asked.

"Chartreuse," I answered.

"And what is 'Chartreuse'?" she inquired.

"Guess," I said.

Now, nothing annoys my estimable spouse more than being requested to guess at a matter of which she possesses no knowledge. It almost invariably has the effect of causing her either to leave the room in an abrupt manner, or else to effectually close her lips for fifteen minutes. In the present instance, however, thinking she might possibly be correct, she responded, after a brief pause, "Why, it is, I presume, somewhat of the nature of a *charlotte-russe*, — at all events, it sounds similarly."

"Wrong, my dear," I said, "but ingeniously answered; Chartreuse is a *liqueur* made in the Alps, from various herbs which grow just below the boundary where vegetation ceases and snow and ice commence. There are three kinds, of which the best is amber-hued, oily, and possessing a delicious perfume. It is usually sipped after dinner, and follows the coffee. A thimbleful is sufficient. It is made by the monks who dwell at Chartreuse."

"For my part," remarked Mrs. Gray, "I think the monks might be better employed."

"You would not say so, my dear," I replied, "if you had tasted it. Some day, when my ships come home, I will bring you a flask of it, and though at first you may not receive it with favor, — for, after all, the taste for it is an acquired one, — you will, in a brief time, deem it a most delicious beverage."

"Mr. Gray," said my wife, "I do not think I care to taste Chartreuse. You like it because it is, probably, an expensive *liqueur*, and not because you really relish it. You have a *penchant*, I think, for all kinds of viands that are costly and rare."

"This, doubtless, was the reason," I said, "why I preferred you, my dear, to the many other charming beings who, in the days of my bachelorhood, crossed my path."

"I would I could believe it, Mr. Gray," she replied; "but how often have you addressed any love-poem to me like those you used to write to the Fannies and the Annies, and the little Southern maids of your boyhood's days?"

"Not often," I responded; "but ask yourself if, after all, such sentimental tokens of regard can be placed in the balance to outweigh those words of love I uttered at the chancel-rails? No! a thousand times no! my dear, I know you will answer."

"You are certainly very kind to reply for me," my wife said, "and I will not say but that you are correct; still I would like to have you address some verses to me, on the anniversary of our marriage, such as you did on my last birthday."

"Suppose," I replied, "I write a Christmas carol for you, in which I praise your beauty and virtues?"

Mrs. Gray assumed an injured air, and turned over the leaves of her book, without replying. After a pause, during which I sipped the contents of my goblet, I added: —

"The truth is, that the verses I wrote to my early charmers were flippant, foolish, and unworthy of being addressed to my wife. For instance," I continued, turning to my scrap-book, and taking therefrom the following lines, entitled —

THE LOVER'S APPEAL.

I LOVE thee! and my heart is proudly ringing
The endless changes of these words to-day,
While round my pathway Hope is gayly singing
The music which befits a wedding-lay.
The clouds of sorrow which above me floated,
Trailing their sable robes before my sight,
In thy sweet presence, silently, unnoted,
Have vanished, and bright day succeeded night.

I love thee! 'T is no weak or foolish dreaming,
The passing fancy of an idle hour;
But like the sunshine, full from heaven streaming,
In all its noontide glory, pomp, and power,
It fills my being with a deep devotion
Which only those who truly love can know,
And, as the moon affects the tides of ocean,
So causest thou my love to ebb and flow.

I love thee! and my thoughts are fondly turning
To when within thy presence I was brought,
And, all unconscious, happily was learning
A lesson which in Eden first was taught.
That blessèd hour with many a joyous vision,
Most happy dreams, fond hopes and pure desires,
Within my memory's bright and fair elysian
Is lighted now by love's warm, quenchless fires.

I love thee! Do not, dear one, I implore thee,
Turn from my words disdainfully away,
Nor doubt my truth when saying, I adore thee,
And shall as long as reason holds its sway.
My heart, with all its deep and true affection,
I lay confidingly upon thy shrine;
Accept it, and through life the recollection
Shall be to thee a joy almost divine.

"That is not so bad," my wife said, "and I only wish you would address as pleasing ones to me. Your passionate pleadings, though, I presume, had no effect on the young lady addressed?"

"Well, I don't know about that," I replied. "The truth is, I met you shortly after I sent them, and — well, I did n't follow up any advantage I may have gained thereby, nor pressed my suit as I would otherwise have done."

"Which, doubtless, you have since regretted?" my wife said inquiringly.

"No," I replied, slowly, uttering my words as if I were considering the matter. "I am not certain that I regret it in the least. If you, now," I said, speaking more briskly and decisively, "had turned away from me, I might have regretted the course affairs took, and taken to billiards or some other disreputable games."

"Is billiards a disreputable game?" asked my wife. "I was under the impression that it was of an innocent character."

"Oh," I replied, "one of the newspapers has recently discovered that it is entirely unworthy of a gentleman's attention. Though, when I witnessed Monsieur Berger's playing a few years ago, I thought there was poetry in billiards."

"And who, pray," asked my wife, "is Monsieur Berger?"

"Monsieur Berger," I replied, "is a Frenchman, a native of Lyons, and a man of considerable weight, doubtless, in his own country, as indeed he is in this, since he weighs — or did, when in this country — about three hundred pounds. Of course, his figure is rotund, and seems like an immense billiard ball, crowned with a smaller one, which represents his head. He is quite bald; his eyes are small, black, and sparkling; his mouth large, and his countenance, when in repose, uninteresting; but when he is speaking, or engaged in his favorite game, it lights up with a smile that attracts and rivets attention. There is, doubtless, much humor in his composition; and that he is kind and generous in disposition, his career here fully proved. He regards the ivory balls, with which he plays, almost as a father does his children, addressing them by pet names and terms of endearment, as they move, seemingly endowed with life, here and there, at his bidding. What Morphy is in the world of chess, that is Berger in the realm of billiards, — king, emperor, czar over all competitors. Marvellous, ay, almost miraculous, is his play; and yet, though every one sees how it is done, none are able to follow it. He causes the balls to accomplish wonderful feats. At his bidding, and simply at the touch of his cue, they run along the elevated edge of the table; they move half-way across the table, and then return to the point from whence they started; they gather together in one corner; they revolve around a hat; they leap into a hat, and perform other strange and curious feats."

"Have you seen all this, Mr. Gray?" asked my wife, incredulously.

"I have, my dear, and more," I replied.

"When?" she demanded.

"You remember, perhaps, the afternoon I left you at the door of your cousin's house in Tenth Street, saying I would return in ten minutes?"

"I should think I ought to, Mr. Gray," said my wife, somewhat reproachfully; "for you kept me waiting from five o'clock till ten in the evening, before you returned. I am not apt to forget such acts of impoliteness, even after the lapse of years."

"But I apologized to you, my dear, for my dilatoriness, I remember," I said.

"Apologized! You only told me you met a friend who asked you to dine with him, and you went. I don't regard that as an apology."

"Well, never mind about it now, my dear," I said; "it's long since past, and, I trust, forgiven. At any rate, that night I met Berger. I dined at a French restaurant with Gignoux, the artist. The great billiard-player also dined there; and after dinner, which was an hour and a half long, and consisted of ten courses, — first, soup; second, fish" ——

"Never mind about the courses, Mr. Gray," interrupted my wife; "tell me about Berger."

"Well, after dinner," I repeated, "I was introduced to Berger. His hand was as soft and plump as a woman's, my dear, and he wore a ring on the middle finger of his left hand, a diamond, set around with blue stones: what do you call them?"

"Turquoise, I presume you mean," replied Mrs. Gray.

"Yes, I think you 're correct. Well," I continued, "although Berger spoke scarcely a word of English, and my knowledge of French is not very extensive, we managed to hold a brief conversation together, by the help of Gignoux, who stood near. Afterward, we went to Phelan's room, and saw Berger play a game of billiards with one of our best American players, Phelan himself, who made, however, but thirty-three points to Berger's one hundred. Now, what do you think of that, my dear?"

"As I am unacquainted with the game, my opinion would be worth nothing," she answered; "but if you will explain it to me, I shall be perhaps better able to answer."

"Billiards, my dear," I said, taking a position before the fire, on the rug, from which I had retired when the ten-minute business came up, — "billiards," I repeated, impressively, "is an ingenious kind of game, invented, I believe, by a Frenchman, and played on a rectangular table, with white and red ivory balls, which are driven by a cue, — a stout stick, five or six feet in length. This instrument the player holds in his right hand, resting it over the left, supported by the forefinger and thumb. The table on which the game is played is about twelve feet long and six wide, or, rather, in the exact form of an oblong. The bed of the table is generally of marble or slate, covered with fine green cloth, and the edge surrounded with elastic cushions, to prevent the balls rolling off and to make them rebound. There are six holes, or pockets. These are affixed to the four corners and midway of the table, opposite to each other, to receive the balls in playing. The Frenchman's table, however, — which he brought with him, — was without these pockets, the disuse of which makes the game more scientific and difficult to play. Indeed, Berger's game, on his own table, was as much superior to the game as usually played in this country as the American game is to the schoolboy's game of marbles. Still the American game has its votaries, and there are those who believe that the great Frenchman would be conquered if he played the usual game of the country and on American tables. Berger's table, I think, was larger than those used in this country."

"But you have not yet described to me the game itself. I know no more what constitutes the playing and winning of the game than if you had not spoken a word about it. Do you play it, Mr. Gray?"

"I confess that I do not. My education in that respect has been sadly neglected, so that it is little wonder I cannot make the game clear to your understanding."

"Well, no matter," replied the amiable woman. "I have at least been interested in what you have told me respecting this wonderful player, and his powers."

"Since Berger was here, another celebrated French player has visited us. His name is Pierre Carme," I said; "and though he failed to play with Kavanagh, a celebrated American player, yet he is probably an equal in the game to Berger himself. And now, my dear, as the fire is getting low, and the voice of my pet chanticleer warns me that daylight is approaching, I think we had better retire, and endeavor to get a few hours' sleep."

And we retired.

CHAPTER XXVI.

A Rainy Sunday. — An Equinoctial Storm. — Van der Palm. — A Comfortable Feeling. — Gathering my Harvest. — A Biblical Reference. —A Catalogue. — Gold-diggers *vs.* Potato-diggers. — A Doubter.—Thomas. A Barrel of Ale. — Aleing. — How to open a Barrel of Ale. — A lively Mood. — Breaking a Commandment. — "Ha! ha!" — October's Brewage.

IT was a rainy Sunday. One of the half-dozen equinoctial storms that always come in the autumn was raging. The wind was stripping the leaves from the trees in the most summary manner. The russet, golden, and scarlet robes which the forest had worn were being torn into shreds and patches, and scattered broadcast over the land. Only the woodbine clinging to the veranda in front of my cottage retained its green leaves, and even a sprig or two of fresh blossoms scented the air. The "melancholy days" had indeed come; and though out-of-doors it was sad enough, within nothing could be more cheerful. The fire blazed on the hearth; Mrs. Gray was reading a sermon by Van der Palm, an erudite old Dutchman, who was born a hundred years ago in Rotterdam, and who afterward became a professor in the University of Leyden, and was greatly esteemed for his piety and learning; and the children were variously engaged in reading, roasting chestnuts, and the Biblical play of Noah's Ark. I, in a somewhat contemplative mood, stood at the window gazing upon the dreary landscape, and contrasting the without with the within.

The feeling I possessed was a very comfortable one, for I knew that my crops were safely housed; that there was a barrel of ale in my cellar; several tons of coal and cords of wood in my woodshed; and a happy household under my roof-tree.

"In regard to getting in my crops and opening my barrel of ale, I desire," I said to Mrs. Gray, "to say a few words."

My wife gave me to understand that I might say as many as I liked.

"I think I told you," I said, "that I remained at home yesterday expressly to gather my harvest. I am happy to say, my dear, that I fully accomplished it. In the morning, after reading the papers of the day, I proceeded to take a view of the garden. I walked around it several times, and took an accurate memorandum of its contents. Then I came into the house, and drank a glass of ale and cut a pie, for I was alike thirsty and possessed of a good appetite. Then I added up in my memorandum-book the entire quantity of vegetables to be harvested. And what do you think was the result?"

"I am certain," Mrs. Gray replied, "I cannot tell; but I suppose no large quantity, for I notice our barns are not bursting with plenty, neither are our presses running over with new wine."

Now, as we have only one small shed, and not a barn, on the premises, and as all the presses we possess are the few contained in the house, and which are termed clothes-presses, this Biblical reference did not strike me as being particularly applicable. But I said nothing in reply thereto, and contented myself with reading aloud from my note-book as follows: —

14 heads of white cabbages.
3 " red "
6 dozen ears of sweet corn.
4 " " "pop" " for the children.
8 " " yellow " for the fowls.
2 pecks of onions.
10 large pumpkins.

17 small pumpkins
4 bushels of turnips.
15 " potatoes.
1 quart of nasturtiums.
1 peck green tomatoes for pickling.
2 bushels of carrots.
1 bushel of parsnips.
1 " beets, and
5 bunches of grapes, slightly frostbitten.

"Not a bad show," I said, "for less than an acre of ground, and considering, too, that we have gathered through the summer many vegetables for our table, not, of course, enumerated in this catalogue."

"It certainly sounds very largely," said my wife, "and I only trust it will turn out as well."

"It has," I said; "every article therein enumerated is already garnered, and, if there be any difference, it is that some of the quantities overrun my estimate. Yesterday afternoon, although you may not be aware of it, I worked like a farmer. I literally gained my bread by the sweat of my brow. Gold-diggers may know pleasure in their occupation, and grave-diggers may even find a kind of sad amusement in their business; but I doubt very much if any one ever took any delight in digging potatoes. It gives one an awful crick in the back; and then the process of stooping down to pick them up after they are dug, is very much, to my thinking, like what warping the spinal column over a low fire would be. I confess I would much rather lose all my potatoes than have the same labor to go over again."

"But I thought," said my wife, "that Michael dug the potatoes, and that you did little more than direct him in his operations. I am sure you passed the greater part of the afternoon in the house."

"Oh, there you are greatly mistaken," I said; "for I am quite certain that, with the exception of the little time I was with my savage literary friend, I was digging potatoes."

"Well, as you went to your friend's," said the matter-of-fact woman, "at about one o'clock, and did n't return home until nearly five o'clock, it certainly appears to me that you could have given little attention to getting in your vegetables."

"Pooh, pooh!" I replied; "by-and-by, perhaps, you'll question the fact of my having got in any vegetables at all."

"Well, the truth is," she answered, "I shall be in doubt in the matter until I see them."

"Perhaps," I said, somewhat vexed, "you would like to put your fingers upon the potatoes and taste of the cabbages before you will believe. And perhaps, too," I continued, "you will doubt whether I have a barrel of ale in the cellar?"

"No," she replied, "for of it I have tasted."

"And a very good reason it is for believing," I answered. "But if you had assisted in opening it, you would have received much more positive proof of its presence."

Mrs. Gray simply said "ah?" interrogatively, and commenced laughing.

"October ale, my dear," I continued, not heeding her laughter, "when it is new, is exceedingly lively, and in tapping a barrel of it, you should be lively yourself. I had much trouble, as you are aware, in getting that barrel into the cellar. I think I was two hours about it. Then I waited two days for it to settle before tapping it. I should not have opened it then, but that you said you would like a glass of it at lunch. I was just ready to go to the city, but, having five minutes to spare, I consented to employ that time in tapping the ale. I afterward wished I had not; for, when I attempted to insert the wooden faucet into the barrel by driving in the spigot, whether the cunning of my hand gave out, or whether past successes in this line begat carelessness on my part, I cannot tell; but, although the plug went in, the faucet somehow refused to follow, and the jolly ale, finding a vent, came flying out in the liveliest of moods, knocking the faucet out of my hand, and pouring itself in a foaming stream over the cellar floor. I tried to stop it by placing my hand over the hole, but with little success; for the ale forced its way through my fingers, spirting in many streams over me, and blinding me with its spray. The lighted candle, which the gloom of the cellar made it necessary for me to carry, was put out, and I was left in comparative darkness. My position was an unpleasant one, and what to do puzzled me sadly. If I took my hand off of the vent to grope in the dark for the faucet, I should lose all my ale, and to remain in the position I was much longer, was but doing little better. I endeavored, by shouting, to make myself heard above stairs; but, whether the baby cried so loudly as to prevent you from hearing me, or what it was, I do not know; but, at all events, I failed in bringing to my aid any assistance. I endured this position of affairs patiently for a few minutes longer, hoping for the best, until I heard the whistle of the approaching train which was to have carried me to town; then, rendered desperate, I wished the ale in Jericho, and taking my hand from the vent, went up-stairs, leaving the ale to flow in peace. The result was that I lost a half-barrel of ale, ruined my clothes, missed my train, and broke — what was worse than all — into a great many pieces the Third Commandment. I don't know that I should have broken it as extensively as I did, if you and Miss Floy had not laughed at me so provokingly when I made my appearance and told you what had happened."

"It was too bad," said my wife; "but you did, look so funny. Your hair and whiskers were covered with foam, and your clothes were dripping wet. You seemed half-drowned, and a more beery-appearing individual I never beheld. I have to laugh every time I think of it."

And my wife "he! he'd!" in a miserable little way, which was even then exceedingly provoking. I said nothing, however, but stood quietly at the window and gazed upon the wet and dreary landscape.

When Mrs. Gray had exhausted her risible efforts, she asked me how I managed to save half a barrel of the ale.

"Because," I said, "the barrel of ale the Taylors sent fortunately came in two half-barrels, and, as I only tapped one of them on that occasion, the other remained full."

"And you were more careful, I presume," she remarked, "when you came to open that than you were when opening the first."

"I was. And now, my dear, if you have no objection," I said, "I will draw a pitcher of October's brewage, pure and creamy, fragrant of hops and malt new made, and we will together drink thereof."

And we drank.

Later in the day, when it had ceased raining, and a dim, gray mist lay softly upon the earth, wrapping the landscape in its chilly folds, I took a walk down to the Bronx. A thin veil hung over the water, and the trees bordering its banks loomed spectrally through the fog, their slender limbs bare of leaves, and their trunks moist and slimy. Everything bore an ashen hue, save where the earth, showing through the wet and rotting leaves, appeared brown and dingy. Not a sound arose to break the silence of the scene, and the very water of the stream lay under the fog with a sense of weight, as it were, upon its bosom. All the scene was one of gloom, and I thought that nature had indeed spread her pall upon the earth for the dying year to rest herself under. The landscape oppressed me with sadness, and I was glad to return to the warmth and light of my cottage.

A WINTER MORNING. R. GIGNOUX.

CHAPTER XXVII.

Evacuation Day in Town. —The Twenty-fourth and the Twenty-fifth. — The Veterans of 1812. — How my little ones celebrated the Day. — Raising the Flag. — Muskets and Swords. — A War-horse.— A New Recruit. — Her Banner. — A Scramble. — High Pay. — Rations. — Drafted Boys. — Tin Drums. — A March. Disbanding.— A Girl's Tea-party. — A Boy's Circus. — A private Box. — The Eighty-second Anniversary.

Y little ones celebrated, in an appropriate manner, at Woodbine Cottage, Evacuation Day. There was a slight confusion in their minds as to the proper day whereon to celebrate it. This arose, doubtless, from the fact that the commanding general in town, who had an engagement to attend an afternoon tea-party on the twenty-fifth instant, which he wished to keep, had, in consequence, ordered his soldiers to celebrate the day on the twenty-fourth. My young folks had become acquainted with this circumstance through the newspapers; and, as they believe everything that they read in the papers, they naturally supposed that the latter was the proper day, and that I was mistaken in proclaiming the former to be the right one. When my savage literary friend, who had been a captain, or something of that kind, in the old Sixty-ninth Regiment, assured them that the twenty-fifth was the day, they agreed to accept it as such, and duly keep it.

It was with pleasure I observed that the Veterans of 1812 also kept, with music and flying colors, the proper day in town. That handful of graybeards, some with old regimental cocked hats and epaulets, others in citizens' attire, as they marched down Broadway that pleasant afternoon, was a sight worth beholding. As they moved along, two by two, to the inspiriting sounds of the drum and fife, they seemed to have renewed their youth; and, scorning the usual support of their canes, they shouldered them, as they did their muskets fifty years ago, and, with brisk steps, marched gallantly along. There was no tottering nor feebleness apparent in their movements; the bent backs were straightened; the dim eyes regained their brightness; and the wrinkles of age were smoothed upon their faces, while the spirit and courage of brave soldiers shone on their countenances. Some of these veterans were close on to a hundred years of age, and, though I believe none of them had seen service in the Revolutionary War, yet a few of them had lived in those days, and had fathers and brothers in its battles.

The sight of these veterans reminded me of a poem, written by my friend Seyton May, on the occasion of some of the soldiers of 1812 visiting Washington city, on January 8th, 1855, to celebrate the anniversary of the battle of New Orleans. As I walked along the crowded street, after they had passed, I repeated to myself the following verses of the poem: —

"March on! ye are not old to-day!
The lofty music's cheering sound
The echo of the past hath found!
Ye are not old to-day!

"Yon banner in your line is old,
'T is torn and faded — pierced by balls;
It waves — and all your youth recalls —
And so ye are not old!

"But yesterday your step was slow,
But yesterday each form was bowed;
To-day, — of well-won victories proud,
Ready again for war!"

When I told my little ones, on my return home, that I had seen these brave old soldiers, they grew quite excited, and said that I ought to have taken them into town, that they, also, might have seen them. They would have preferred it to going to Barnum's Museum, where I had promised to take them, Saturday afternoon. They proceeded to tell me how they had celebrated the day, and, as I am writing this chapter especially for the entertainment of small readers, I think I can do no better than give the account as nearly as possible in the language of the little boy who related it.

"You know, papa," he said, "that the first thing I did this morning, when I got up, was to raise the flag on the staff down at the foot of the garden, and the next thing was to eat my breakfast. After breakfast, I got Em. and Sis to assemble round the flag-staff, where I drilled them with muskets and swords, — only we did n't have muskets and swords, you know, but just canes and such kind of arms. Em. had your charter-oak cane that the good old soldier, who died at Hillside, left you, and Sis had the gold-headed one, made from 'Old Ironsides.' I was the general, and so I had a sword, — not a real one, but just the carving-knife, not the best one, but the other one; and, then, what do you think I got?"

"Why, I think," I replied, "that you got a whipping from the cook."

"No, I did n't, though," he answered; "and I 'd just like to see her try to give me a whipping — that 's all. No; I got the goat and made a war-horse of her; and, I tell you, she was gay. It was just as much as I could do to keep on her — she danced and jumped about so. We marched in procession up to Mr. Jack's, and there we got a new recruit, Florry. She carried a flag made out of a silk apron, and she forgot to take some chestnuts out of the pocket; so, when she unfurled it, and the wind waved it about, they all fell out upon the ground, and then we broke ranks, and scrambled for them."

"Yes," interrupted Em., "and you and the goat got the most."

"That 's so," said the boy, "and generals ought always to have the most. They get more pay than privates, you know."

"But the goat was n't a general, was she?" asked Em.

"No, not exactly," he answered; "but never mind talking about that now. Papa don't care anything about what the goat did; he wants to know what we did. Don't you, papa?"

"Yes," I replied, "I am much interested in your account of the day's proceedings."

"Well, after we got Florry," he continued, "we marched down again to the house, where I dismounted, and went and got some rations, — hard tack, you know, and cheese. Then I drafted a couple of little boys who came along, and made 'em drummers."

"Yes," said Em., "and you 'd better tell pa what they did."

"Oh, hush! do, now. If you keep talking so much, I shall never get through."

"But what did your drummers do?" I asked.

"Oh, nothing much; they just drummed, that 's all," he replied.

"Yes," said Em., "and they drummed holes in the bottoms of two tin pails. That 's what they did."

"Oh, they were old pails, papa," the boy said; "they were n't good for much. Em. is all the while telling everything. Ma said she did n't care" ——

"Oh!" exclaimed Em., "what a story."

"Much," added the little rascal.

"It is very improper," I said, "to drum holes into the bottoms of tin pails, — very improper, indeed. Tin pails cost money, and I can't afford to have them destroyed in that way," I said.

"Well, you see, papa, they did n't mean to do it — but the pails had poor bottoms. They ought to have been strong enough to stand a little beating on Evacuation Day."

"Well, well," I said, "I suppose I will have to overlook it."

The boy gazed at his sister triumphantly.

"After we 'd eaten our rations, we marched up the hill; and then we marched down again. And then we hurrahed ever so many times. And then the goat ran away with me, and Gumbo ran after the goat, and I fell off; and the dog and the goat had a fight, and Gumbo whipped Nan; and then we disbanded, and came into the house. And I cracked some nuts, and Em. had a tea-party; but she would n't invite me to it, so I had a circus out in the barn, and I guess I did n't ask her to come to it."

"That was not right," I said; "Em. should have asked you to her party, and you should have been kind enough to have invited her to attend your circus."

"Papa," said Em., "I would have asked him, but he said he did n't want to go to a girl's party. And I am sure I did n't care about his coming; for he always wants to drink the tea out of the teapot, and pocket all the sugar from the sugar-bowl, and eat the butter off of the plate."

"You have such a little bit on the table," said the naughty boy, "that, when I am hungry, all of it don't seem but a mouthful. But I 'm going to have another circus next Saturday, papa, and then, if Em. wants to come to it, she can. She can sit in the private box all day, if she likes, and see me stand on my head."

"You don't mean to say that you intend to stand on your head all day?" I asked.

"Oh, no; only a minute or two at a time, you know," he answered; "but she can sit in the box all day if she wants to, and watch me when I do it."

"Now, papa," said Em., "will you tell me what Evacuation Day is for? — for I am sure I don't know."

"Evacuation Day, my little ones," I said, "is so called because, on this day, eighty-two years ago, the British troops evacuated or marched out of the city of New York, of which they had possession, and the American troops marched in. Since then, every year, with few exceptions, the day has been appropriately celebrated. If you will read your "History of the Revolutionary War," you will find the account fully recorded. And now, my children, we will go to dinner.

CHAPTER XXVIII.

Birthday Dinners. — the Pilgrim Fathers. — Yankee, Southern, Indian, Puritan, and Cavalier Blood. — Mary Morey. — Pies and Puddings. — The Tenth of December. — A Second Centenary. — A Golden Wedding. Indian Cruelty. — Blind-Man's-Buff. — Asleep. — Arrival of Visitors.

"WELL, my dear," I said, as I lighted the lamp in the library, "no crowned head in all Europe has had a better dinner this day than I; and I even doubt if one of the descendants of the Pilgrim Fathers — those individuals who are supposed to do their utmost in the way of eating on Thanksgiving Day — will rise from the table to-morrow, more satisfied with his meal, or better filled than I now am. Still, I would not have you to understand, my dear, that I do not feel called on to do my best day's eating on Thanksgiving Day, though I regard it simply as preparatory — a getting the house into order, as it were — for that greatest of all feasts, a Christmas dinner. You, Mrs. Gray, who have the blood, not only of the hero of Bennington, but of one of the noblest of Virginian families, in your veins, can easily understand why I, of Indian, Puritan, and Cavalier descent, should readily accept and celebrate, not only Thanksgiving Day and Christmas, but such festal days — as nearly as I can learn when they occurred — which the original inhabitants of our country were wont to celebrate."

"This is first time, Mr. Gray," said my wife, "I ever heard that you were part Indian, though I have always thought your complexion was tawny. When, pray, did you learn this interesting fact?"

"Oh, years ago, my dear," I replied; "if you will turn

to the registry in the old family Bible — the large one in the corner of the room — you may read, in the handwriting of one of my respected progenitors, a marriage between an Indian woman, whose baptismal name was Mary Morey, and Hezekiah Gardner, which took place December 20th, 1665. Unfortunately, the place where it occurred, and the name of the officiating minister, are not recorded. It must have taken place, however, in the Province of Massachusetts, and the bride probably belonged to the Narragansetts. For aught that I know, she may have been a daughter of Massasoit, and, consequently, a princess. If so, I should have met the Prince of Wales, when here, upon more equal ground than I did. Had I thought of it in time, I should have claimed the right of our little daughter — whose birthday dinner we have just assisted at — to open the ball at the Academy of Music with the youthful prince."

" Now, my dear," interposed my matter-of-fact wife, " you speak ridiculously. For my part, I am very thankful that birthday dinners do not come every day. I think hereafter I will not use brandy in the mince-pies, nor put wine into the pudding-sauce. You partake too largely of both, and the liquor in them seems to affect you, — making you talk nonsense."

" A capital idea, Mrs. Gray," I replied ; " the pie and the pudding will be the better for the children without these additions ; and as for me, I prefer my liquors plain, without being united with pastry or sauce."

" I fear, Mr. Gray," she answered, " that you are incorrigible, and that it will be better, after all, for me to have the pies and pudding-sauce as I now do."

" If you suit yourself, my love, in this matter," I said, " you may be assured of its pleasing me."

Mrs. Gray simply smiled.

" The dinner," I added, " was really admirable, and if the one on the twentieth of December be equal to it, I shall be perfectly satisfied."

"Why," asked Mrs. Gray, "do you name the twentieth of December?"

"Because," I replied, "it is the second centennial anniversary of the Indian marriage referred to a few minutes ago."

"And do you think, Mr. Gray," she inquired, "that it is worth our while to celebrate that event at this distant day?"

"Certainly, my dear," I replied.

"Why, what have we to do with it?" she asked.

We may not have a great deal to do with it; but individually, my love," I said, "I, being a lineal descendant of that couple, am probably indebted to them for existence. I have, of course, no desire to celebrate the anniversary of their marriage every year, and would do so now only because it will be the two hundredth anniversary. Just think of it for a moment, my dear! It is better than a golden wedding in one's family."

"Suppose, then, we term it," suggested Mrs. Gray, "a copper wedding?"

"Mrs. Gray," I uttered, in a measured tone, as I rose from my chair and took my favorite place on the rug before the grate,—"Mrs. Gray," I repeated, "if you wish to affront me, you may call it a copper wedding."

And I jingled half-a-dozen pennies within my pocket.

"Why, the truth, notwithstanding your remark, Mrs. Gray, is, that a more noble, ingenuous, and faithful race than the Indian never run its course on the globe."

"I have been told, on the contrary," she said, "that they were cruel, vindictive, and treacherous; that they had rather meet an enemy than a friend: as in the former case they could exercise the natural propensity that led them to delight in bloodshedding; while in the latter event occurring, they could enjoy only a moderate degree of pleasure in the smoking of a pipe of peace. A human being's scalp was more prized by them than a costly gift of furs or rarest plumes."

"Wrong, my dear," I answered,—"all wrong. As nature made him, before the white man invaded his hunting-grounds, there was no truer being on the earth than the Indian. As primitive in his habits and simple in his desires as our first parents before the fall; courageous as a lion and docile as a lamb, as occasion demanded, he was, in many respects, a better man than any of the followers of Columbus when they landed on the shores of this Continent."

"Very well spoken, Mr. Gray," said my wife, approvingly; "I like to see men stand up for their kin, even if they be Indians. It shows—if you will excuse the expression—pluck."

"Well," my wife added, after a pause, "as the repetition of this dinner will not occur in a hundred years, and as neither you nor I will be here to partake of it at that time, I will consent to your celebrating the anniversary on the twentieth instant."

"Thank you," I replied; "and if you will only let it be equal to Em.'s birthday one, it will be worthy of the occasion. And now, little ones," I continued, turning to the children, who were playing at "making visits," in a corner of the room, "what do you say to a game of blind-man's-buff?"

Of course they were all delighted with the suggestion, and Em., the eldest of the three, immediately bound her eyes with a handkerchief, and proclaimed herself to be the blind man. Then ensued a half-hour's play, during which time *pater familias* was blinded—with the exception of one eye—more than once, and succeeded in catching Miss Em. several times, though she hid behind fire-screens, and crept under chairs, to avoid him. The lad in boots, and the eight-years' old girl, were like crickets, chirping and jumping about the floor. Finally, the boy rolled himself up in the carpet-rug and went to sleep; little Mary climbed into her mother's lap, and, nestling her head amidst rich laces, also went off into dream-land; only Em. and myself were left to keep up the game, which was brought to a close by the entrance of my savage literary friend who came to pass the evening with us.

Then the maid appeared, who carried the children away to the nursery; and as they vanished, I said softly to Mrs. Gray, "The meeting of the club for the evening is ended."

CHAPTER XXIX.

Thanksgiving Day; its Origin; its Elasticity. — The Puritans; their Descendants. — The Christian Church. — The Day in New England and New York. — A Cruel Hoax. — Home! — Our Poor Brother. — Our Neighbor, the Widow.

"THANKSGIVING Day, my dear," I said to my wife, as I went into the library from the Thanksgiving dinner-table, "like Christmas, as the old song has it, comes but once a year."

"I don't know about that," answered Mrs. Gray. "I think I remember of celebrating two or three Thanksgiving days in one November, not many years ago. The Governors of the several States of New York, Massachusetts, and Connecticut each appointed a different day; and it was my good fortune, Mr. Gray, to keep it in each of those States."

"That may all have been, my dear," I replied; "but the fact as to there being but one Thanksgiving Day a year, except under extraordinary circumstances, still, in my opinion, is incontrovertible. Each State has been accustomed to keeping it but once a year; and though every one might have selected a different day, yet the rule as to there being but one Thanksgiving Day still holds good. Again, you might assert, with the greatest truthfulness, that every day in the year is a Thanksgiving Day; and I am certain you, my dear, should be thankful every day you live that you have so good a husband as I am, even as I am thankful that I have so good a wife as you."

My wife smiled, and drew her chair a little nearer to where I was sitting.

"Like Christmas, too," I continued, "it is a day of prayer and feasting. Originating in New England, where it was instituted by the Puritans, at a time when the festival of Christmas was by them not only neglected but actually denounced, it answered a widely felt requirement. It was the single holiday of the year, — the sole really enjoyable day, out of three hundred and sixty-five, that the *May-Flower* Pilgrims and their descendants had to look forward to, and enjoy when it came, as a national holiday. Still it was little more — hedged around as it was by puritanic customs and blue laws — than a Sabbath day dovetailed into the working-time life of the colonists, possessing in a slight degree an India rubber-like capacity, that allowed it to contain the few innocent pleasures which were denied to them on all other occasions. Little by little, however, as the strictness of the Puritans' character dissolved before the more genial nature of their descendants, rural delights and worldly amusements — the apple-bee, the husking, the candy frolic, the quilting-party, the sleigh-ride, and even the theatre and the ball-room, with their separate enticements — crept in among the sacred offices of the day, and increased its popularity and the welcome accorded to it. Nearly, if not all, of the States in the Union, now celebrate, with due observance, this excellent and peculiar New England festival."

"My dear," my wife said, as I paused to take breath, "you talk quite like a book."

"While the Christian Church throughout the world," I continued, not heeding her interruption, "and in all ages, has never been without some festal anniversary, — a day not chosen from the Sabbath, but selected from the working-time, and set apart for purposes of praise and thanksgiving, — the Puritans of New England, Pilgrim Fathers, as they are reverently and lovingly termed, were, until the appointment of Thanksgiving among them, possessed of no holy festival. In the Protestant-Episcopal and in the Roman Catholic Churches, such festivals are of frequent occurrence. The Christian Year, commencing at the season of Advent, has its calendar thickly studded with similar festivals commemorative of God's gracious protection of, and his goodness as displayed in his bounty to, man. Although to these Churches, therefore, the observance of Thanksgiving might be deemed unnecessary, yet it is, I rejoice to perceive, as duly celebrated and as dearly prized by them as by other Christian sects. It is in New England, however, and among the lineal descendants of the Pilgrim Fathers, that Thanksgiving Day in its perfection is to be found. As a national holiday, it is there regarded as being almost if not quite equal in importance to the Fourth of July. On this day, more than any other, do families, long separated and dispersed abroad, reassemble around the festal board and about the blazing hearth under the parental roof. This day do fathers and mothers select to call their wandering children home; and they, bringing with them their sons and daughters, obey the call. Once more brothers and sisters meet; once more the old homestead resounds with the merry laughter of childhood, and the elders live over again in their offspring the days of their own departed youth. At these reunions old memories arise, calling up old tears or old smiles; old topics are discussed, old stories told, old hymns sung, and old prayers — such as only can be uttered when the whole family reassemble in the old home — are offered."

"You almost make me wish," said my wife, now close beside me, "I were a New Englander by birth, that so I might the more enjoy her peculiar festival. What other day does she celebrate so cordially as this?"

"Oh," I replied, "you forget there is Forefathers' Day, which commemorates the landing of the Pilgrims, or Puritans, as it would be more correct to term them. Do you know I once recited some verses of mine at a New-England festival held in commemoration of this day?"

My wife said that she did not, and she quite doubted whether I, who was not a New Englander, had ever done so. Thereupon I turned to my scrap-book, and found the following lines, which I read to her, as a proof of my assertion: —

THE LANDING OF THE PILGRIMS.

They were a sturdy race of men —
  A small but dauntless band —
That sailed along New England's coast,
  And viewed the promised land.

Two hundred years ago and more,
  These pious Pilgrims came,
To build, upon a savage shore,
  A Church, a home, a name.

For months their little bark has sped,
  The sport of boisterous winds,
Until, at last, with tattered sails,
  An anchorage it finds.

Then, on its deck glad hymns of praise,
  And voices loud in prayer,
From earnest men and women rise
  Upon the frosty air.

The falling snow is drifting deep,
  The wind is fierce and high,
When from the *May-Flower's* icy deck
  They view their haven nigh.

No verdant landscape meets their gaze,
  Nor flower, nor foliage bright;
A wild and snow-clad wilderness
  Is all that greets their sight.

While, here and there, amidst the trees,
  Strange forms and shadows rise,
That come and go, with catlike tread,
  And watchful lynxlike eyes.

But hark ! above the ocean's roar,
  A thrilling cry they hear ;
It is the Pequot's ringing whoop
  That fills their startled ear.

For one brief moment shrinks in fear
  The bravest of the band,
Till, sword in rest, Miles Standish speaks, —
  " God holds us in his hand ! "

Then back again to trusting hearts
  Their flying courage turns ;
Each soul upon that vessel's deck
  With zeal and glory burns.

What tempted these brave Christian men,
  With brave and Christian wives,
To leave behind them home and friends,
  And peril thus their lives ?

For conscience' sake, for peace, for faith,
  This noble little flock
Crossed o'er a wide and stormy sea,
  To land on Plymouth Rock.

And there, amidst December's snows,
  They kneel them down to pray,
And thank their God who, safe thus far,
  Has brought them on their way.

And there, amidst December's snows,
  Their humble homes they rear,
And teach their daughters and their sons
  The Lord to love and fear.

And there, amidst December's snows,
  A goodly seed was sown,
From which there sprung a race of men
  Our land is proud to own.

And there, amidst December's snows,
  This night our thoughts will stray,
To linger near our mother's shrine,
  And bless her Pilgrim-day.

"So much, my love," I said, "for my appreciation of Forefathers' Day. But, to come back to Thanksgiving Day. In town, though duly observed, it has not half the significance which it possesses in the country. The city simply regards it as a day of release from labor. Wall Street speculators don't go down town; the Custom-House, the Sub-Treasury, the banks, and many places of business are closed. The clinking of gold, and the rustling of greenbacks in these places of the money-changers are unheard, and the ways leading thereto are quiet and deserted. Many good people go to church in the morning, to dinner in the afternoon, and to the theatre in the evening. Base-ball and cricket and billiard clubs have 'tournaments', and military and target companies display their skill in hitting the 'bull's-eye;' and Jones, Brown, and Robinson come into the country for a day's fishing or shooting."

"What! — our Jones, our Brown, our Robinson, do you mean, my dear?" asked Mrs. Gray. "I am certain I've seen none of them go past Woodbine Cottage, and I've been sitting at the window ever since we returned from church."

"They probably went by while we were in church, my dear," I answered.

"Oh," said my wife, "that may be."

"Every one, in short," I continued, "who could, doubtless kept the holiday appropriately; while those who could not, declared the day to be a Yankee innovation, and not to be compared with the Fourth of July or the First of January. But even these poor fellows — working editors, I imagine — managed, no doubt, to get a tenderer slice of turkey, a thicker piece of pie, and an extra bottle of Catawba, than fall to their lot at common unthanksgiving dinners."

"Poor fellows," said my wife, sympathizingly, "how I pity them. You ought to ask them all out to Woodbine Cottage some day, Mr. Gray. Will you?"

"Oh, yes," I replied, "often. Do you remember, my dear, the bitter hoax that a young lad, a few years ago, in a spirit of thoughtlessness, perpetrated on Thanksgiving Day?"

Mrs. Gray said she did not.

"Well," I continued, "he caused to be inserted in several of the newspapers, a notice to the effect that bread and meat would be given to such of the poor of the city as might desire, and would come for it on Thanksgiving morning, at Union Square. At the appointed hour, hundreds of poor, forlorn creatures appeared with baskets, prepared to receive the thanksgiving offering. Bitter the disappointment and great the sorrow among them, when, after patiently waiting beside the equestrian statue of Washington for hours, for the distribution to take place, they were compelled to believe themselves the victims of a cruel and unexampled hoax, and that neither bread nor meat would be given them that day. Slowly and reluctantly the vast assemblage dispersed; and it was not until late in the afternoon, that the last mendicant, who had hoped even against hope itself, drawing her thin shawl around her shivering form, took up her empty basket, and, bearing a heavy heart in her bosom, wended her trembling steps to her humble home. Her home! yes, if a damp, dark, and ill-ventilated cellar, or a garret with a leaky roof and broken windows, can possess that thanksgiving-like name. To her home, however, she went, where were expectant and hungry little ones, perhaps, who, after long watching for their mother's coming, were at last doomed to go dinnerless and supperless to their beds of straw. A card published in one of the daily newspapers stated that the boy was penitent, and sorrowed for his cruel act. Let us hope that this was so; and may the lesson his thoughtless and cruel deed taught, keep him and all others for the future from violating the golden rule, which saith, 'Do unto others as you would that others should do unto you.'"

Here I observed that my wife wiped her eyes, as if a tear or two had dimmed their sight, and straightway she said that it would also be well to invite these poor people out to Woodbine Cottage. When I invite the first-mentioned "poor fellows," I will also invite the last-named "poor people."

"Thanksgiving Day in the country, my dear," I said, "is quite different from what it is in the city. It must appear to every one who tills the earth, and plants and reaps thereof, that he should give thanks for the full harvest which has been granted him; that he should give praise to God that his barns are filled, and that the work of the year is nearly ended, and that a season of rest from toiling in the fields is to be his. He can go to church, I trust, with a clear conscience, — if he sent a fat turkey to the parson before going, I am sure he will, — and, after listening to a sermon tending to illustrate God's wonderful love and goodness, as vouchsafed to the children of men, in bringing peace to our land, and causing our harvests to be plentiful, can return home and partake of a dinner, such as only his wife, a thrifty housekeeper of twenty or more years' reputation, can cook, and the greater part of which is the product of his own land, without fear of indigestion, or the many ills which are too often the attendants of city-made dinners, following. In the afternoon he will go and talk with his neighbors, and learn for how much they each sold their hay, and oats, and corn, and wheat; and then he will come home to tea; and, perhaps, in the evening, he will have a quiet rubber of whist, and smoke his pipe, and drink a mug of ale or cider; and later he will have family prayers, and sing a hymn, and go to bed."

"A very good description, my dear," said my wife, "of a farmer's Thanksgiving Day."

Which sentiment Miss Floy echoed, and Miss Em. declared the whole account was almost equal to a story.

"Thanksgiving Day," I said, much elated, and feeling as

if I were addressing an audience, "is but the forerunner of Christmas, — the most joyful festival in the calendar. Let those of us, then, who have pity for the poor, and who say to ourselves, on next Thanksgiving Day we will fill the basket of our poor brother with bread; we will kill the fatted calf, and send a portion of it to our neighbor, — the poor widow down in the cellar, — remember that, before the year goes round, and Thanksgiving comes again, our poor brother may be dead, and our neighbor, the widow, with her children, perish from starvation. When Christmas arrives, however, our poor brother will doubtless be alive, and our neighbor, the widow, still remain in her cellar, surrounded by her little ones. On Christmas, then, let us make glad their hearts by crowning their boards with plenty."

CHAPTER XXX.

An Early Tea party. — Rappings. — My Neighbor Joyce. — Celebrating a Birthday. — A Search. — A Hot Punch *vs.* a Cold Punch. — Twenty Minutes. — Ungrateful. — A Toast. — "Never again." — Rejoice. — A Pleasant Walk. — A Glorious Fire. — A Package of New Books. — A Hot Punch.

I AM passing the day at home, by myself. The children are shut up in the nursery along with Miss Floy, who is teaching their young ideas how to shoot. My esteemed wife has gone to visit a neighbor. Singularly enough, she received her invitation at a very early hour this morning. Indeed, it came before any of my family were out of bed. It is not usual, I know, to ask visitors to one's house before the moon goes down, and while the morning-stars, peering through the keen atmosphere, are still singing together in the heavens; but circumstances sometimes make it necessary to invite, even at three o'clock A. M., a lady friend to do so. My neighbor himself, a respectable man of forty years of age, came with the invitation. At first when I heard the knocking at the door and saw that it was far from being daylight, I thought it was "spirit-rapping;" afterwards, I wondered if the house were on fire, and an early traveller going by had not stopped to tell me of it. When I woke Mrs. Gray, however, and called her attention to the disturbance, she very coolly said it was Mr. Joyce, and immediately proceeded to arise and dress herself. How she knew who it was I cannot tell; but when I, opening the window, put my head out into the frosty air, and asked, "Who is there, and what do you want?" the reply came back: "It 's me, neighbor Joyce, and I want Mrs. Gray."

"What for?" I asked.

"Mr. Gray," said my wife, "will you stop asking such foolish questions, and close that window, for I'm catching my death-cold with that wind blowing upon me."

"Certainly, my dear," I replied, "in a minute. Hark! neighbor Joyce is saying something, and your talking to me prevents me from hearing him. "What did you say?" I asked outside; "I did n't catch your reply."

"We're celebrating a birthday at our house," he repeated.

"Whose?" I shouted.

"I don't know," he replied; "I want your wife to come and find that out."

"My dear," I asked, bringing my head inside, "what the deuce does that fellow mean? Is he crazy?"

"Mr. Gray," said my wife impressively, "will you do me the favor to close that window?"

"Certainly, my dear," I answered; "but what the dickens brings Joyce here, at this hour, to celebrate a birthday?"

"It is all proper, Mr. Gray," she replied; "I know all about it. Now, do close that window."

"Yes, yes, in a minute. Joyce," I cried, thrusting my head out of the window, "does your invitation extend to me and the children?"

"I guess not," he replied; "it's only an old woman's tea-party."

"A tea-party," I echoed; "well, I'm fond of tea-parties myself; but is n't it a little early in the day to give a tea-party?"

"Oh, don't bother me," said Joyce; "you don't know how badly I feel. Is n't your wife most ready?"

"I'll see," I answered. "My love," inside, "are you nearly ready to go to this tea-party? Joyce is getting impatient."

"Well, he'll have to wait until I find my Balmoral skirt, at all events. I laid it on the outside of the bed, just at the foot, when I undressed, and now it 's gone. I can't find it anywhere, neither in the bed nor under the bed. One of those blessed children must have been cold in the night, and come and got it to cover over themselves. I do wish you 'd buy more blankets and quilts; here 's winter upon me, and I 've not half sufficient for all the beds. Goodness me! what can have become of that skirt?"

"Oh, here it is," I said; "I put it over my shoulders, to keep me warm, when I went to the window to talk to Joyce."

"That 's just like you, Mr. Gray," my wife replied. "Will you please to close that window? I am shivering with cold."

"Certainly, my dear," I replied; "but you can't be colder than Joyce, outside there, pacing up and down the veranda. Don't you hear him? Hark! he is calling to me."

"Well!" I cried, putting my head out of the window, "what do you want?"

"Is Mrs. Gray nearly ready?" he asked.

"Yes," I answered; "she has found her skirt now, and has only to put on her shoes and some other things, and she 'll be down in about twenty minutes."

"Twenty devils!" he shouted — let us hope spasmodically — "I can't wait all that time. I shall go crazy if she don't come sooner."

"It is pretty cold out there, Joyce, — is n't it?" I asked. "How would a hot whiskey-punch go?"

"Hang your punch!" answered Joyce. "Ask Mrs. Gray to please hurry."

"My dear," I said, bringing in my head, "Mr. Joyce wants to know if you 'll please hurry."

"I am hurrying as fast as I can," my wife, somewhat excited, replied; "you surely don't wish me to go without being dressed, — do you?"

"Certainly not," I answered. "I 'll go down-stairs and let Joyce in."

"Do so," she replied; "and tell him I'll be ready in five minutes; but please shut the window first."

"Joyce," I cried, putting my head out of the window, "I'm going down to let you in, and my wife will be ready in five minutes."

"Good!" cried Joyce, cheerily.

And then I did close the window, and go down-stairs.

"Joyce," I said, when I had opened the door, and taken him into the comfortable library, "excuse my appearance, old fellow; I did n't stop, as you see, to array myself in purple, as I thought the fine linen would answer, especially as I did n't want to keep you any longer out in the cold."

"You 're very kind," said Joyce, "but you might have thought of asking me into the house fifteen minutes ago."

"Look here, Joyce," I replied, "don't be ungrateful now. I did think of it; but what with your talking to me outside, and Mrs. Gray inside, I really had no opportunity."

"Humph!" ejaculated Joyce.

"Joyce," I said, "I don't think we've time enough to heat water, so we'll take it cold. Here's a bottle of choice whiskey; help yourself." Joyce did so.

"Joyce," I said, "a toast, — Many happy returns of the day."

"No," he said, gloomily, rubbing his hands; "never again, never again."

"Oh, I've heard husbands say that before, Joyce. Saying so don't amount to anything. They always forget they've said it."

"But I never shall," said Joyce.

"All right," I answered; "but, Joyce, you now have occasion to rejoice."

"Hang your bad puns," said Joyce; "give me some punch."

"That is worse yet," I answered.

"I did n't mean it," said Joyce; "I did n't, upon my word."

"All right," I said, "I did n't suppose you did; but here comes my wife. Don't let her drink too much strong tea, Joyce; it is apt to make her nervous."

"Oh, bother!" cried Joyce; "how can I help it, I should like to know?"

"Well, I don't know that you can," I replied. "The fact is that we husbands can't help a great many things which our wives do. If they will, they will, and that 's an end of it."

"That 's so," said Joyce, "you 've hit it there;" and my wife appearing at that moment, I said good-by; and, wishing them a pleasant walk and my wife a quick return, I let them out into the cheerless dawning, and, coming back myself to the library, stirred up the buried embers on the hearth, and, putting some fresh wood above them, soon had a glorious fire blazing before me.

It was scarcely worth while, I thought, to go to bed again; therefore I resolved to examine the new books which I had brought from town the night before. So, after finishing my toilet, I opened the package before me. To me there are few pleasanter things in this life than to open a bundle containing new books. And how plentifully, in these holiday times, do new books make their appearance! They fall around one as thickly as leaves in Valambrosa. "And what," I ask myself, "can be more appropriate, at this season, for a gift to a beloved friend, than a book? Mothers, wives, sisters, daughters; fathers, husbands, brothers, and sons, individually and collectively, find delight in a new book. A book helps to lighten the weariness of convalescency, the dreariness of sorrow, the tediousness of idleness; it makes more cheerful the honeymoon, adds greater lustre to happy homes, and crowns the enjoyments of the holidays.

"Now, there is my savage literary friend," I say aloud,

the while carefully undoing the paper which enwraps my books, "who, if I should ask, which do you prefer, a book-store or a library? would probably answer neither, but that he preferred a bookstall, filled with what I would term second-hand rubbish, dusty and musty, and among which one might rummage half a day without finding a single book worth the carrying home; but, if found, it would seem to him most valuable, and one, he would declare, that could be obtained neither for love or money at a regular book-store. Probably it would turn out to be a mutilated copy of a collection of Irish plays, written by some old buffer who had been dead a hundred years, but who, in his day and generation, had a certain reputation as a playwright, surpassed only by that which he possessed of being able to brew and to drink a better and stronger hot whiskey-punch than any other man in Dublin."

Being thus reminded of a punch, I get the little copper kettle in which my wife boils water for her tea, and place it on the coals in the chimney-corner; then I hunt sharply around for a lemon and white sugar, and, having found them, place them on the table beside the bottle of Glenlivet.

Then, thinking aloud again, I say, "There is to me something exceedingly pleasant in possessing a fresh book, with its leaves still uncut, and its contents still unknown, which is eminently gratifying to my feelings. It gives me the impression that I am, in some sort of a way, a literary Columbus, about to discover a new country; and when I sit down, and take my paper-knife in my hand, I feel confident that I am going to consummate an important act."

Thereupon I draw forth from the package a copy of "Æsop's Fables." There was a time, years ago, when I was a youngster, that I had great faith in Mr. Æsop, and believed that he really was acquainted with animals possessed of the faculty of speech. It was a shock to my feelings, I remember, when I discovered that, after all, the stories were nothing more than what they purported to be, — fables. I never was able, afterwards, to read them with the same zest; and, though I take kindly to them in their new dress, yet I endeavor to make myself believe them literally, and always skip the application. I have not, however, and I hope I never shall, lose my interest in, and enjoyment of, the next book I draw forth, which is "Robinson Crusoe." How the very name recalls the days of my boyhood! What plans I formed, after reading it, for getting shipwrecked on Rocky Island! And I did one day drift off alone in an old scow, and came to grief before I reached my desert island, through being overhauled by a party of shad fishermen, and ignominiously towed back, notwithstanding my protests, to my starting-place! How I longed for a goat-skin dress, and a parrot, and a man Friday! My faith in the truthfulness of that book has never been shaken; and now, when I find it so nicely printed, and embellished with a hundred pictures, I am more than ever convinced of its truth; and I should be sorely tempted, I am certain, to punish very severely any one of my boys or girls who did n't believe in it implicitly from beginning to end.

"And here," I say, bringing forth the last volume, "is 'The Children in the Wood,' told in charming verse. The story carries one back, in imagination at least, to the days of good Queen Bess, when young Sir Arthur and little Lady Jane — for these were the names of the two children — lived and died, and were buried by the robins, who

> 'Strewed, with pious care, the leaves
> On cheek, and brow, and breast,
> Till they had raised a funeral mound
> To mark their place of rest.'

"Ah me!" I exclaimed, taking the kettle off the fire, and pouring a small quantity of hot water into a goblet which contained some white sugar, that had been bruising itself against a bit of lemon-peel for the past ten minutes, and to which I added, after the sugar was thoroughly dissolved, a modicum of Scotch whiskey, which I thereupon stirred with a spoon, and partook of unctuously and appreciatively, — "ah me!" I repeated, "I almost wish I were a boy again, that I might once more have the pleasure of reading, for the first time, 'Robinson Crusoe,' and all other juvenile books."

CHAPTER XXXI.

An Investment. — Trumpets. — A Deaf Girl. — Horns. — A German Fashion. — Tooting. — A bewildered Party. — Silver-plated and Tin Trumpets; the Family supplied. — A Jolly Sight. — Foremen and Captains. — Broken English. — Gabriel. — Two Horns. — Another Kind of a Horn.

HAVE been investing considerable money, recently, in speaking-trumpets. My wife has a silver-plated one, and the rest of the family tin ones. The reason of this is that the nursery-maid, a young German girl of pleasing appearance, and who only partially understands the English language, is almost as deaf as that popular object of comparison, — a post. We had all made ourselves hoarse with shouting at her, and I determined to endure it no longer; so I suggested to my wife the propriety of discharging her and hiring a young woman whose ears had not been corked up. But so many good traits were discovered in Bertha, — she was so willing to do anything you required of her, and so quick to accomplish it, after she understood what it was you desired; in fact, so quick that she goes off sometimes half-primed, thinking that she clearly knows what you wish, and does exactly that which you do not wish her to do, — that my wife preferred to endure the existing evil rather than risk finding something worse in a girl of whom she knew nothing. Desiring, however, to alleviate, as far as practicable, the annoyance which the retention of Bertha made necessary, I purchased and brought home, much to the astonishment of my wife and the delight of the little ones, a dozen trumpets, assorted sizes. Of course my family cannot make use of them all; but, in case of visitors, I tnought, for supplying them with, they would be handy to have in the house.

"What in the world, Mr. Gray," my wife asked, when the expressman, having deposited at the door one evening, just as we were finishing our dinner, the package containing them, which I immediately had brought into the dining-room, where I unpacked and exposed them to view, — "what in the world," she reiterated, "are you going to do with all those horns?"

"Well," I replied, "as New Year's Day is coming, I thought, since we had a German girl living with us, it would be polite in us to adopt the German fashion of blowing on horns as the old year goes out and the new one comes in. This is done, I believe, to frighten away the ghost of the dead year, and to encourage the spirit of the new year to approach."

"I, for one," said my wife, slightly bridling up, "don't desire to accept that fashion. I am satisfied to let the ghost of the old year go and the spirit of the new come without such foolery on my part, even if it be a German fashion. I 'd look well, would n't I, and Miss Floy, and the children, too, going out into the street, in the middle of a cold winter night, tooting on one of those concerns?"

"Well, my dear," I said, "if you do not wish to do it, you know you need not; but, from your desiring to keep Bertha, I really thought that something of this kind, which would be gratifying to her sense of nationality, as it were, would meet with your cordial approval. If I have been mistaken, why, I am sorry."

"You certainly are," said my wife, "the strangest and most foolish man I ever met. Now, what shall we do with those horns?"

"They are not horns, my dear," I said, "but trumpets; though never mind that. An idea has struck me. See." And, seizing one of them, I shouted through it, "Bertha!"

Bertha, who was up-stairs in the nursery, immediately made her appearance.

"Bertha," I continued, still shouting through it, "go down into the cellar and draw me a pitcher of ale."

Bertha took the pitcher, and disappeared.

"You see," I continued, addressing the slightly bewildered party who sat around the table, and who were convulsed with laughter, "to what excellent use these trumpets can be applied. Bertha, who has not been known to hear anything you might say to her until it had been repeated at least a dozen times, and each repetition of which it was necessary to yell louder and louder, until you almost cracked your skull and nearly raised the roof off of the house, now hears and understands at the first bidding. My dear," I continued, selecting the silver-plated trumpet, "allow me to present you with this magnificent affair; and you, Miss Floy, another, equally effective, but not so high priced; and you, my little ones," handing each of them one, "small, smaller, smallest. And now your papa will take this; the remaining ones we will reserve for invited guests."

It is a very jolly sight, to see each member of my family going about the house with a trumpet slung at her side, for all the world like so many foremen of fire-engine companies, or sea captains on the quarter-deck, and to hear them given their orders, in stentorian voices, at the breakfast and dinner table. They appear to have an idea, too, that, by talking to Bertha through the trumpets, she will the more readily understand the English of what they are saying. This may or may not be so; but, at all events, she does seem to more fully understand what is said to her, and is, moreover, highly delighted with the success attendant upon the use of the trumpets. Indeed, she is so pleased with them that she carries two herself, and nothing delights her more than to shout back her answers, in broken English, with a vehemence and rapidity quite appalling, at my wife, who, at times, I am sorry to say, is quite crazed with the tumult, and wishes the trumpets in Jericho, or some other equally agreeable place.

Miss Floy very wickedly says that the trumpetings now going on in Woodbine Cottage are calculated to make even Gabriel jealous, and she much doubts whether he will be able to create a louder noise when the time comes for him to wake the sleepers. Miss Floy further says that it will no longer be necessary for me to go round the corner, to the old sea captain's, late at night, as I have been accustomed to do, to "take a horn" with him before going to bed, as the prevalence of horns in my own house will be all-sufficient; indeed, she thinks that I might ask him to come to Woodbine Cottage and take several with me, without any perceptible loss of quantity or of detriment to the discord.

Since those horns came into the house, the baby has slept scarcely a wink, except at night, and at least three servants have come and gone, giving, as the reason for their departure, that their nerves could not stand the racket. One good thing, at least, has been accomplished by the introduction of those horns, in that the German girl, who walks around the house with a trumpet at each ear, is now able to hear the baby cry, which, previously, she was not able to do.

CHAPTER XXXII.

The coming of Christmas. — A Christmas-tree. — A Party of Little Folks. — Several New Books. — A Christmas Story. — "Santa Claus's Visit." — A Cold, Still Night. — Mary and her Lover. — The Old Man. — Nicholas. — Santa Claus. — His Portrait. — Pictures. — Rejoicings. — The Lovers' Arrival. — Happiness Complete.

"MY dear," I said to Mrs. Gray, as, with the children nestled around us, we seated ourselves near the centre-table, in the library, "are you aware that Christmas is almost here, and we are not provided with a Christmas-tree, or any presents to hang on it, for the little folks?"

Here the parties interested opened wide their eyes and mouths, as if to see and swallow everything, in the way of toys and candies, that the occasion could possibly bring forth.

"Yes," she replied; "but I have been waiting for Miss Floy, who has promised to assist me in getting up a Christmas-tree. Captain Jack's little ones have been asked to pass the day with ours, and great preparations are being made by them, in view of this circumstance."

"Why, we shall have quite a party of little folks," I said, "and it will be my duty to see that as many juvenile books are provided as will enable each of the children to have one. Let me think, which of my friends, the publishers, shall I call upon, on this occasion?"

"Why," interposed Mrs. Gray, "there are the 'Five Little Pigs,' and 'The Fox and the Geese' books, with nice illustrations, just published, for the younger; and 'The Adventures of a Little French Boy,' and 'Robinson Crusoe,' for the boys."

"True, my love," I replied; "nor can any be better than these."

"Except some fairy books," exclaimed Em., "and a doll, and a skipping-rope."

"And oranges, and a rocking-horse," chimed in the boy in boots.

"And me wants 'tandies,'" lisped the youngest.

"To be sure," I answered; "all these matters are important, and shall be attended to in due time. It is a pleasant occasion, my dear, this, which so delights the little ones, aside from its historical interest as the Christian's most solemn festival. I do not know what we should do without Christmas, and its attendant saint, good old Santa Claus.

"And this reminds me, my dear," I continued, "of a story which I have written, which, if you will permit me, I will read to the club, this evening — even the little ones may take pleasure in hearing it; so, if they will be very quiet, they may remain up beyond their usual bedtime, while I read it."

Mamma consenting, and the children promising to be "good," I read the following, entitled

SANTA CLAUS'S VISIT.

It was as still and cold — on Christmas Eve — as it could well be; so cold that the very moon-beams, as they came struggling against the window-pane, seemed to congeal, and appeared like lines of silver wire drawn out into the icy air. The trees were covered with a coating of ice, which gleamed and glittered in the moonlight, as if their branches were studded with precious stones; icicles, like pointed spears, hung from the eaves of the cottages; and the smoke which rose from the hundred chimneys of the village, passed, like pious incense, upwards into the still air, bearing in its quiet folds kind thoughts and grateful words from the loving ones clustered around their hearth-stones.

The snow lay deep upon the ground, and was covered with a thick crust, which bore up the children when from the beaten track they turned aside, chasing each other over the frozen surface, as they came home from school. Lights gleamed from the windows of every cot in the single street of the village, and voices of young and old mingled with song and laughter. At one end of the village, within a cottage, a little apart from the others, are seated an old man of seventy winters, his wife, and his granddaughter, Mary. The room is one of those antique rooms which answer alike for the parlor and kitchen; the floor is of oak, and sanded with clean white sand, which was sprinkled by Mary's own hands. Pictures adorn the walls, descriptive of "The Prodigal Son," in four distinct illustrations, — his going, his folly, his poverty, and his return. On the dresser are ranged pewter platters and numerous plates; while mugs of goodly dimensions hang from pegs, and reflect the flame of the fire. Curtains of white, as pure as the snow in the meadow, are drawn at the windows and fall in graceful proportions; on one side of the wainscot, a little away from the dresser, hangs a cage of woven willow and wire-work; within it a robin — that bird of the homestead — gladdens the house with its music. On an ancient carved table, drawn out in the middle of the room, lies the Bible, unclasped, and wide open, and the eyes of the matron are fixed on the passage before her, — "We have seen his star in the east, and are come to worship him."

The old man is seated within his arm-chair, with his feet to the fire, where the yule-log is burning, and he watches the flame and the smoke as they dance and play with each other, while his thoughts are wandering back to the time of his youth, when he danced and joyed with the maidens. Oft doth his eye seek the face of his grandchild beside him, with a look of the kindest inquiry. Sad, sad is the heart of the maiden, though her lips wear the smile of happiness; yet oft doth she start and sigh as footsteps glide on past the doorway. Thus sit they in silence, each wishing, yet fearing, to utter the thoughts that have birth in their bosoms, till the clock in the corner, grown bold by the stillness, chimes loudly the hour of seven. Then the cat by the fireside, dozing, awakened by the sound, answers, by purring, the chirp of the cricket, and the dog, with a wag of his tail, looks up to the face of his master. Then rises the old man, and paces the floor of the kitchen ; his face has a look of trouble, and the eyes of the maiden are downcast; while the matron wipes the mist from her glasses and lays them within the book, on the page that tells of the birth of our Saviour. Still paces the old man backward and forward, like a pendulum weary with going ; but, anon, he stops at the window, and drawing the curtain aside, looks out on the village ; the street is deserted, and he hears not the sound of a footfall. Then he turns to his granddaughter Mary, and says, —

"Why is it, my child, that Nicholas comes not hither to woo thee on this holiest of eves? Surely thou canst not have driven him from thee in anger?"

Then sighed the maiden, and answered as follows : —

"Truly, my father, I know not the reason that keeps him away ; 't is now three days since I have seen him, though he hath not been out of the village. There are maidens more beautiful, father, than I, and richer by far. Man's heart is a changeable thing, and perhaps my love is forgotten."

Then paced the old man backward and forward, while dark grew his brow, and the feeling of wrath was upon him. At last he lifted his hand and said : —

"Never shall Nicholas" ——

Suddenly paused the old man, and his hand fell down on the table — while the matron looked over her glasses, and opened her mouth as astonished — while the maiden rose from her chair and was fixed like a statue — the dog cowered in the corner, and the cat crept under the dresser, while the clock ceased its ticking, and held up its hands in amazement. But the cricket kept up its chirping and sang louder and louder; brighter grew the fire, and the burning brands crackled and snapped, as if giving a welcome, while the flame and the smoke rose higher and higher, and wreathed together fantastically.

The door stood open, and there, on the piled-up snow, was a sleigh, carved out from an oak of the forest. Coursers were there, with stately horns, that resembled the reindeers of Lapland: they pawed the snow with their hoofs, and scattered it high in the heavens; icicles hung from their antlers, and their backs were covered with snowflakes; they were fastened to the sleigh with links cut from the icebergs, and their saddles were carved out of ebony, inlaid with hailstones; their reins were of crystallized moon-beams. The sleigh was filled with presents of all kinds, — toys for the children, and candies and books in profusion. Then from out the sleigh there arose a being of jovial appearance. He winked to his steeds, and then entered the cottage. His face was the face of the moon seen through the mists of October; his eyes were like stars of the night, and his mouth was made for feasting and drinking; his hair was white as the snow, and his beard like the hoar-frost; his looks were quizzical, and jollity shone in each feature; he was short in stature, though broad in his girth, while his walk was a roll and a caper; his coat was the skin of the polar bear, and hung round his body, — alas, ere the morning, it would be black with the soot of the chimneys; leathern breeches adorned his limbs, and fitted his person *exactly;* moccasons covered his feet, and he bore in one hand a three-cornered hat, in the other a flagon of home-brewed. Closing the door, he sat down in a chair, and placed the flagon beside him; not a word did he speak, but, taking a mug from the table, he filled it, and handed the same to the old man. Trembling, he drank; but when he had finished he smacked his lips, and vowed it was as good as the best,—even that which his old wife had brewed him.

Loudly old Santa Claus laughed (for it was he), till he shook "like a bowl full of jelly." Then he sung an old song, till the rafters resounded, and the old man joined in with the chorus: —

> "Both back and side go bare, go bare,
>   Both foot and hand go cold;
> But on Christmas give us good ale enough,
>   Whether it be new or old."

At last Santa Claus rose, but no word did he speak as he pointed to the flagon; and there, as if in a mirror, they saw the inside of a cottage, and heard the music of voices, — young men and maidens were gathered together, and linked hand in hand in the dance. But Mary saw not in the group the one she so longed to behold, and her heart grew light as she gazed. Slowly the picture faded from sight, and now they looked on another, and heard the faint murmur of bells.

Rapidly over the frozen ground came a party in sleighs; and as each passed along, the light of the moon shone upon them. Mary's heart beat faster and faster; many among them she knew, but nowhere saw she her lover. Slowly the picture faded from sight, and now they looked on another, and heard men's voices in anger.

In the village inn, in the bar-room, were grouped together a party of men, drinking and gaming. Mary hid her face in her hands, for her woman's heart dared not to look on the picture. But she thought of her lover, of his goodness and kindness unto her, and she knew he could not be among them; and she gazed with calm heart and clear eye on the semblance before her; but no shade of her lover was there. Slowly the picture faded from sight, and now they looked on another, and heard the faint chirp of a cricket.

'T was a chamber, alone and deserted; no light and no

fire gave warmth to the picture, and Mary knew 't was the room of her lover. Unpressed was the bed, and the curtains were drawn at the window, and shut was the chest and the clothes-press. But he was not in the chamber. Slowly the picture faded from sight, and now they looked on another, and heard the low stroke of a hammer.

There, in his workshop, she saw her lover, and his eye was lit up with a smile. Beside a carved wardrobe he stood, and was inlaying her name in the panel. Hard had he worked, day after day and night after night, to finish it for her by Christmas, and now he put the finishing touch, and gazed on his work as gazes an artist. Beat Mary's heart lovingly faster, tears overflowed from her eyelids, as water bubbles up from the fountain, and she sank on her knees by the hearth-stone, while her hands were clasped o'er her bosom. The old man bowed his head on his breast, while his silver locks shrouded his eyebrows, and his wife opened the Bible, her thin lips parted in prayer. Oh! filled were their hearts with joy at the instant. But ere they looked round, Santa Claus had departed, and the soot dropped down from the chimney.

Soon a step on the snow outside was heard, and Nicholas tapped at the doorway; he entered, and Mary was clasped in his arms, and a kiss was impressed on her forehead. A grasp of the hand did the old man give, and the matron murmured her blessing. So happiness dwelt in the household this night, and the Christmas that followed thereafter.

When I had finished, the children clapped their hands, and said it was a very nice story; and then, as they showed evident signs of sleepiness, Miss Floy very kindly consented to see them to bed.

CHAPTER XXXIII.

Buckwheat Cakes. — Sausages. — Confidence. — How to make Sausages; how to cook them. — Opening a Cook-house. — Miss Floy's Management of Children; her Play; its Progress.

THE season of buckwheat cakes has arrived. With buckwheat cakes, country-made sausages, a delicate roll or two, and a cup of Mocha coffee, with cream, one can make a very comfortable breakfast. But the cakes must be light, nicely browned, and hot from the griddle; then eaten with plenty of fresh, golden-hued butter, — and, for those who are not particular about the flavor of their coffee, a spoonful or two of refined syrup may be added; and, for my part, I am sorely tempted, I confess, to use maple-syrup, — and you have a dish good enough for any one. The sausages, too, must be well cooked; if they incline to be a little crispy, reminding one just a trifle of the cracklings of roasted pig, it is not amiss. You should be cautious though, as to where you obtain your sausages; if you have ever so slight an acquaintance with the woman who makes them, it is well, provided you have confidence in her. Confidence in your sausage-maker is an excellent thing. One of the best ways for possessing this confidence is to have your sausages prepared in your own house, with materials furnished by yourself. Pork, two thirds lean and one third fat, chopped finely, is, of course, the foundation for all sausages; but a boiled beef's tongue may, with a good result, be added. Salt, pepper, summer-savory, and sage should be the chief seasoning, though curry and spices may be effectively joined thereto. The mixing of these various ingredients — so that no one savor predominates — should be as carefully wrought as in making a salad. It is not every one who can properly accomplish this, any more than can every one create a salad. It requires judgment in preparing the combinations, skill in putting them together, and an appreciative taste. Then it should be made into small cakes, and fried slowly and kindly in its own fat. For a long time it seemed to me as if this making them fry themselves, as it were, was a little ungenerous; so one day I told the cook to fry them in olive oil. She did so, and, though I pronounced them to be very fine, my mother, in whose house the experiment was made, and all of my juvenile brothers and sisters, failed to take kindly to them, and when we next had them for breakfast they were cooked in the usual way.

Something very similar to the above I spoke to Mrs. Gray the other morning at breakfast, whereupon she asked me if I had been to the French cooking academy.

I answered I had not, but that I had serious intentions of visiting it; for I thought I could put the professor up to one or two ideas in the matter of preparing certain new dishes, which would be of benefit to him.

"What, if you will allow me to ask," said my wife, "are the dishes to which you refer?"

"Well," I replied, "I dare say I can instruct that *chef-de-cuisine* how to concoct a green-corn pudding among other dishes."

"Probably you can," my wife replied; "but I would not advise you to do so."

"Why not?" I asked.

"Because," answered Miss Floy, "you cannot tell how soon you may desire to open a cook-house for the sale of corn-puddings in New York. If Uncle Samuel should turn the cold shoulder upon you, and literature should fail, why, you may have to turn your talents to — not take them out of, observe — the white napkin, and knife, fork, and spoon business."

My wife nodded approvingly, and the little ones, without knowing why they did so, laughed merrily.

"Children," said Miss Floy, who, since she has undertaken to instruct them in the multiplication-table, seeks also to improve their manners at the breakfast-table, and generally has a rod in pickle for them in the form of an exhibit to me of their day's shortcomings, which she produces at the dinner-table, — "children," she repeated, "do you know that it is extremely rude to laugh aloud during your meals? The table is the place where you should eat, and not chatter or laugh. William Howard," addressing my eldest boy, "will you do me the favor not to put such great pieces of food into your mouth? And you, Mary Allen, stop sipping your coffee with a spoon, — it is quite improper."

"It is n't coffee," answered the pert young miss; "it 's only milk and water. I wish it was coffee, though."

"There, say no more," said Miss Floy. "It is highly improper for you to reply to me in that manner. Children should be seen, and not heard."

"Perhaps, then, you 'll see me recite my lessons, and not hear them," said Miss Em.

"Miss Emma Louisa," — Miss Floy, I observe, likes to address the children by their full Christian names, — "I shall be compelled to ask you to leave the table if you speak in that way again. You will oblige me by holding your peace."

"Piece of what?" asked Em.

"Piece of tongue," said Miss Floy, getting provoked.

"Emma," said her mother, reprovingly, "don't be rude."

Miss Emma bowed her head, and was silent.

Miss Floy looked numerous daggers at the three children, and then turned to me and — winked.

It is my private opinion that Miss Floy is not the proper

person to manage these children. She is too much of a child herself, — a somewhat wilful, giddy creature; and, though she strives to govern them properly, she is prone to be too exacting with them at one moment, and too lenient the next. The result is such episodes as the above.

Miss Floy continues to work on her play, and has completed the second act; but, owing to the disturbance which resulted from her reading the first to me, she has forborne to favor me with the hearing of the second. When the five acts are completed, I shall doubtless be treated to the play entire; but, before that time arrives, I am afraid that the season of buckwheat cakes will have ended.

CHAPTER XXXIV.

The Twentieth of December. — The Indian Dinner. — Prominent Dishes. Another Christmas Story. — My Children in Utopia.—Mary and Fanny. The Old Saint. — A Christmas Hymn. — A long Time ago. — An Old-fashioned Chamber. — Poor Old Lady. — My Grandmother. — Prayers. Arrival of Santa Claus. — A Jolly-looking Gentleman. — Merry Christmas.

"AND you really believe, Mr. Gray," said my wife, continuing a conversation which our rising from the dinner-table had interrupted, "that to-day is the two hundredth anniversary of the Indian wedding?"

"Most certainly I do," I replied. "The date of the marriage is distinctly stated in the old Bible, and I know of no reason to doubt its correctness. I wish I knew whether any one would celebrate the third centennial anniversary of this couple, and if so, whether the dinner will be equal to the one we have just eaten. Your idea of adding hominy and succotash to the bill of fare, Mrs. Gray, because of the probability of these having formed prominent dishes at their wedding-feast, was worthy of you, and, in the name of the Indian woman, I thank you."

"Nonsense, Mr. Gray; no thanks are necessary. If my efforts in getting up this dinner have been successful, and if it has met with your approval, I desire nothing further."

"You are too kind, my dear," I answered; "and if you will tell me what you would like in the way of furs for your Christmas present, I will promise to purchase them for you. Speaking of furs and Christmas, reminds me of a story I wrote when I was a bachelor, and my family existed only in Utopia, which, if you would like to hear it, Mrs. Gray, I will read aloud to you and the little ones."

Mrs. Gray acquiescing, and the children, who, at the word story, had left their play of "hunt the slipper," and had gathered around papa's knees, showing their willingness to listen, I drew from my desk a small roll of manuscript, somewhat faded with years, which I unrolled, and, taking my usual place on the rug before the grate, read the following

CHRISTMAS STORIES.

It was Christmas Eve, and I was seated in my easy-chair, drawn up before the blazing wood-fire in my quiet study, lost in a golden reverie. Beautiful pictures of long ago, kept green in memory through many twilight musings, were passing before me. The present, too, with its cheerful realities, and the far-off future, with its hopeful plans, came to fill my heart with happiness. How long my reverie lasted I scarcely know, but I was suddenly aroused from it by seeing the old oak-door — that door which had been closed for many a year, that passed into the chamber where my mother died — slowly open, and timidly and noiselessly come forth my two little ones, Mary and Fanny. By what means they had obtained ingress into that long-deserted room, the key of which I keep in the private drawer of my secretary, I never thought to ask. I seated them, one on either knee, while they twined their little arms caressingly about my neck, and, kissing me with their red lips, said they had come for papa to tell them some Christmas stories. I felt that God had been very kind in bestowing upon me two such precious gifts.

Mary, my elder child, has the dark hair and the sparkling black eyes of her mother, and the very look which in my early manhood had such power to draw me to that mother's side. Fanny, my baby-girl, has light hair and mild, blue eyes, and resembles — for so I think when in a musing mood — a fair dream of my boyhood, which faded into the shadow-land long before I knew how to distinguish between love and sisterly affection. Mary is all vivacity and life; Fanny is reserved and quiet. Mary laughs aloud; Fanny only smiles. Mary moves about our home like a singing-bird; Fanny, like a gleam of sunshine.

"And what," asked I, "shall papa tell to his little daughters?"

"Oh," said Mary, quickly, "first of all tell us those funny verses about Santa Claus coming down the chimney, dressed in furs, carrying a big pack on his back, and with a pipe in his teeth, to fill our stockings."

"And then," said Fanny, "please repeat, papa, that pretty hymn of the shepherds sitting on the ground, watching their flocks by night, when the angel appeared and told them of Christ's coming."

And so, while I repeated Clement C. Moore's well-known Christmas verses, they listened quietly, and when I ended Mary exclaimed, clapping her hands with childish glee:—

"Oh, how I should like to see Santa Claus and the reindeers! And don't you think, papa, that if I should sit up to-night for Saint Nick, and ask him to give me a large wax doll, with eyes that open and shut, just like the one Cousin Nina has, he would do it?"

"And me a book, full of pictures and pretty stories?" chimed in Fanny.

I had not the heart to tell them that Santa Claus was but an imaginary being, for I consider that these mysteries of our childhood — this belief in fairies and good spirits — are of too poetical and beautiful a nature to be rudely disenchanted of at an early age. The ideals of our childhood disappear fast enough before the actualities of life. So I promised my little ones that I would speak to the old saint in their behalf, while they, nestled snugly in bed, should be dreaming of dolls and books, and I doubted not but their wishes would be gratified. Here Mary kissed my cheek, and called me her good papa; while Fanny laid her head upon my shoulder and looked up into my face, her mild eyes beaming with gratitude.

They were both very quiet and attentive while I repeated the Christmas hymn; and when I had finished it, they asked me for another, and then another, till I quite exhausted my stock of hymns and carols, and had to bring my inventive powers to the task in conjuring suitable stories for the Christmas Eve. I remember I told them tales wherein the words plum-pudding and mince-pies, roast turkey and flagons of ale, the yule-log and wassail-bowl had prominent place. But I found that they both loved best to hear me tell of things that happened to myself, many long years before, when I was a little boy, and hung up my stocking o' Christmas Eves; and, among other stories, I told them how, when I was a very small lad, not bigger than Fanny, I had gone with their great-grandmother Gray to the house of an old friend of hers, who lived in the country, to spend the holidays. It was Christmas Eve when we arrived; and as we had ridden a long distance in an open sleigh, I was very tired and sleepy, and so, soon after supper, I asked to be put to bed. Here Mary interrupted me to say that I must have been a very, very little boy indeed, to want to go to bed so early on Christmas Eve, and that, for her part, she should n't have been sleepy in the least, but would have liked to sit up all night. This I knew was intended as a hint for me to allow both Fanny and herself to stay up beyond their usual bedtime; so I let the hour go by without dismissing them, and continued my story.

The chamber which I was to occupy with my grandmother was a very large one, filled with old-fashioned furniture; and I remember she told me that the greater part of it came over in the *May-Flower*, along with the Pilgrim Fathers; and while she undressed me she told me a long story about Captain Miles Standish, and Governor Carver, and the Indians, and Plymouth Rock, the greater portion of which I can still recall to mind. Here Mary wanted me to tell her what it was, but Fanny said:—

"No; wait till papa has finished telling us about himself."

So I continued as follows: —

"There seemed to my sleepy little eyes to be quite an army of chairs ranged about the room, and, with their high, straight backs, and long, slender legs, they looked so strange it was difficult for me to keep from watching them. I half expected to see them step out into the middle of the floor and make formal bows to each other. There was a large black-walnut bookcase on one side of the room, filled with great dusty volumes, that looked as if they could never have been read; and I recollect walking boldly up to it in my nightgown, and finding that the books on the lowest shelf were just as tall as I, and wondering whether I would ever be able to read such huge volumes."

Here Fanny clapped her hands, and wanted to know if, when I came to be a man, I had ever seen these great books again; and whether or not they had many pictures in them. So I told her that some of those same books were now in my library, and that they were the very ones she and Mary so often, on rainy Sundays, were fond of looking at, and having me explain to them the pictures. This piece of news seemed to astonish them very much, so they both got down and went to the bookcase to look at those wonderful books which, so many years before, I had wondered at when a little boy. They were very anxious to know how it came to pass that I now owned them, and I told them that one day the good old lady, their great-grandmother's friend, who first possessed them, died, when all her furniture and books were sold, and I had bought these with many others. Here Fanny said, "Poor old lady!" and crossed her little arms meekly over her breast, looking up into my face most piteously, while her eyes filled with tears. But Mary asked, "Where was her husband? why did n't he keep her books?" So I had to tell her that he had been a soldier, but was killed at the battle of Bunker Hill, soon after their marriage.

At length I continued : —

" Among other things in the chamber that particularly attracted my attention were several portraits in gilt frames upon the walls, so old and dusty that I thought to myself, 'They, too, must have come over in the *May - Flower*.' There were two oval-framed mirrors in the room, and a great bunch of peacocks' feathers in one corner. But the bedstead itself was the crowning wonder; so grand and gloomy did it look, that I quite feared to sleep in it. Heavy blue silk curtains surrounded it on every side, upheld by four tall posts at the corners. When my grandmother, however, parted the curtains in the middle, and looped them up at the sides with the great silk tassel, thereby revealing the white counterpane and lace-edged pillow-cases, I began to think that there might be a worse place for a little boy to sleep in than that would prove to be. So raised was the bed from the floor that I had to be lifted into it, as it quite excelled my powers of climbing, even by the aid of a chair. When I sank down amidst the feathers, I could but just see the top of my grandmother's turban, as she stood at the bedside smoothing the coverlet about me.

" After I had repeated my prayers, and my grandmother had gone down-stairs, and I was left alone, with only the ticking of the clock upon the mantel and the light of the blazing wood-fire upon the hearth to keep me company, I remembered that it was Christmas Eve, but that, occupied as I had been, I had forgotten to hang up my stocking."

Here Mary got down from my knee and crept quietly to the chimney-corner, where she hung up a clean white stocking, with which her mother had provided her, and, coming back laughing, said she would n't forget such a thing for all the world.

" Nor will I," said Fanny, " so soon as papa finishes his story."

So I kissed my little daughters, and continued : —

"What to do I did not know. I could not get out of bed with any certainty of being able to get back again; and as for going to sleep, with never a stocking hanging for Santa Claus to fill, it was not to be thought of. So I determined to keep wide awake till either the good saint or my grandmother should arrive; but I found it very difficult for my sleepy eyes to remain open, as every few moments the old sand-man came along and dropped black sand into them, till first one closed and then the other, and at last, in spite of all I could do, they both shut up tight, and I went to sleep."

Here Mary opened her large eyes very widely, as if to let me see that no sand-man had come to trouble her yet.

"After I had slept what seemed to me a long time, I was suddenly aroused by hearing the tinkling of sleigh-bells; and as I raised myself softly in bed, I saw, just by the fireplace, Santa Claus himself, like as he is described in the Christmas verses."

Here Mary clapped her hands; but Fanny nestled closer to my side.

"He appeared to be looking for my stocking, which he could not find; and just as I had mustered courage to tell him where it was, he stepped up before the portrait of a grave-looking gentleman, who wore a powdered wig and displayed an abundance of ruffles to his shirt-front and around his wrists, and asked him, — these were his very words, — could he tell where little Barry's stocking was hung? But no answer came from this fine gentleman; he only shook his head, and seemed to draw back into the depth of the canvas. So Santa Claus put the same question to the next portrait, which was that of a prim and starched gentlewoman, evidently the wife of the first; but she only pursed up her lips and said nothing. So he questioned the third, a jolly-looking person, with a red nose and yellow waistcoat with gilt buttons, who nodded and winked in return, but spoke not a word. At last, in despair, he turned to the portrait of a dainty-looking creature, dressed in white satin, with a red rose on her breast, and who had golden hair and blue eyes, and a delicate pink nose that turned up towards the ceiling very prettily; but she only simpered and cast down her eyes, and evidently wanted to get up a flirtation with the good saint. But he seemed so indignant at the treatment he received, that he turned his back upon her, and would have gone off in a rage, had I not softly wished him a merry Christmas."

"O papa, how brave you must have been," said Fanny. "I am sure I would n't have dared to speak to him."

"Pshaw!" exclaimed Mary. "I would; and I 'd have told him, too, exactly what I wanted."

"Well, my children," I continued, "my greeting acted like a charm, for he instantly opened his pack and took from it toys, and books, and candy, which he put upon the table at the bedside. Just as he finished, a loud gush of music came up from the rooms below, and, quickly shouldering his pack, he passed, with a 'Merry Christmas' on his lips, directly up the chimney, and the next moment I saw the shadow of his sleigh and reindeers glide across the frosted window-panes, while, with a beating heart, full of wild wishes for the morrow to come, again I fell asleep."

As I finished my story, a soft hand was placed over my eyes, and a fond voice exclaimed: —

"Ah! what a sad romancer you are! How can you fill our children's minds with such foolish tales?"

But I soothed my wife with the promise of a set of furs on the morrow, and, taking her hand in mine, drew her to the chair beside me. Fanny crept close to her mother, and putting up her rosy lips for a kiss, told her not to scold dear papa. And so, with the firelight still flickering on the wall, and the wind roaring and blustering without, we passed our Christmas Eve. And still I repeated many a pleasant tale, and my sweet wife sung many an olden song, and the children prattled on my knees.

But as the midnight came the light grew dim, the fires smouldered on the hearth, the songs and stories ceased, and the children's prattle died away. And as I stretched out my hand to take my wife's in mine, I groped about in vain; my little Mary's arm no longer clasped my neck, nor Fanny's head rested upon my shoulder. I started up and found that all had been a dream, that wife and children of mine lived not yet upon the earth, but had place only in that far-off and sunny land of Utopia, where so many men's possessions and treasures ever remain.

But I heard the church-bells ringing midnight, and proclaiming to all the world the glad tidings, that "Unto us this night is born, in the city of David, a Saviour, which is Christ the Lord." And my voice joined in the mighty chorus, which from all Christendom arose, "Glory to God in the highest; and on earth peace, good-will towards men."

When I finished, my wife said it was a very pretty story, and the children were urgent for me to tell them another. But as it was time for them to go to bed, and their mother expected me to go out with her to make a call on a young bride, I was compelled to decline the honor of telling another, and to declare the meeting around the library lamp to be ended.

CHAPTER XXXV.

Christmas Eve. — No Christmas. — Another Story. — Holiday Nights' Entertainments. — Good Children. — Utopia. — An old Bank Clerk. — Striking a Balance. — Old Tom. — Mary and Fanny. — Hanging up Stockings.

"CHRISTMAS must be here, Mrs. Gray," I said, as, looking up from the book I was reading, I observed the little ones engaged in hanging their stockings beside the blazing grate, with evident faith in Santa Claus.

"Not quite," she answered, "although Christmas Eve may, after all, be designated as such. The children, evidently, believe it to be already here, and will go to bed with all manner of fancies in their little heads."

"Nothing can be better," I said, "than to have this holiday come once a year, as it does. Suppose, though, through some unforeseen circumstance, — an actual impossibility, however, — the present month should pass away, and the year 1865 close without Christmas making its appearance."

Here the children opened their eyes and looked frightened.

"How severely, in the future," I continued, "we would criticize — and with justice, too — the year that had no Christmas in it! How the little ones, who hang up their stockings on Christmas eves, and dream beautiful dreams on this night, would shudder and turn pale as their nurses recounted to them the frightful epoch bereft of Santa Claus, and, as a matter of course, of the numberless gifts which the old saint, who is no niggard, freely dispenses to all good little boys and girls."

Here the little folks looked sorrowfully at each other.

" Once there was a time, strange as it may seem, when the years really possessed no Christmas ; but this was long ago, in the dark ages, before our Saviour's day. Now we, who live in the Christian era, need not fear that ever a year will pass unhallowed by Christmas and ungladdened by Christmas cheer. Oh, it is excellent to live in these times, and be a little boy or girl, and have presents given to you, and take sleigh-rides," ——

Here the three little ones clapped their hands in glee.

" And go to church, where you may hear sweet anthems sung, and listen to the story — which all have heard told over and over again, but which ever seems new and beautiful — of the shepherds on the plains of Bethlehem, who, while watching their flocks by night, beheld the Star in the East."

" Now, papa, do please," cried Em., " tell us something more about your children in Utopia."

" Well, if you will be very good little ones, and not go to sleep while I am telling it, — though Miss Floy, I 'll warrant, will see to your not doing aught so impolite, — I will promise to relate all I know about the precious family in Utopia, which was mine long before I knew your dear mother, or had such good little bodies as you are to get my slippers and easy chair ready for me when I come home. But this story is a very long one, and as I shall not be able to tell it all in one evening, I will divide it up through the Christmas week, and will call it the Holiday Nights' Entertainments."

" Oh, that will be nice," said Em.

" It will be nice," echoed Mary.

And " That 's bully," said the boy.

" William Howard," said Miss Floy, reprovingly, " I am astonished to hear you utter such a coarse expression. How many times have I cautioned you against speaking in an improper manner ? "

"Nary time," he replied.

"There it is again," she continued; "you certainly are incorrigible. I shall have to give you a long lesson in your spelling-book to-morrow as a punishment, if you make such a remark again. Miss Emma Louisa, now, is behaving herself like a lady, and, when Saturday comes, if she continues to be good, she shall come to my room and hear me read some of my play."

Em. frowned and looked cross.

"I am sure," said Miss Floy, observing her, "it is quite as interesting as, and much more instructive than, the foolish story your papa is going to read."

"It ain't, is it, papa?" asked Em.

"It may not be to you, my child," I replied, "but to me it is much more so."

This acknowledgment quite pleased Miss Floy, who smoothed out the creases in her silk dress, and then, with a smiling countenance, sat down near Mrs. Gray to listen, with the children, to the story of—

MY FAMILY IN UTOPIA.

Mine is a precious family. It consists of a wife and two children. Some of you, perhaps, may remember having heard of them. Their residence, I am happy to state, is in Utopia. I manage to see them several times in the course of the year. Sometimes they come to me, but oftener I go to them. Of an evening — especially a winter evening — it is my delight to visit them. There is no stage-line, nor canal, nor railroad leading to Utopia; only a balloon flies occasionally from a chateau in Spain, where I pass many of my evenings, to the vine-clad cottage in which they live. I have never been able to learn exactly where Utopia is situated, though I have made diligent search for it on many maps, at various times. I have often thought that if any one were capable of giving me information regarding its locality, it would be Sinbad the

Sailor. I once wrote him a letter of inquiry concerning it, but when I came to superscribe his name, I could not, for the life of me, tell his place of residence; nor, by referring to his biography, as reported in the "Arabian Nights," could I obtain any clew as to his whereabouts. So the letter to him was never mailed. If I could remain awake when journeying to Utopia, I think I might, without doubt, settle to my perfect satisfaction both its latitude and longitude; but I invariably go to sleep on my way thither. I have heard of men who spent their lives seeking in vain to locate it. There is something, I confess, a little strange and misty in all this, — something I do not quite understand, and I fear I never shall. I used to puzzle over it a good deal at first, when I was young; but now, grown older, I think it better to strive more to discover the exact spot where great peace, and contentment, and righteousness dwell, than to be wondering and worrying any more about the position of Utopia.

Few persons of my acquaintance suspect my being at the head of a family. There are no signs to denote either the husband or father in my appearance. No lines of care are traceable on my brow; no white hairs mingle with my brown locks; no sighs rise from my bosom, nor is my form less erect than when I was a bachelor. On the contrary, there is much to convince my friends that I am unmarried. I am well preserved; my constitution is unimpaired; my step as elastic as it was twenty years ago; and, I am gratified to be able to say it, I whistle as I walk. Sometimes, even, I find myself singing, not in a low tone, but loud enough to be heard above the city's din. It is well that the fact of my being a husband and father should remain a secret to the bulk of my acquaintance. I am very glad that the directors of the bank where I hold a situation as clerk, regard me as a single man. Should they ascertain my true position in social life, they might wonder how I contrive to support myself and family on the slender salary I receive. They would, doubtless, think it well to examine, oftener than they do, my accounts. Not that I should object to their doing so, — for I have no fears but they would find each quantity correct, — yet their wonder would thereby be the more increased, and they might think I was too crafty for them; and, their suspicions once excited, it would end in my dismissal. Were they to know the truth, even, that I add a few pennies to my scanty wages by occasionally contributing an article to the magazines, this, in itself, would be a sufficient reason for dismissing me from the desk I have so long occupied. These Wall Street directors, I have observed, with some exceptions, are amazingly shy of all who, like myself, delight to dabble in literature. It does not appear proper to them for a book-keeper to be, even in a small way, a book-writer. Therefore it is that with the wily public I choose to pass for an unmarried man, having no desire to rise higher in the social scale than just what I am taken for, namely, a solitary, ill-paid bank clerk. In Wall Street during banking hours, I am neither more or less than this. My intimate friends — I have some intimate friends whose positions in life are humble as my own — regard me in a somewhat different light, for the reason, it may be, that they look at me from a directly opposite point of view. The directors behold in me simply a dependent; my friends consider me their equal, perceive a few good points in my character, and speak of me with praise — somewhat qualified, however.

Sometimes, when I have been detained at the bank till late in the evening, I have astonished the Custom-house, as I passed it, with a series of whistles so jubilant and shrill, that the weathercock above its roof has whirled around in affright, to learn what was in the wind. But such proceedings, on my part, within the dollar-getting precincts of Wall Street, do not often occur. It is only when I step into the shadow of the cross that surmounts

Trinity's spire, that I put off, as I would a garment, the mildewed air of a bank clerk, and assume the sunshiny lounge of a man of leisure. I do not, however, suppose that my assumed character imposes on any one. I feel the disguise is altogether too feeble. I can detect such in another as quickly as I do a counterfeit bill. I take the character simply to please myself, and, as I stroll up Broadway, among gayly attired ladies and well-dressed men, I forget that I am nailed, like a spurious coin, to a bank desk, while I revel for a time in the brief Arcadian dream of happiness I conjure up.

On the last day of the year just passed, when I glanced over my private account with the bank, preparatory to striking a balance, I was surprised to find that a sum which the figure X would cover, and leave a wide margin, was all that would be coming to me. I examined my pass-book several times very carefully, to make certain I was correct. I even hoped that, somewhere, I had made a mistake in my calculations. Though I pride myself on my accuracy as regards balancing other people's accounts, yet, in my own case, I should have been pleased to detect an error, if in my favor, though it were at the expense of my pride. I confess I was exceedingly disappointed in the result before me. I had expected that at least five times that trifling sum would have been my due. Visions of several unpaid accounts rose up before me, — accounts which I had promised to settle early in the new year. I felt quite unnerved when I thought of them. I really pitied the holders of those little accounts. Especially did my pity flow towards my landlady. I knew she quite relied on receiving from me full twenty dollars. I thought, at first, that I would give her my note at thirty days; but then I felt certain she would ask the bank to discount it. And the idea of having "our directors" sitting in solemn council over my poor note, was ridiculous. "No, no," I said, "a bank clerk must n't give notes, — that 's certain."

When the hour for closing the bank came, I found that I was behindhand with my work. I hastened, therefore, to finish it. It was long, however, after the other clerks had gone home that I brought my duties to an end. At length my year's work was finished. And as I laid my weary head on the desk, over which I had bent for more than a dozen years, I thought how like an arithmetic had been my life! Nothing but figure added to figure in all those years. I had fingered gold, and silver, and notes, — an unknown but vast amount, — and now, of all this, what was mine? I crumpled the note I held within my fingers with a nervous grasp, which, had it been a living thing, would have made it shriek aloud. I gazed about the apartment, as though I should have liked to find the president, or cashier, or some one of the directors, on whom I might vent my anger; but my eyes only encountered the wrinkled face of the old black man, who sat beside the stove, patiently waiting my departure, that he might bar the window-shutters and lock the outer doors.

As I passed out, the hearty "Happy New Year" uttered by faithful Old Tom, helped to lighten my grief. I felt still more relieved when, just as I stepped on the sidewalk, I heard the bells of Trinity chiming the hour; for they recalled to my mind the hymn which on Christmas Day the same chimes rung forth, proclaiming "on earth peace, good-will to men." With this remembrance, joy returned to my heart, and it was with a light step that I mingled with the crowd which glided up Broadway.

It was dusk when I turned down the side-street wherein is located my boarding-house. As I mounted the three flights of stairs leading to my room, I thought — why, I cannot tell — of my family in Utopia. It had been long since I had seen them. I had been so engrossed by my daily labors, that I had scarcely given them a thought. Now however, — perhaps because the year was so nigh its end,

— I recalled my wife's sweet looks, and my daughters' charming ways, and I resolved to pass New Year's Day with them.

When I entered my apartment, I found a bright fire burning within the grate. My easy chair was drawn in front of it; my dressing-gown rested across its back, and my slippers lay on the soft rug. I felt that fairy fingers had been at work. I stopped in the centre of the room, and gazed curiously about. It seemed to me that pure spirits were near. I thought I could detect the sound of their rustling robes. I listened attentively, when forth from the shadow of my great arm-chair sprung towards me, encircling my neck in their fond embrace, my two children, Mary and Fanny.

How they had found their way to my apartment, from their far-off home, I did not think to ask. I did, however, for a moment, wonder whether they had escaped the prying eyes of my landlady, in their passage through the halls and staircases. But this was all forgotten in my joy at beholding and clasping them to my heart. After they had taken my hat and over-coat, and brought me my slippers and dressing-gown, they seated me in the easy chair, and then, climbing upon my knees, they placed their little faces close to mine, and kissed me, first, as they said, for dear mamma, and then, afterwards, for themselves. When I asked why their good mother did not come with them, Mary exclaimed, quickly, that mamma had sent them to take papa to her; while Fanny, laying her soft hand on my cheek, whispered, "Dear papa will go with his little darlings, — will he not?" Then Mary wanted to know whether I knew that it was New Year's Eve, and straightway proceeded to inform me that last Sunday night was Christmas Eve, but that she did n't believe it, hardly; for, though both Fanny and herself hung up their stockings, Santa Claus failed to put anything in them; and, for her part, she thought that if it were really Christmas, the old fellow would have given them something. Fanny was quite shocked at hearing Mary call Santa Claus "old fellow," and said that she knew it was Christmas, for mamma had said so; and if Santa Claus had n't given them anything, she supposed it was because they were such very little girls, that maybe he 'd forgotten them. And besides, she added, they lived so far away from New York, that perhaps he had no time to go to them. "Any ways," said Mary, pouting her lips, "it was real mean in him." This speech greatly frightened Fanny, who clung closer to me, and asked if Santa Claus ever got vexed with what little girls said of him? I replied that he sometimes did, but he was of such a gentle disposition that he soon forgave whatever naughty things they uttered. Mary hereupon evinced quite a penitential spirit, and remarked that she was sorry for what she had said; but added, after a pause, during which she seemed to have been considering the matter, it was mean anyhow. I then told them I thought the reason why they had obtained nothing on Christmas was, that the good saint had not time to go to Utopia; "But I have no doubt," I continued, "in regard to his filling your stockings to-night."

Here Fanny, I perceived, glanced about my room, and, seeing no fireplace, immediately wished to know if Santa Claus could get through the bars of a grate. After I had satisfied her on this point, Mary immediately inquired whether the old saint could become little, for I had once told her that he was as large as Grandpa Gray. When I had explained this matter to their entire satisfaction, they desired to know where would be the best place to hang their stockings. Having decided this important matter, Fanny exclaimed, with considerable feeling, that they had forgotten to bring clean ones with them. This for a moment cast a shadow over their fair faces. Mary, however, was the first to recover. "Ho!" said she, "these I 've got on will be good enough for me." But Fanny's lip curled, the tears sprung to her eyes, and her voice trembled, as she said that she could n't bear to have Santa Claus see her soiled stockings. No! she 'd rather go without anything than have him. Then I promised them both that we would go out into Broadway, so soon as the gas-lamps were lighted, to buy each a pair of nice new stockings; and in the mean time I would tell them a story. This proposal so delighted Mary that she clapped her tiny hands, while Fanny kissed me on the lips, and called me her good papa.

"And here closes, my little ones," I said to the children grouped around me, "the first part of our Christmas Nights' Entertainments. To-morrow evening I will tell you a story within a story, being that of 'Merry Clochette,' which I related to my children in Utopia."

CHAPTER XXXVI.

Story within a Story. — "Merry Clochette." — Misses Vane. — Lite Rod, Esquire. — A Yellow Gown. — Messrs. Chimes. — A Young Clergyman. Two Pigeons. — Monsieur Horloge. — Keeping Watch.

THE following evening, as soon as we had gone to the library from the dinner-table, Miss Em., even before I had lighted my cigar, importuned me to go on with my story of "My Children in Utopia," and especially to remember that I promised to tell them a story within a story, entitled, "Merry Clochette." So, as the little ones were all ears, I commenced as follows: —

"Once on a time, no matter when, there dwelt, no matter where, a young lady of French extraction, named Clochette, — Merry Clochette, the good neighbors, who loved to hear her voice, called her. There were others, however, not so partial to her, who spoke of her as noisy Clochette; and a few, even, I am sorry to say, who said that, after all, she was no better than a brazen belle. These last were certainly ill-natured persons, and ought to have been ashamed of themselves."

Hereupon Fanny said she thought they would have been.

"Strange as it may seem," I continued, "the home of Merry Clochette was high up in the tower of an old church."

"How nice that must have been!" said Mary.

"Here, indeed, she passed all her time; but, though she led so solitary a life, Mademoiselle Clochette was a very talkative little body. Her tongue was in almost constant motion. If there were anything of importance going on in the neighborhood, she was sure to be the first to bruit it abroad. No one could get married but she learned the news as soon as any; and then you could hear her voice ringing through the clear air, telling it over and over to every one who would listen. Or, if a baby were to be christened, she had its name at her tongue's end, only she could n't always pronounce it properly, though she often came pretty near to doing so. Then, too, when any one died, she was about the first that told it, and would name with great accuracy, the number of years the deceased had lived."

Fanny here remarked, she thought Miss Merry must have been a very curious lady to have known all these affairs; while Mary said she guessed the lady must have been very inquisitive, and asked a great many questions. I answered simply by telling them to listen, and proceeded.

"On all occasions of rejoicing — on May-days and on Christmas — Mademoiselle Clochette was certain to be very merry and talkative; and if at any time a house, or even a rough shed, chanced to be on fire, she made noise enough to wake everybody within hearing. Dwelling so high above the earth, she had a fine opportunity to behold all that went on below her; so that it is not to be wondered at that she talked a great deal. Yet it is conceded by all that she never uttered a sound unless she was requested so to do."

Mary thought this very strange; but Fanny said not a word.

"Oh!" I continued, "she was very much of a lady, and belonged, I assure you, to a high-toned family, — one that occupied rather an exalted position in society. She was connected, too, with the Vane family, — very aristocratic people, — some of which held the highest places in the church. They are, however, rather a fickle, changeable set, and would be likely any day to turn on her a cold shoulder. She is connected with them by marriage. Her cousin, L. Rod, Esq., a tall, thin young man, who rose from a position far below her, had succeeded in consummating a matrimonial connection with one of the Misses Vane, a young lady bedizened with a large amount of gilt. Lite Rod considered this a great alliance, and often, especially on windy nights, alluded to it in the presence of his cousin Merry. She was not, however, too well pleased with his boastings, and used sometimes to tell him that, though his head might be in the clouds, yet his feet were, nevertheless, in the earth; which was true enough. Whenever Merry said this to him, he retorted by replying that she herself owed the position she occupied to a scaffolding and a rope; which, lamentably enough, was just as he represented. But I cannot now explain this matter, for 't is a long story, and, indeed, will scarcely bear repeating."

Mary here expressed considerable curiosity to know why it would not bear repeating; but Fanny cried, "Hush! listen to what papa chooses to tell us." So I kissed little Fanny on her lips, and patted, half reprovingly, half caressingly, my Mary's silken hair.

"But for all this," I said, continuing my story, "Miss Merry was quite a lady, and wore always a yellow gown, nearly the color of gold, which, when the sun shone full on it, you would have declared was really made from that precious metal."

"How fine a sight she must have been!" exclaimed Mary. "And so lady-like," added Fanny.

"Of course, Mademoiselle Clochette, who had been a belle a great many years, had not been without many admirers. Yes, there were the three brothers, the Messrs. Chimes, who lived in a new stone tower, about half a mile distant from Merry, who were all desperately in love with her. Such delightful serenades as they gave her on summer evenings, and such strange, wild stories as they told her o' winter nights, were very wonderful. But these serenades and stories had no effect on Merry Clochette. She either turned quite a deaf ear to them, or else she mocked them with such silvery sounding laughter as made them believe their singing was most discordant. Poor fellows! they took her coolness quite to heart; and one by one their voices became cracked and harsh, till at last they fell from the tower, lost the use of their tongues, and never uttered a loud word afterward. When Merry heard of their accident, she was quite doleful for three whole days, and then, on the fourth, she forgot all about them."

Fanny thought this very cruel in Miss Clochette, and came near crying; but Mary shook her curls, and laughed outright.

"Then again," I went on, "there was the old sexton, who lived close by; he used on sunny afternoons to climb up in the tower, and, sitting by her side, rest his poor old head on her breast. Though he never really told her that he loved her, yet she knew it by the glances and sighs he gave her. But, because he was an old man, gray-haired, and wrinkled, and bent, and, moreover, had buried such a number of wives, — more than a hundred, I have heard, — she never gave him the least encouragement. Still, she enjoyed his society very much, and often beguiled his weary old heart from sadness by her merry tones."

Fanny said that she should have dearly loved the old sexton, if he were anything like dear Grandpa Gray. But Mary remarked that she should n't care to marry him for all that, for he was too much like Blue-Beard.

"Besides him, my little ones," I continued, "there was the young clergyman that officiated in the church, who, in the early mornings, often visited her, and read aloud his sermons for the coming Sabbath. These were very instructive and interesting for Merry to hear; but I don't think she profited by them one bit."

"How shameful in her," said Fanny.

"Because," I continued, not heeding the interruption,

"she was so much occupied in watching his handsome face. Then he possessed such mild looks, and his voice was so soft, and he had such winning ways, withal, that she was quite charmed, and became, before she was aware of it, very much in love with the gentle clergyman. But he did not once suspect this in her, because he was so much engaged doing his Master's work."

Mary spoke here, and said that she could have loved him, but not the old sexton.

"Merry Clochette, I think, acted very wisely in the matter, and when she perceived that he cared not for her, she straightway determined to forget him. To enable her the sooner and better to do this, she resolved to occupy her time in some cheerful manner. Luckily for her, two pigeons had built their nest on the cross-beam just over her head; and it became her great delight to watch them, and study their life and habits. Oh, they were a source of great comfort to Merry Clochette, for

> 'Summer and winter those birds were there,
> Out and in, in the morning air.'

And so, little by little, she came to forget the young clergyman.

"Yet, poor little thing! she could not help but feel lonely, sometimes, up there in the old tower, and greatly desired some one to love."

"Had she no papa, or mamma, or grandpa, whom she could love?" asked Fanny.

"No," I said; "she was all alone, and never knew what it was to have a parent."

"Poor Merry!" cried Fanny, and the tears stood in her eyes; while Mary exclaimed, — "Poh! don't cry, Fan.; it 's only a story."

"Simpleton! that Merry Clochette was," I proceeded, "she did not know that in the apartment directly below her dwelt a gentleman, — Monsieur Horloge, — who for years had thought and spoken only of her. But, as he was a most bashful youth, he had never dared to show his face in her presence. Indeed, he kept his hands constantly before it, and no one could prevail on him to take them away."

"What a foolish man!" exclaimed Mary.

"Sometimes he was quite run down and low-spirited; besides, he was disposed to be quarrelsome, and never hesitated to strike one, if he thought proper so to do. So that, after all, it was just as well, perhaps, that little Merry did not know him; for I don't believe they would, if they had married, have dwelt happily together. He would, I am certain, have been always striking; while she, for her part, would have told something concerning him every hour. Still it was sad to hear him muttering to himself all day and all night, never ceasing a single minute, and all because he was so desperately in love with Merry Clochette."

"How very pitiful!" said Fanny, clasping her little hands, and looking into my face.

"At last, one Christmas Day, a personage, very grand-looking, wrapped in costly furs, came in a sleigh, drawn by reindeers, to visit Mademoiselle Clochette. Her cousin, Lite Rod, Esq., led him up to her room. Here he sat by her side so long, and laid his gloved hand so caressingly upon her yellow gown, that all the neighbors, who, of course, were watching, declared that Merry Clochette had a beau."

Fanny hereupon clapped her hands, and said she was glad of it; while Mary added, she guessed Miss Clochette was glad enough too.

"Through the short afternoon, and far into the cold night, the idle neighbors kept watch; some, provided with spy-glasses, and *lunettes*, and bits of smoked glass, stationed themselves at their windows, and gazed with earnest eyes into the tower. Others, still more curious, sent their little boys to climb the tall trees that grew beside the tower, where, lodged in the branches, they could note all that passed; but none of them, I am happy to state, saw anything improper, or which the most fastidious maiden would not have permitted her lover.

"At length, however, the neighbors grew quite sleepy, and one by one they put out the lights in their houses; and the little boys, numb and chill, slid down the trees and went home, and soon all the village were in bed. Then, when everybody was asleep, the grand personage in furs — it was no other than Santa Claus himself," (here Fanny clapped her hands, and Mary shouted with glee,) — "took little Merry by the hand, dressed in her yellow gown, which looked like gold, and assisted her down the winding stairs, and placed her safely in his cushioned sleigh, amid the costliest furs. Only the Man in the Moon looked down on them. Monsieur Horloge held his hands steadily before his face, and did not give them so much as a parting glance. Mr. L. Rod and his pretty wife — lately Miss Vane — were dreaming, one of the wind, and the other of thunder-clouds. The young clergyman was kneeling at the bedside of the old sexton, who was just breathing his last; while the two pigeons, with their heads folded under their wings, were resting side by side.

"Little Merry's heart beat fast as the sleigh glided swiftly away from the foot of the old church-tower; but Santa Claus drew her closely to his side, and, whispering softly in her ears, declared that she, and she alone, should ever be his bride.

"Then he loudly exclaimed, ere they vanished from sight, 'Little folks, peace be with you! Good-night, oh! good-night.'

"And here closes," I said, rising from my chair and taking a position on the rug, with my back to the fire, "the second part of our Holiday Nights' Entertainments; and now I desire to say a few words."

"Mr. Gray," interrupted my wife, "pray don't destroy the pleasant impression left on our minds through your story, by getting off anything prosaic in the way of a speech. I can always tell, when you assume that not very polite position on the rug, that you are intending to deliver something very dull and stupid."

Miss Floy, too, seemed to have the same opinion regarding the affair as my wife; for she, while Mrs. Gray was speaking, without giving the children an opportunity to thank me and say good-night, hurried them out of the room, and went herself along with them.

Thereupon, having no audience, I yielded to my wife's entreaties, and forebore to make the learned remarks concerning the festival of Christmas, its origin, antiquity, and the manner of keeping it by different nations, which I had proposed to myself to set forth.

As I passed to my own room an hour or two later, after having seen that old Santa Claus filled the children's stockings in an appropriate manner, I stopped in the nursery, and kissed the two little girls asleep in their bed, and the boy asleep in his, and wished them, and all good children everywhere, a merry Christmas.

CHAPTER XXXVII.

Christmas Day. — Utopia. — Our President. — Gold *vs.* Greenbacks. — In the Toy-store. — Prayers. — Night. — Morning. — A Pleasant Check. — Our Bank. — Breakfast. — Off to Utopia. — The Balloon. — "Tress." — The Dead Babe. — Mamma. —Carol. — The Awakening.

CHRISTMAS Day came and went, and the children, who had enjoyed themselves exceedingly in examining their various presents, in going down to the Bronx to skate, and in doing much snow-balling and sliding down-hill, were so wearied when evening came, that they failed to ask me to continue the story commenced the night before; but the following night they were wide awake, and, shortly after dinner, before I had finished reading the evening papers, gave me to understand that they were waiting for me to celebrate another Holiday Evening's Entertainment. Thereupon, putting aside the evening paper, I began as follows: —

MY FAMILY IN UTOPIA.

"WHAT nice stories you tell, papa," exclaimed Fanny, as soon as I finished; "how I love to sit on your knee, and listen to you. Don't you think they are beautiful, Mary?"

"Yes," replied Mary; "but I think I like Hans Andersen's better. His are much more funny; and then, you can read them yourself; and his book, too, is full of pictures. Pa, tell another one; will you?"

But I pointed out to my little daughters the gas-lights shining in the streets, and told them we would now go to

Broadway, and make our Christmas purchases. So, quickly they wrapped their pretty mantles around themselves, and, each placing a trusting hand in mine, we descended to the street. As we turned into the noisy thoroughfare of Broadway, I nearly upset "our President," who, with his fur-caped cloak gathered about his face, rushed blindly towards me. He paused a moment; adjusted his hat, which the encounter had slightly displaced; peered at me a moment through his gold-bowed spectacles; apologized for his part of the accident; wished my little ones a "Happy New Year," and passed on his solitary way. I say solitary, because he is a bachelor, and possesses neither wife nor little ones. It was evident to me that he failed to recognize, in the proud father with the two little girls, a toiling clerk of the bank in which he held the highest rank. He was rich in worldly goods; but, poor as I was, I deemed myself wealthier, in the possession of my two priceless jewels, than he would dare dream of being.

Somewhere about Houston Street we stepped into a hosiery establishment, to purchase the new stockings. It was amusing to me to notice the airs Miss Mary put on while making a selection. These were too coarse; those too large; and others, again, not long enough. Fanny, on the contrary, was pleased with the first pair shown her. "They matched," she said, "so well her blue dress and hood."

At last Mary found a red pair, just the color of her cloak; and so, having paid for them out of my slender purse, we passed down Broadway. As we went on our way, there was scarce a window ablaze with light before which we did not stop. Had my purse been filled with gold instead of the few "greenbacks" it contained, it would not have bought all my little ones desired. Now it was something I must get for "dear mamma;" then something for myself; while Mary must needs want a whole window-ful at once, often containing articles which she never would have known what to do with. Fanny, however, was more moderate in her desires, and only wished for particular articles. I noticed, though, that she always selected such as were the most costly, while Mary wanted everything, with little regard either to quality or cost.

When we reached the toy-store, my little ones were half crazed with delight. Such wonderful wax-dolls, and tea sets, and bureaus, and bedsteads, and hundreds of other things, were, surely, never before seen. I managed while they were both engaged in examining a miniature play-house, to make several purchases, unseen by them; and placing the dainty packages in the capacious pockets of my coat, we turned to retrace our steps. After a slight halt at a confectioner's, and a further pause at a book-store, where, at each place, I secretly added to my hidden hoard, we reached again my boarding-place. To be sure, my purse was now very light, but my pockets were heavy, and my children's hearts were full of happiness. I felt pleased, however, that I did not encounter the landlady, on my way up the stairs. The sight of her pale, careworn face would have sadly discomforted me. It would have reminded me of my bankruptcy. Though such thoughts as these came across my mind, they were quickly put to flight, when I reached my room, by the merry laughter of my precious ones.

When the new stockings were carefully hung up, and I had arranged a bed on the lounge for my little darlings, I seated them on my knees, and told tales of the old years past. I told what I did, when, a little boy, I used to hang up my stocking, and believed in good old Santa Claus.

Mary wanted to know why I did n't hang it up still; and Fanny asked whether I had ceased to believe in Santa Claus. When I had satisfied them on these points, it was time to go to bed. So, after they had repeated their prayers — prayers their mother taught them — and had sung a little hymn, — I heard the echo of that mother's voice throughout it, — they kissed me a good-night kiss, and a few moments afterwards were nestled snugly in their bed. When the sand-man — who always goes before Santa Claus — had dropped sand upon their eyes, and before I had myself gone to bed, I beheld the old saint carefully fill their stockings, and then, directly after, I myself retired.

But I never shall forget — not if I live to be very old indeed — how singularly Santa Claus was attired. He had on a long white robe — perhaps it was trimmed with fur — that almost reached the floor; a pair of blue velvet slippers, embroidered with gold braid, were on his feet; while his head was adorned with a red silk cap, ornamented by a gilt tassel. When he had performed his allotted work, he kissed my little girls, put out the gas, and that was the last I saw of him for that night.

With the first rays of the morning of the new year, I was aroused by soft whispering; and then I heard the patter of bare feet on the chamber floor, as my little girls hastened to their stockings. I remained very quiet; for it was pleasant to hear their expressions of delight and astonishment as they drew forth from their stockings the various articles they contained.

"See," exclaimed Mary; "here is the very wax-doll that we saw at the toy-store. I know it," she continued, "by its pink dress and blue eyes. Is n't it beautiful?"

"And here," shouted Fanny, "is the work-box we admired so much. Don't you remember the little round piece of looking-glass in the centre of the cover? How kind in Santa Claus to get us exactly what we wished for! is n't it, Mary?"

"Yes," answered Mary, "if it were really Santa Claus who gave them to us; but don't you believe, Fan., that, after all, it was papa?"

Fanny had never considered the matter; it was something to think about; so she simply replied, she did n't know; she was evidently very much perplexed and disturbed in her mind by this new suggestion of Mary's; so a silence ensued, and during its continuance I again fell asleep.

When I awoke, the sun was shining into my room, the children were dressed, and had arranged on the centre-table their various gifts, for my inspection. It was delightful for me to hear their many expressions of pleasure, as they showed me their new treasures. They were in haste, too, to get home, so that mamma could share in their pleasure. There was enough left in my purse, I found, to treat them to a simple breakfast, and pay for our conveyance to my castle in Spain, from whence the balloon started. From there to Utopia no money is required. The balloon is, with one exception, free for all who choose to travel in it. The exception is this: no man who has much money in his pocket is permitted therein. In fact, the less wealth a man has, the better the accommodations that are given him. I felt certain that that morning I should be received with much honor and a cordial welcome, and would be shown to a very distinguished place. This thought made me feel very proud, but, as I descended the staircase, my pride was doomed to a sad fall. I regretted it more than I rejoiced over the receipt of that which caused it. Just as I was going down the third flight of stairs, I encountered Old Tom, the porter of "our bank," coming up. He held a letter in his hand, addressed to me. My hand, I remarked, trembled almost as much as did his, at the moment I took the letter. I feared that I had run my course as a bank clerk, and that the letter contained my dismissal. I was afraid that, somehow, my literary labors had reached the ears of the directors, and I knew what such knowledge would result in. It was, therefore, with a somewhat quickened pulse that I tore open the envelop, and unfolded the sheet within, when, to my astonishment, there appeared, with the bold signature of the president at the bottom of it, a check on the bank for one hundred dollars; accompanying which was a communication, to the effect that, in consideration of the strict attention I had given, and the correct manner I had performed, for many years, that particular part of the business of the bank which it was my duty to look to, the directors had, at a late meeting of the board, unanimously agreed to increase my salary, and, at the same time, had voted me one hundred dollars for a New Year gift.

When I had fully assured myself that this good luck had really befallen me, I emptied what little money my purse held into Old Tom's open palm, and at the same time gave him to understand that I considered the directors of "our bank" had performed a very handsome act. When I told my little ones, who had stood by me all the time, what had befallen me, they evinced their joy in a very simple yet happy manner; they remarked that such news would please their dear mamma, and both wished to be the first to inform her of it.

I could not resist stepping into the breakfast-room, as I passed along, to assure my good landlady that her little bill would be paid on the morrow. Her countenance brightened as I spoke, and a smile hovered about her pale face, as she replied that it would be of great assistance to her. She had feared, she added, from not having seen me at supper the night previous, that, perhaps, I would not be able to pay her. I suspected, from this remark, that she had been a boarding-house keeper many years. It betrayed experience in such matters; her conclusions were logical ones; she reasoned from the effect back to the cause.

Then, wishing the quiet, but somewhat shrewd, woman a merry Christmas, I rejoined my little ones, and, giving each of them a hand, proceeded down Broadway to a quiet saloon where we partook of a Christmas breakfast, made merry to me by the joyous prattle of my children.

Where we started from, or how we journeyed going to my castle in Spain, I have no remembrance. My impression, however, is, that we went in a one-horse gig, — though the horse may have been a pony, — for the girls, I think, drove him all the way. Had I been alone, I should doubtless have borrowed the horse which General Washington rides daily in Union Square. Perhaps some one can tell me the course we took. I know we passed several objects and places of note, — the Castle of Indolence, the Village of Dreamland, Reverie Lake, the Island of the Seven Cities, the Valley of Poppies, the Mansion of Happiness, the Vale of Arcadie, and El Dorado. Fortunately, there was a balloon just on the eve of starting for Utopia when we reached my castle in Spain. Directly, therefore, taking our places in it, we found ourselves, in an incredibly short space of time, — as it seemed to us, for we slept most of the way, — hovering above Utopia. There it lay, in the soft sunshine and roseate light, nestled between green hill-sides, — it is always summer time in Utopia, — a picture of loveliness. There were to be seen woodbine-covered cottages, and ivy-clad towers, and white, tapering spires, and mirror-like lakes, and roaring brooks, and rustic bridges, and a May-pole, and gayly robed children dancing round it. As we drew nearer, sounds of music and singing reached our ears. We could discern the features of friends and neighbors; and, by-and-by, Fanny exclaimed, "See, papa! see! there's mamma crossing the green by the May-pole; she has recognized and is coming to meet us." And Mary leaned far over the side of the balloon, and waved her silken sash — and mamma saw it, and, in turn, waved her handkerchief and wafted kisses to us with her hand. A few minutes more, and we stepped from the aërial car, and were welcomed with kindly greetings and cheerful words by those around us. Something more than these, however, were mine, when I clasped my wife's hand; for in Utopia 't is not considered either indelicate or out of place to kiss one's wife, when meeting after a long absence, even though you be not sheltered beneath the roof-tree. So, then, I kissed my wife, and she kissed me. The children, too, were kissed; and then, with our little packages of gifts for mamma in our hands, we hastened home. Home! 't is a goodly word to speak. It does not mean hotel or hospital, boarding-place or restaurant, where you can simply eat, drink, and sleep — where you can keep your extra wardrobe, and spend your rainy Sundays; but it means the spot you were born in — the house of your childhood — the place which contains your wife and all most dear to you, and near to which, in the dim and far off future, you pray that your grave may be. All this, and nothing less, is home; and to such a home we and our children went.

Of course, there were many things which had occurred in the months past that my wife and children found to tell me. Changes had taken place in our little home, and changes had occurred outside the garden palings. The cat that had been ours from kittenhood, and portraits of which the little ones had worked, with various-colored worsteds, on magnificent samplers, was dead. The canaries, however, had thrived wonderfully, and raised two full broods of young since St. Valentine's Day. And old "Tress," the faithful Newfoundland dog, that had summered on the front-door mat for many a year, had grown lame and blind, and scarcely recognized the hand which fed him.

Then, too, there had been marriages and deaths, — for people marry and die even in Utopia. My neighbors had lost their little boy, just the age, when he died, of an angel-child of ours; and, as my wife told me of his death, the tears traced each other down her cheeks, and I knew she was thinking of our blessed boy. Years have gone by since we laid him in his little grave, and Mary and Fanny have both been given us since then; but neither, nor both of them, can ever fill the void in his mother's heart which the death of our precious boy caused. When she rocked the other children in *his cradle*, she tried to make herself believe that it was he who lay therein. Months after his death, when the grass was green on his little grave, she accidentally discovered behind the lounge, in the closed and deserted nursery, a small red and white worsted sock, which the baby, some day, in playing, had kicked from his tiny foot, and which had there fallen and been forgotten. My loved one nearly broke her heart afresh, weeping over that bit of colored worsted.

And then, after a short pause, my wife told me of another neighbor, whose daughter, — a fair, blue-eyed girl, — on Christmas Eve, had become a bride, and left her mother's hearth and home for a hearth and home of her own. And straightway my mind went back to the day, years and years agone, when I led my bride from the shelter of her father's house to the low-roofed cottage where I dwelt. And, looking at her, the bride, the wife, the mother, I asked myself if she had been happier in her wedded life than she would have been had I not sought her hand? She seemed to read my thoughts; for, raising her dark eyes to me, she smiled one of her old sweet smiles, and placing her hand in mind, with the other pointing to our little ones, she said: "Children make a woman's life complete; the bride is happy, but the mother happiest of all." Then, taking them by the hand and laughing, often looking back and nodding in a merry way, she led them from the room and me.

When they had gone, a cloud seemed to have swept across the sun's disk; shadows came out into the room where before the sunshine lay, and wild, sharp pains shot through my heart and brain. I thought, what if she and they have passed from my sight forever! I tried to drive away the idea as foolish; but it would not be driven away. I tried to whistle it down with an air from "*L'Elisir d'Amore,*" but 't would not be whistled down. At last I took a prime Havana, and, lighting it, essayed to smoke it out. This had the desired effect, and quickly soothed me to a happy mood. Seating myself, then, in my easy chair, I indulged in a little reverie: "Of a certainty," I thought, "my lines have fallen to me in pleasant places." I, though a simple bank clerk, am blessed with a fair and loving wife, and two beauteous and dutiful children. The latter are to me as milestones placed in the journey of life: I have but to look at them, as year by year they advance towards womanhood, to perceive how swiftly I am moving on through life; while the former, like the genial sun, sheds a light on my path, and makes easy to walk what would otherwise be a dark and rugged way. True, it is seldom that we meet; often months go by without our seeing each other; but then I enjoy with greater zest, I suppose, their society, than I otherwise should. How much better it is, too, for them to be here in Utopia, with its delightful climate and sunny skies, than in the unhealthy city, with its noise and dust, where I pass my days. They live in a continual sunshine: no clouds gather over their blue sky; no harsh November winds drive the dry leaves about the garden walks; nor do the frosts and snows of January come to chill the currents in their veins. Ah! this Utopia is a delicious spot; but, then, — *quien sabe?* — perhaps 't is just as well for me not to be here alway. I live, I know, a very stupid life in Gotham; but it has its advantages. There are there some bits of sunshine. I find them when I go to the opera; I basked in them while Jenny Lind was there; I mellowed in them, like a peach, when Grisi cast a tuneful glory round; and lately, while listening to Thalberg's magic touch, a genial glow pervaded my frame, and there was summer in my heart. 'T is something, too, — not much, perhaps, but something, — to go to the anniversary dinners given by the various societies, and hear the toasts and speeches. I certainly do miss, however, on my return to my solitary quarters, the voice of welcome from my wife; but then, too, there is no one to ask me where I have been, or what kept me out so late. Oh, I am convinced that my "lines have fallen to me in pleasant places."

At this moment the music of a sweet song reached my ears. It was a carol for the New Year, sung by my wife and daughters in the adjoining room. 'T was a simple melody, — an old, old song, — one with which mothers, for generations back, had hushed their babes to sleep; yet it brought the tears to my eyes, and wakened memories which had lain dormant in my bosom, hidden beneath cares, and jealousies, and disappointed hopes, and broken resolutions, and unfulfilled acts, since I sat at my mother's feet, a child in mind and years. What, to me, was the "Echo Song" of Jenny Lind, or the "Casta Diva" of Grisi, compared with this humble melody? Unconsciously, my voice united with my loved ones in that childlike song, and I was on the point of joining the singers, when a hand was laid on my arm, and a voice exclaimed: "Mister Gray, you most got dem figgers added up, so dat dis ole darkey can go long home to him wife Charity? She bin 'spectin' me now dis night more'n one hour. She and me got 'siderable marketin' to do for de-morrow, and I sartinly 'spect I can't go from dis bank till I'se locked all de doors."

"Where," said I, turning round on my seat, and seizing hold of Old Tom, —"where is Mrs. Gray and my children?"

"Lor bless me, Mister Gray," shouted Thomas, "you be crazy for sartin! you got no Missus Gray, and no children, conskently you must be berry crazy for to talk dis fashion. I guess you bin sleep and dreaming, sir."

"Thomas," I asked, now fully awake, — "Thomas, what time is it?"

"Just 'zactly seven o'clock P. M. by de Trinity Church, tho' my 'ronometer," answered Tom, "make it ten minute more."

I started up from my desk, put my books carefully away,

placed what little money I possessed in my pocket, remembering, as I did so, that my landlady was paid a month in advance only the week before, and that sundry other little bills were settled; and, giving Tom a quarter, I drew on my gloves, and the next moment was walking briskly towards Broadway.

That evening a cosey, bachelor party assembled in my rooms; a few games of whist were played; a few bowls of punch were brewed; and, though wifeless and childless, yet, when I came to lay my head on my solitary pillow, I could not but own that "my lines had fallen to me in pleasant places."

"My dear," exclaimed my wife, the moment I finished reading the above, "why will you forever be talking about punches in your writings, when, if you were to tell the truth, you would say that punches, either hot or cold, seldom are to be found on our mahogany?"

"Well," I replied, "if you fail to observe them, I shall not call your attention to their presence; but the fact is, that most of these punches are concocted when you have retired from the scene of your daily labors, and are quietly enjoying that repose which arises from possessing a clear conscience. And now, my dear, as I know that you and Miss Floy and the children must be wearied and sleepy, I would advise you and them to retire to your virtuous couches, while I remain up to attend to balancing the year's accounts."

Miss Floy hereupon said that she feared I would not be able to balance myself when I went to bed, if they should, thus early in the evening, leave me to my own devices.

My wife and little ones also protested against deserting the library thus early in the evening; and so, to keep them awake, I consented to engage in a game of blindman's-buff, which we pursued, much to the endangerment of our several heads and the damage of sundry pieces of furniture.

CHAPTER XXXVIII.

Around the Library Lamp. — Utopia again. — Ten Years ago. — Louise. Days of my Boyhood. — The old, old Story. — "A Tress of Golden Hair." — Foolish Memories. — "Our Florence." — The Old Chateau. — The good Old Man. — "Beyond." — The Churchyard. — Ebb and Flow. "Marriage-bells." — A little Discourse.

NO sooner was the evening lamp lighted in the library the following night, than the little folks besieged me with entreaties to finish the story of my family in Utopia, and as their mother and Miss Floy joined them in asking me, I put my newspaper aside, and, lighting my cigar, prepared to continue it.

Miss Em. whispered to me as I was waiting for them all to get properly seated and quiet, before commencing, that she hoped it would end well, as she very much disliked to have a story end badly.

I promised her that the end should be satisfactory, and if only Miss Floy would stop rustling her silks in the frightful way she was then doing, and would sit quietly in her chair, I would commence.

Miss Floy evidently overheard me, for she immediately rustled her dress still more, and moved her chair to the opposite side of the room; then, as if perfectly satisfied with having sufficiently annoyed me, she said, "Now, Mr. Gray, that we are ready, why don't you begin?"

"Yes, my dear, begin," cried my wife.

And "Begin," echoed each of the children.

And as I could do nothing else, I proceeded as follows:

More than a year, my little ones, is supposed to have elapsed since I last visited my precious family in Utopia.

My duties as a bank clerk in Wall Street have been so arduous during the past season that I have had scarcely a day in the whole period which I could call mine own. Once, during the month of June, on the anniversary of my marriage, I was on the point of starting for Utopia, and had even placed in my hat a clean collar to take with me, and purchased a pair of white kid gloves, and silk stockings, striped with blue, for the same purpose, when I was debarred from going by being subpœnaed as a witness in an important lawsuit, wherein our bank was the defendant. Had it not been for this, I should have visited my family the fifteenth day of last June. Ten years ago, from this very date, I married my sweet wife, the mother of my children. I sometimes doubt whether so many years have elapsed since that happy event, fraught with numberless blessings, transpired. It is only when I look on my two children, Mary and Fanny, and mark how rapidly they are approaching womanhod, (Mary, the elder of the two, can but just pass under her mother's arm, when raised, without disturbing the smooth and evenly parted hair, while Fanny's flaxen curls reach that mother's waist,) that I fully realize the flight of time.

Dwelling, as I do, apart from my family, and months often elapsing without my beholding them, doubts sometimes arise in my mind, whether, after all, I am really a husband and father; or, if it be not simply a dream, — well defined, indeed, and like reality; but still only a dream, a very myth. At such times I have recourse to the old family Bible, which, for safety, I keep at the bottom of an oaken chest that one of my sailor progenitors — a very sea-king he was, too, hailing from the island of Nantucket — carried with him during many voyages around the world, and turning to the record of births, marriages, and deaths, I read there, in my proper handwriting, the date of my own marriage, and likewise the record of the birth of each of my three children, and also of the death of the eldest born. Even this evidence fails to satisfy me altogether, and I am disposed to question my senses, and ask of myself whether there be not an error in the dates, and if there did not once exist another than myself who bore the name I bear, of whose marriage and children I am reading.

Of course, too, at such times I fall to speculating as to who I really am, and wondering whether or not Louise, my early love, — who died years on years ago, and lies buried far away in a southern clime, in an old churchyard, under a spreading palm, which is ever green, as is my memory of her, both summer and winter; and whose grave is marked by a marble slab, on which is carved, in raised letters, simply her name and the number of years (eighteen) she dwelt on earth, — be not, after all, my wife; and whether we do not live together in the cottage, down in the Valley, where once we hoped to dwell, about the porch of which trailing vines, and roses, and honeysuckles cluster, and where wild bees hum all the summer through, and robins and orioles sing; and whether there be not two brave and sturdy boys — the comfort and pride of their mother, and the pride and comfort of their father — who are our sons; and whether, moreover, my own surname be not the same that she, the vanished hope of my early manhood, bore, ere she became an angel among angels.

But such fancies as these do not often come to perplex me; they arise only when I, in a dreamy mood, am seated alone in my own apartment, in the fourth story of our boarding-house, on summer nights, listening to the pleasant rustle of the leaves on the trees just outside my window, and watching the white-winged clouds that, like fairy ships, float in the quiet moonlight. Then it is that I, on these sailless and oarless vessels, fantastic and ever-changing in their shapes, having no chart or map by which to sail, possessing no compass or rudder with which to guide their course, and bound to no known port, go back over oceans of departed years, and rounding capes of half-sunken memories, enter, through narrow channels of thought, havens of blessed rest; and there, in these olden resting-places, do I find my Louise, and, sitting beside her as of yore, clasping her hand, I listen to words such as no earthly voice can utter.

Then the days come back of my boyhood; then, too, the days return to her girlhood, and again we seem to wander in the woods together; we gather wild flowers on the hill-sides and on the borders of the running brooks; we search for strawberries along the edges of the woods, while I cavalierly fill her basket in preference to my own, and receive a smile for my reward. I help her to cross the stream, laying down stepping-stones for her to pass it without soiling the soles of her little shoes, and still my guerdon is a smile. I assist her to scale rail-fences, moss-grown and decayed, and to scramble through thickets of tall underbrush, dangerous with sharp thorns and prickly briers, and to step carefully over beds of tangled grass and waving fern, made fearful through truant school-boys' stories of poisonous snakes therein encountered, and my only guerdon still remains a smile. But, by-and-by, seated on a gray rock beneath a leafy elm, I tell her tales which smack of the marvellous, and are redolent of fairies and such ilk; and, little by little, I draw nearer to her side, and let my arm slide softly round her yielding waist, and, clasping her little hands in mine, then and there I tell her, in a boyish fashion, shamefaced and stammering, how much I love her; and she, the while blushing as rosy as the berries in her basket, pouts her red lips and taps the green turf with her dainty feet, until at last, half coaxed by me, half of her own accord, she turns her peach-bloomed cheek for me to kiss.

From that same hour, eight years, through summers and through winters, in sun and in storm, was she the sunshine of my days, the starlight of my nights, till, passing hence through doors that only open outward, she became the bow of promise to my future life.

I have a tress of golden hair, —
  I keep it hidden in a book;
And this in turn is hidden where
  No eye but mine may on it look.

It ne'er belonged to my sweet wife,
  Her raven curls knew not its birth;
Nor to the blessings of my life,
  The household jewels around my hearth.

But down a girlish neck it fell,
  My sainted love's of former years,
And never has it lost the spell
  Of calling forth my holiest tears.

I sometimes leave my precious ones,
  And go where orange-flowers bloom,
Amidst the warmth of southern suns,
  To muse beside my darling's tomb.

Long years have flown since there I laid
  Her body softly down to rest,
And turning from that grave new made,
  Left therein all I loved the best.

But time has healed the wound I thought
  Could never during life be healed,
And seldom is a lifetime fraught
  With greater joys than mine doth yield.

Yet oft I seek to count the days
  That must elapse before we meet,
Ere I may tread the milk-white ways
  Which she has walked with shining feet.

But away with these foolish memories that, in spite of my manhood, in spite of my present happiness, come to dim my eyes with tears, and fill my heart with thoughts of bitterness. Let them vanish and return no more, even as *her* form has vanished from my sight, — her footprints from the green turf which once she trod. Let other memories arise. The memory of the day when I led my sweet-voiced wife, a young and blooming bride, out from her father's house. Ten years have passed since then — ten years with, here and there, in the otherwise bright woof of happiness, a grief heavy with tears. Sickness and death have caused our tears to flow. Our boy — the only boy we had — sickened and died. Our second child, with fever burning in her heart and brain, lay tossing long weeks upon her little cot, hovering 'twixt life and death, while every moan and sob she uttered went like a sharpened arrow to our very souls; but, God be praised! a mother's prayer was heard, and Azrael's hand was stayed. Then it was that I, my heart moved by hopes and fears and joys, wrote, —

OUR FLORENCE.

WE 'VE a tiny, helpless, wailing one, whose age by weeks we number,
A blue-eyed babe, a little girl, whose presence fills our life
With such happiness and pain as only parents' hearts encumber,
For we know that she has entered a world of sin and strife;
Where thorns spring up with flowers, and where shadows chase the light,
Where for every day of summer comes a chilly winter night.

But with true and earnest thankfulness, her mother and myself
From the good and gracious Giver receive the precious one,
And to our bosoms tenderly we clasp the dainty elf,
And think 't were hard to give her up and say, "Thy will be done."
For of our love the baby has so great and rich a share
That it seems to us she ever had our watchfulness and care.

Oh, 't is sweet to watch our baby and perceive how, day by day,
The light breaks through the darkness of her mind so infantile,
And shows itself to lookers-on in many a cunning way, —
In playing with her fingers, or in learning how to smile, —
Till we even think the pretty one begins to know and bless
The loving arms that hold her and the voices that caress.

And when her little spirit seems within her breast to flutter,
  And the golden bowl seems broken, and the silver cord seems
    loosed;
And while, amid the darkness, seems Azrael's voice to utter,
  In tone of warning, that our babe to us on earth is lost;
We fail not to remember those glorious words of His,
Our *Christ,* who said of children, *Of such my kingdom is.*

But with our prayers all answered, comes the morning soft and
    bright,
  And like the dews of evening-time our tears have ceased to fall,
While the warm and precious sunshine makes a glory in our sight,
  And the baby smiles and wonders at the shadows on the wall.
And I say unto her mother, as the tiny form I raise
From the couch where it is lying, Let us give our Maker praise.

Oft we look upon our baby, and we ask ourselves if she —
  Should she live to be a woman, with a woman's heart and mind —
Will e'er as firm and faithful, as good and patient be,
  As the one for whom we've named her, the best of womankind,
Whom all the world is praising, who has found the Holy Grail,
While performing deeds of mercy, — sweet FLORENCE NIGHTIN-
    GALE.

But more of sweetness than of bitterness has mingled in our marriage-cup, and with hopeful and rejoicing hearts do we look forward to future years, and beyond them to eternity. But my thoughts glide on too fast. I would go back again with memory to my wedding-day.

The father of my bride let not his only daughter pass undowered from the shelter of his roof. She came to me not penniless, but bringing with her, as a marriage portion, a small estate — a hundred goodly acres — on which the father, at some future day, purposed erecting a *chateau,* something more stately than the home from whence she came, in which we were to dwell, and wherein he — for age was stealing on him, bending his form and silvering over his head — could come to pass his last remaining days.

The *chateau* never was built. The future day the old

man looked for never came, though years flew on, and he, seated within his easy chair, warmed his slippered feet before my fire, rubbed his thin hands approvingly together, pleased with the genial warmth, and drank with relish of my wines, praising the same with every glass he drained. Much talked he, too, of the proposed *chateau*, and weeks and months he passed in drawing plans of it on paper. He even went so far as to consult a noted architect regarding it. A structure that this gentleman had built — the Castle, I believe, of Indolence, it is called — seemed similar, so far as I could gather, in many a feature, to that my wife's good father thought some day to build. I have no doubt myself but that, in twenty years or more, he would at least have laid the corner-stone, provided that his life thus long were spared. The generous, kind old man — appreciator of good wines and many other things as good — lived not to finish what was never begun, but died one Christmas Day, eight years and something more after I had made his only daughter wife.

I would myself have built the *chateau*, as the old man thought of doing, in strict accordance with the best-drawn plan his trembling hand had made, if I could find the title-deeds to the estate, or register of them, in any hall of record. But the whole matter seems tangled and dark, and wrapt in mystery; nor can a living soul in all the land tell aught concerning it. It is true, I hold the place, and it is mine by right possession gives, but who knows? if I should build thereon a charming *chateau*, with pinnacles and towers, turrets and battlements, arched windows and oak doors; and, within, tall casements, wainscots curiously carved, ceilings fretted and groined, and floors with jasper and with sandal-wood inlaid, and many other things of rare and strange device, — whether, some rainy day or other, there might not come from over seas, even perchance from mountains in the moon, a stranger learned and versed in all the law's strange quips and quirks, and oust me out of this my fair domain; or else a neighbor, one I call my friend, might, peradventure, rise and claim the whole, substantiating it with mouldy parchment deeds! Alas for me and mine if this should happen! and certain am I that it would, if I should ever build; and so, in all this broad demesne, I dare not lay one stone above another.

I will mention here that the estate itself lies at the distance of a swallow's flight, be the same more or less, from dear Utopia, within the boundaries of the country known among landless but aërial proprietors as Spain.

A few months prior to the old man's death, I wrote, at his desire, the lines below, descriptive of the country wherein lay a goodly portion of his large possessions. My wife has told me that he used to sit at twilight, with our little ones upon his knees, before a deep-bayed window looking west, within my cottage at Utopia, and then and there repeat aloud — his gaze fixed on the sunset clouds — my simple lines; and thus, one Christmas Day he died.

BEYOND.

There is a country lying far away,
  Beyond the outer bounds of this our earth,
Where never comes a dark or rainy day,
  But where each hour is fraught with joy and mirth.
Fair palaces, and stately, crown its hills;
  Its streets are broad, and paved with costly stones;
And down their sides flow cool and crystal rills,
  That murmur sweetly in a thousand tones.
Its men are brave, its women pure and fair,
  And art and song are handmaids in the land;
While holy hymns, and blessed words of prayer,
  Show that the nation is a Christian band.
This is the bright Utopia of our youth, —
  The *El Dorado* of our hopes and fears, —
And when in age we come to learn the truth,
  A Spanish castle crumbling like our years.

After her father's death, my wife, still grieving over

our earlier loss, passed many an hour within the churchyard, training the roses and sweetbriers growing upon our dead boy's grave over the marble slab which marked the spot where lay the good old man. There, too, she led our children, and, seated within the shadow of a drooping willow, told them stories, old and true, drawn from the Book of books, — of little Samuel and the stripling David, and the child Jesus disputing with the doctors in the temple; and, also, pretty hymns she taught them, which they sung beside their brother's grave, so that the passers-by along the dusty highway, hearing their song, nor knowing whence it came, — for broken wall of stone, lichened and green with moss, hidden from sight in thick-set privet hedge, kept them from view, — would pause and listen, thinking the music heard from chanting cherubs rose. There also did they learn their simple prayers, which, night and morn, kneeling beside their mother's knee, they humbly said. So filled with love and thankfulness was little Fanny's heart, that she was quick to utter, in season or out, at home or abroad, within her chamber or without the house, a word or two of prayer. Success in overcoming the smallest things of life would call one forth. After her hands were washed, her shoestrings tied, her lesson learned, or many another daily act performed, would she repeat some simple, childlike prayer. Once, in the street, for having crossed dry-shod a little pool of water, she, in the fulness of her heart, gave thanks aloud. Then Mary, standing by and hearing her, exclaimed, "I'd not be such a Pharisee as you, Miss Fan. for all the world." Mary's rebuke cut Fanny to the heart, and made great tears roll down her tender cheeks, while sobs, so big they choked her utterance, forbade her to reply. My precious child never forgot it, and prays now only at home or in the village church.

But again I wander — again my thoughts, on the topmost billow of the flood, glide forward to the present.

Let the tide ebb once more, while memory sails backward in the current.

Ten years ago — it seems not that to me — standing beside the altar in our village church, I called for the first time my sweet one wife. Until I heard the man of God this question ask, "Ruth, wilt thou have this man to thy wedded husband?" with more that follows after, and also had heard her sweet reply, "I will," I scarcely could believe that she indeed was mine. Not till the ring was on, the blessing given, and we had turned together from that spot, did the truth in all its beauty break on my wedded heart.

There are some tones in marriage-bells,
  Which, falling on my list'ning ears,
  Awaken thoughts of other years,
That to my heart are potent spells.

They bring, from o'er Time's wid'ning sea,
  Fair visions, pictured on my brain,
  Of scenes and days that ne'er again
Shall come with joy to gladden me.

Once more with Ruth I seem to stand
  Before the altar and the priest;
  Once more I taste the wedding-feast,
While she presides at my left hand.

I see the wreath that binds her hair;
  I hear, as 't were a golden lyre,
  The rustle of her rich attire,
And mark her coy yet gracious air.

I note again her winning ways,
  I hear the music of her voice
  In songs that make my heart rejoice,
Because they were my bridal lays.

And yet, I feel the present times
  Are not without their due delight;
  For my two children bless my sight,
And Ruth herself extols my rhymes.

And thus, with soft regrets behind, —
With hopes and fears before me spread, —
In manly confidence I tread
The paths through which go all mankind.

"Now, my dears," I said, when I finished the above, "thus ends the stories of my Family in Utopia, and with it comes the end of our Holiday Nights' Entertainments."

"Oh, no, papa," shouted the little ones, "don't, please, say that. There are three more days left before New Year's, and you must have some story or other to tell or read to us every night till then. Must n't he, mamma?"

Mamma nodded her head.

"Well," I replied, "if you insist upon it I will see what I can do, but you must not be disappointed if what I may provide shall prove uninteresting."

"If you will promise not to tell us anything more about boots and shoes," said my wife, "I think we shall be able to keep awake under the infliction; but if you attempt anything more in that line, I, for one, shall be privileged to leave the room during the discourse."

"And I," said Miss Floy, "shall also depart and take the children with me."

"Which will give me an opportunity," I said, smiling, "to mix and drink a strictly private brewage which will not be tea."

CHAPTER XXXIX.

Two Essays. — Something Fearful coming. — Miss Floy's Skirts. — Relief of the Little Ones. — "Winter in Town." — "Now," with More thereto pertaining. — A Call for More. — Lamb or Hunt. — "Winter Out of Town." — More "Nows." — A Panorama.

Y dear," I said to Mrs. Gray, as we drew around the centre-table in the library, "I have written two essays to read to the club this evening, and, as the lamp is lighted, suppose we begin."

"Very well," my wife replied; "children, be attentive; your father is going to read two essays.

The children looked very blank.

"Sit well back in your chairs, children; fold your hands on your laps, put your feet down on the floor, and give great attention to your father, for he is going to read two essays," said Miss Floy, slightly improving on my wife's commands.

The blankness of the children seemed to increase.

"For goodness' sake," I exclaimed, "don't frighten the children out of their wits. Little ones," I continued, in the most conciliatory of tones, "your dear papa is about to" —

"Read two essays," broke in my wife.

"Two essays," echoed Miss Floy, putting her eye-glasses over the bridge of her nose.

The children fairly trembled.

"Will you be quiet a minute or two," I cried to the two feminines, "and let me explain to the children what I am about to do?"

"Certainly," my wife answered, "but I thought you said you were going to read two essays."

"Two essays," croaked Miss Floy.

"Good gracious!" I exclaimed, "do you want to drive me mad with your confounded interruptions. Won't you let me say a word to the children?"

"Certainly," my wife replied.

"Of course," said Miss Floy; "go on."

"Proceed," said Mrs. Gray.

"I'll be hanged if I do," I said; "I am not going to be driven into 'going on,' or 'proceeding.' I choose to take my own time about it. Em., ring the bell for the servant to draw me a mug of ale."

There was quiet for a brief space of time. My wife looked mischievous, Miss Floy looked vicious, and the children looked glum. After I drank the ale, "Children," I said, "your dear papa is going to" — I paused a moment, but there was no interruption — "read two essays. Your dear papa, my beloved ones, thinks that you will be amused with these two essays, and if your dear mamma and the amiable Miss Floy do not desire to hear them, they need not remain in the library."

Thereupon Miss Floy gathered up her skirts and swept like a new broom out of the room. Mrs. Gray, however, who is a sensible woman, remained. The children brightened up after Miss Floy's departure, who, I might as well confess it, has accepted the position, without the name, of governess in my family. I am inclined to think that she leads the little ones anything but a comfortable life, but discipline is everything, and she employs it, in her management, to the fullest extent. They scarcely dare to say, when she is present, that the hair —and they have n't a great deal of it — on their little heads is their own. I remarked something like this to Mrs. Gray; but she said that she saw no occasion for the children to say it. What hair they had, she very justly remarked, was their own; but she saw no reason why they should state that fact to Miss Floy or any other person. Of course my wife is correct, but my expression, as I endeavored to explain to Mrs. Gray, unsuccessfully however, was only a general way of putting the fact that the children stood slightly in fear of Miss Floy.

"Now that she is not present, the little ones," I said, "as you may perceive, have unfolded their hands, have got their feet upon the rounds of their several chairs, and are generally sitting in easy, if not graceful, attitudes."

Mrs. Gray said she noticed it, and she did n't approve of it, and on her threatening to send for Miss Floy to come back, unless they sat up correctly, — I think correctly was the word she employed, though why, I do not know, — they each arranged themselves again in systematic order.

Then I unrolled my manuscript, and declaring the club to be in session, read aloud the following essay on —

WINTER IN TOWN.

Now it is mid-winter. Christmas and New Year have gone by, and now Twelfth Night is here. Now the mercury in the thermometer marks zero. Now the bell rings for us to arise, but now we like to lie in bed of mornings, debating in our minds whether to do so or not. Now, as we peep from beneath the bedclothes, and see the hoar-frost on the window-panes, and watch our breath, like smoke, roll to the ceilings, we conclude to lie still. Now we believe in Jack Frost. Now we place our hands on our noses, and are reminded of icy capes in the Arctic region. Now we draw the clothes closer about us, and build snow castles in the air. Now the shrill cry of the milkman arouses us from our musings, and his morning salutation to the servant as she brings out the pitcher for the lacteal fluid, reaches our ears, and, if she be good-looking, he embarrasses her with a sly joke, over which she giggles as she passes down into the area. Now the light car of the baker, with hot rolls and twists, stops before the door, and we hear him leap from it, and enter the house, while the horse paws with his hoofs the frozen ground and neighs with impatience. Now the newspaper carrier hurries past, and as he throws the paper into the area, he shouts its name. Now we listen to the noise of feet and the crackling of the snow, as the small tradesmen and early clerks and porters hasten "down-town" to open their stores. Now John knocks at our door, and says, "Breakfast is about up, and the Gov'nor 's down." Now we ask John if he thinks ice made during the night? to which he answers with a chuckle, rolling his eyes towards the windows, "Some, sir." Now we tell him, as he places our boots at the bedside, that hot water is a luxury. Now declaring that the Croton is frozen in the pipes, he goes down to the kitchen for the hot water. Now we draw the bedclothes closer about us, and pull our cap further over our ears. Now we grope in the bed for our stockings with our feet, and as they touch the cold sheets we quickly withdraw them, and desire a hot brick. Now we dress and shiver, and now we leave our chamber. Now the little breakfast-room looks pleasant, and the sun shines in at the eastern window, and its rays fall with a roseate tinge upon the white table-linen. Now the fire in the grate burns freely, and the bituminous coal sputters and blazes whenever it is stirred. Now the morning papers send up a steam from their fresh sheets as they are opened before the fire. Now we read accounts of persons being frozen to death, and of poor children perishing of starvation and exposure. Now the coffee-urn bubbles and sings, and the plates are heated before the fire, and the steak and rolls are brought in, and now we sit down to breakfast. Now butter, and flies on the window-pane, grow stiff, and seats nearest the fire are preferred. Now the Governor puts on his spectacles and reads the paper, sipping his coffee between the paragraphs, with the air of a gentleman of leisure. Now sister Mary presides at the urn; and the old lady butters the muffins, while we carve the steak. Now we love to linger long around the table, as the old lady makes out her list of the marketings we are to send home. Now gloves and fur tippets are in requisition, and overshoes and coats are warmed before putting on. Now kisses are exchanged by newly married couples, and the little child holds up its pretty mouth to be kissed by papa.

Now out-of-doors the air is piercingly cold, and our breath freezes as it leaves our lips. Now our beard and mustache are encrusted with ice, and our fingers turn to icicles. Now large men, buttoned to the chin in heavy over-coats, and with fur collars around their ears, hasten over the crossings, heeding not the thinly clad, pale-faced little girls running at their side, imploring a few coppers. Now sleighs glide by, containing ladies richly and warmly clad in velvets and furs, whose horses keep time in their prancing to the chime of silver bells above their saddles. Now huge sleighs, drawn by a dozen horses or more, and filled with the democracy of our city, grate harshly over the pavement of Broadway. Now stray dogs seek sunny doorways, where they may warm their chilled bodies. Now old ladies, unless they be very careful, are likely to slip down. Now boys skate on the sidewalks, and little girls, on their way to school, slide wherever they find a bit of ice. Now the big pond in the Central Park is the place of resort, where skaters most do congregate. Now the sunny side of the street is much frequented, and ragged boys nestle together and sun themselves in corners. Now noses grow red, and eyes water, and teeth are apt to chatter. Now cigars become a necessity, and pipes are excusable. Now hot whiskey-punches are at par and ice-water at a discount. Now itinerant organ-grinders play mournful tunes in the cold winter solstice, and have a hard time generally, and their red-coated, barefooted little monkeys a still harder. Now fat men, and cooks and bakers, are better off than kings and queens, and a tavern kitchen is no bad place. Now stage-drivers may be pitied, and stage managers envied. Now theatres are patronized, and Booth's *Hamlet* and Clarke's *Toodles* are having a run. Now coal-yards are visited and ice-houses shunned. Now Greenwood is not considered as desirable a spot as it is in summer time, and Coney Island and Long Branch are deserted. Now hoops must be cool institutions, and a fan a useless invention. Now dancing and wood-sawing are really enjoyed by those who like them, and bowling is pleasant exercise. Now church-spires glisten in icy mail, and the eaves of houses are warlike with pendent icicles. Now the fountain in the Park ceases to spout. Now the wind sets from the north. Now people eat substantial dinners. Now the sun disappears early in the afternoon, and the stars shine till late in the morning. Now we have brief days, and now nights are allowed an extension. Now much gas is burned, and the gas companies make money. Now young men find time to go a-courting. Now late suppers are patronized, and oysters are in good repute. Now policemen retire from the street and may be found in kitchens and bar-rooms. Now nightcaps and warm flannels are not to be recklessly dispensed with; and now it is time to say our prayers and go to bed.

When I had concluded, the children expressed themselves as much delighted with the first essay, and asked immediately for the second. Even Mrs. Gray said it was not bad, but she thought that there was something similar to it either in Leigh Hunt's or Charles Lamb's writings.

"If there be," I said, "you may find it out. I am not going to point out the page, and thereby destroy the credit of originality which it now possesses in the minds of the children."

The children said they were certain no one had ever

written like it, or could write like it, and that papa was the best writer in the world. After this praise I could not do otherwise than read the second essay, entitled, —

WINTER OUT OF TOWN.

Now, in the country, it is mid-winter. Now the snow lies in huge drifts against stone walls, and beside long lines of fences. Now the wood-pile becomes a mountain of snow, and the well-curb is hidden from sight. Now, on the farm, cattle linger around the barn-yard trough, waiting for a friendly hand to break the ice. Now fowls stand on one leg, with heads sunken in their feathers, and nestle closely to each other when they go to roost. Now peacocks freeze to death, and pigeons fall dead from their perches. Now turkeys, geese, and ducks are apt to go off suddenly, especially about the holidays; and now hens refuse to lay eggs. Now chilly are the sheep in woolly fold, and numb the herdsman's fingers as he fodders them. Now hares and rabbits limp trembling through the frosty snow, and squirrels, all a-cold, run along the fences. Now bears suck their paws, and bees are torpid. Now the air on the hill-tops is piercingly cold, while in the woods it is comparatively mild. Now forest-trees fall beneath the axe of the woodman, and saw-logs are drawn to the mill. Now the report of the hunter's rifle rings out sharp and clear, and deer and foxes give up the ghost. Now snow-shoes are very well in their way, and to walk with them on the deep snow is splendid exercise. Now dancing with stilts on the crusted ground is an impossibility, and to dance without them would be an absurdity. Now barns are cheerless places, and hayricks not exactly the thing. Now the measured strokes of the flail of the husbandman are heard, and fill the ear like a song of thanksgiving. Now oats are oats and corn is corn, and there is no such thing as grass save in the flesh. Now sheep are sheep, and lambs are slowly coming. Now pine-knots blaze in farm-houses, and chips collect in the back-yard. Now seats by blazing wood-fires are particularly affected by old ladies who knit, and children who roast apples. Now barrels of cider in the cellar are tapped, and pork-barrels dipped into. Now potatoes and pumpkins are covered with straw, and bins of apples — rosy-cheeked, russet, and green — are protected from frost. Now buckwheat cakes are at a premium, and maple syrup is better than molasses. Now honey is not bad, nor fresh butter, if one can get it, to be calumniated. Now rooms with northern exposures are to be avoided, and quilts and rose-blankets can scarcely be depended upon to keep away the cold. Now loosely fitted window-sashes shake in the night-time, and the lightning-rod rattles against the side of the house. Now weathercocks are in their glory, and vary with every wind that blows. Now the mercury in the thermometer marks twenty degrees below zero, and now never-failing springs freeze over. Now the Bronx is frozen over, and the little ones going there to skate or slide on the ice, get falls, and come home with many bruises. Now stone foundations of old farm-houses snap, with a report like the crack of a pistol, causing children to start affrighted from their sleep. Now pails of water, inadvertently left out-of-doors, burst their hoops, which are quickly seized upon by little lasses, who insert them in their quilted skirts. Now ice makes in the pitcher, and the oil in the lamp is hardened. Now shaving seems as bad as tooth-drawing, and razors are like icicles. Now slippers almost freeze the feet. Now well-to-do farmers build up their poor neighbors' wood-piles, and their kind-hearted wives send widows, pitiful in rusty crape, great baskets stored with good things. Now spareribs and mince-pies are in good repute, and doughnuts are important institutions. Now quiltings and apple-bees are of frequent occurrence, and sleighing parties often meet with upsets. Now a "dance" at the tavern is a matter to talk about, and the belle of the ball-room — a plump lass in a pink dress — a being to be remembered forever. Now nuts are cracked, and apples are eaten. Now farmers talk about last year's crops, and read the History of the Rebellion. Now singing-schools are attractive, and debating societies are in their zenith. Now donation parties take place, and parsons are affable and contented. Now little girls, when they go abroad, wear mittens, and have stockings drawn over their shoes, and are wrapped in red cloaks; while in-doors, clad in woollen dresses, and with checkered aprons, they delight to sit in the chimney corner and read aloud to their grandmothers, from the Bible, the story of little Samuel. Now small boys like to slide "down-hill" on their sleds, and take much pleasure in snowballing each other. Now large boys go a-skating, and rejoice themselves by cutting figures and letters on the surface of the ice, with skilful manœuvre, and now a plump through an air-hole is highly dangerous and unpleasant. Now the trees are leafless, — save the evergreens, which are refreshing to look at, — and the snow sifts drearily through their naked branches. Now the singing-birds have gone South, and their last year's nests are filled with ice and snow. Now snow-birds chirp, and "the owl, for all his feathers, is a-cold." Now Dinah, the cook, says, "flannel petticoats are in season," and young girls term flannel-waistcoats "delightful." Now flaxen-haired children, hand in hand, with dinner-pails on their arms, and school-books in their satchels, trudge through the snow to the district school-house. Now school-boys model in snow the form of the pedagogue, and take much comfort in pelting it with snowballs. Now they build forts, and fire at each other from behind them, while the more juvenile play at "*track the rabbit.*" Now boys complain of frozen toes and nipped ears; and little girls talk about chilblains. Now even burly men think it chilly, and every one says to every one he meets, "How cold it is!" And now the writer, finding his fingers all thumbs, and his back an iceberg, thinks that he will freeze up and come to the end of his chapter.

When I stopped reading, the children clapped their hands, and Miss Em. said, that while I was reading it seemed to her that one of those panoramas she had seen in the city was passing before her. Both of the essays seemed to be full of pictures. My wife said it was amusing, but that she was going to see if she could n't find something like it among the books of her library, and if she did she should make a note of it.

Then I declared the meeting around the evening lamp to be dissolved, and that the little ones might go to bed. Which they did.

CHAPTER XL.

Miss Em. speaks. — Another Story. — The Little Quakeress. — An Old House. — A Pattern Housekeeper. — Tim Coffin. — Long Sally. — Yarns. — A Libel. — A Strict Friend. — A Little Violet. — Little Ruth. — What all Good Girls should do. — Charlton. — A Bit of Love. A Wedding.

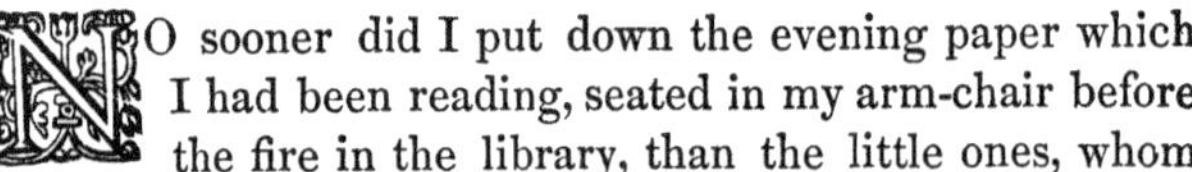

NO sooner did I put down the evening paper which I had been reading, seated in my arm-chair before the fire in the library, than the little ones, whom I had observed earnestly chattering among themselves, in one corner of the room, approached me in a body, and making Miss Em. the spokesman, asked me to tell them another story about my children in Utopia.

I replied that I believed I had nothing more to relate about those precious little ones, but that, if they would like to hear a true story instead, I would tell them one. Thereupon they clapped their hands, and shouting with glee, gave me to understand that nothing would please them better. So, drawing around the library table, I proceeded to unfold the following story about —

THE LITTLE QUAKERESS.

"MANY years ago, when the winters were colder than they are now, and the snow came earlier and remained later than in these degenerate days, — and, moreover, lay deeper upon the ground than at present, — so long ago that only the oldest inhabitants can remember the time, there stood, and is still standing, in the main street of a certain little city, a wooden house, which, though now sadly out of repair, — for the top of the chimney has fallen in, and the window-shutters hang loosely, and creak and groan on their well-worn hinges with every wind that rushes past, — then gloried in a new coat of white paint and bright green blinds, with a highly polished brass knocker on the door; all of which, with the neatness which was visible about it, — for not a blade of grass or a single weed was allowed to come up through the cracks in the pavement, — certainly proclaimed it to be the prettiest house in the neighborhood, and led one to think that its housekeeper must be a pattern for all housewives; and so, indeed, she was. Such extraordinary scrubbing and cleaning as she kept up throughout the week, was enough to drive a poor man, who loved retirement and quiet, quite crazy. Mondays and Saturdays were her great days, wherein she celebrated her love for cleanliness with more ardor and devotion than she was wont to celebrate the anniversary of her marriage. But there were two seasons of the year when she seemed more than herself, as being gifted with supernatural powers, and those were early in the spring and late in the fall, when the house seemed a perfect little bedlam. Such turning upside down of tables and chairs, such taking apart of bedsteads and polishing of bureaus and sideboards, such washing of windows and scrubbing of paint, such shaking of carpets and whitewashing of walls and ceilings, and such quantities of soap and water as were then used, would certainly shock any respectable boarding-house keeper of these days into a premature decline. Truly, she was renowned among the neighbors as a notable good woman, who could wash, bake, brew, scold, and gossip with the best of them.

"Indeed, my little ones, such an exemplary housekeeper is seldom to be found nowadays." Here I looked at Mrs. Gray, who, without looking up from her crocheting, simply said, she should hope so.

"At the time of which I speak," I continued, "this house

was owned and occupied by a jolly little man by the name of Timothy Coffin; though, to tell the truth, Tim was a mere cipher in his household, as meek and patient as a lamb, though out-of-doors Captain Tim was as bold as a lion, and feared no man; but albeit the sight of a woman made his heart quake — his wife Sally evidently being the master. How it happened that Captain Tim came to marry Long Sally Coffin, (for she was also a Coffin, and sister of Long Tom of that name,) will ever remain a mystery; for I have made diligent search throughout many old letters relating to the Coffin family, in the hope of finding some clew by which to arrive at a conclusion; even their family Bible only states, that on such a day, which now matters not, seeing that it hath long since passed away, they were married after the manner of Friends, at the bride's paternal mansion, on the little island of Nantucket.

"Now, though Captain Tim wore the drab coat and the broad brim of the Quakers, yet would he sometimes let fall strange words which were not seeming in one of his persuasion; neither are they, even at the present time, in any one, though I regret to say that some men are prone to use them. But, when we bethink ourselves of the remarkable wife he had, it seemeth no longer of so much wonder that he should once in a while forget himself."

Here Mrs. Gray interrupted me by saying she did not think even that was cause sufficient to make any one use bad language.

"As I said before," I continued, not heeding my wife's remark, "Captain Tim was a jolly little fellow, who liked his pipe and his mug of ale quite as much as if he had been born a Dutchman instead of the sturdy Yankee that he was; and in wet weather, or even when it betokened a storm, he would not refuse a glass of good brandy, which, he said, would not hurt any man *if* taken with moderation; but it grieves me seriously to know that there are some persons even in this age who drink to excess. Now, nothing pleased Captain Tim better than to be seated on a stormy winter night, beside a large blazing wood-fire, smoking his pipe, with a glass of brandy and water by his elbow, spinning to his old comrades long tales about the time when he sailed as master in the good ship *Sally Ann* from the port of Nantucket. Then was he truly in his glory, and his small gray eyes would twinkle with glee, and his rubicund face would shine like polished mahogany, while his bald head glistened like a pewter basin. Although some used to say, more especially the young men of those days, that his stories were without any wit, yet I am inclined to think that his libellers must have been actuated by jealousy; for true it was that at any social gathering, the young maidens, for the sake of hearing his sailor yarns, would congregate around Captain Tim, whom they all loved as a father, though he looked on them with suspicious eyes, for he deemed that all women were alike; and though they might be sunshine and laughter before marriage, yet after would their true characters be unfolded, and the clouds and tears which they had hidden from sight in their courtship days, would reappear, and even with more strength than before. The greatest plague to Captain Tim was his wife's tongue, which he used to say was a more fearful sound to him than the breakers on a lee shore; and, truly, I believe it was.

"Some one has said, that the reason monkeys do not talk, is, that they may not work; but many women, on the contrary, talk twice as much, just because they work; and such was the case with Long Sally Coffin, who, the more she worked, the louder and faster she talked, till it often seemed that she must faint from sheer exhaustion; but such a happy thing for Captain Tim never occurred; so he was fain to content himself with hoping that the time would come when his wife would learn that, to make home pleasant to him, it would be necessary for her to put a bridle upon her tongue. Alas! 't was a vain hope for Captain Tim."

"A worse libel on woman, than all you have just said," interrupted my wife, "I don't think I ever listened to; and I warn you, my children, not to believe what your naughty papa is telling you."

"But you know, ma," replied Miss Em., "that papa said it was a true story."

"Your father, my love," my wife answered, "is prone to declare a great many things to be true which are false, and much that is false he as often pronounces to be true."

"That is a libel on me, at all events," I said; and, without waiting for the smart reply which I saw on my wife's tongue, I continued the story.

"Now, Long Sally, as Captain Tim's wife was called, to distinguish her from others of the same name, was a tall, slim, gaunt woman, the very personification of a scold; and yet at times, when her tongue was still, which, truly, was but seldom, one could trace on her face the remains of great beauty, though almost effaced by the wrinkles and lines of care which now were so visible. It was the last remnant of her girlhood, and no one would think who looked upon her now, that she had once been celebrated for her beauty; but, peradventure, that was the reason why Captain Tim came to marry her. The plain dress, so very neat, which she wore, and the simple thee and thou language which she used, were in strange contrast to the loud voice and shrill tones that were wont to issue from her lips; and one would not willingly believe that she was a strict follower of that gentle sect, the Quakers. But thus it was, and so strict was she, that when her daughter appeared one day with a rose-bud twined in her hair, she rebuked her and told her to put it away, as it was not seeming to be fond of gay flowers.

"Sometimes, my children, when wandering in the woods, I have suddenly come upon a single little violet, raising its head from the tangled fern and long grass which grew around it, apparently more beautiful for being thus alone in the midst of strange and unseemly weeds, than if it had been placed in the *parterre* of some magnificent garden; and I have thought to myself that the sunlight fell more lovingly about it, and the night dews rested more gently upon its leaves, and even the very winds, as they went past, breathed more softly upon it than on the wilder things that surrounded it, while it, in turn, seemed to yield a grateful perfume to the wild and scentless shrubs about it. To me it always appeared that the good Being took more than usual care of such lonely little flowers, and nurtured them as his own especial favorites."

"That's pretty, is n't it mamma?" asked Em. Mamma, however, only smiled in a half-satirical fashion.

"Like such a flower," I continued, "was little Ruth Coffin. Her sensitive nature shrunk from contact with the world, and took refuge in the protection of the rough but generous spirits of her household among whom her lot was cast; they shielded her as the shepherd does the feeble lamb, allowing no wind to visit it too roughly. She was the sweet flower of the garden — the joy, the gladness, and the sunshine of the home. In truth, Ruth was one of those merry little maidens round whose hearts seem to cluster loving thoughts, who have ever a sweet smile and a pleasant word for all whom they may meet, and who come across our paths like stray beams of sunshine, making glad our ways, and giving new vigor and fresh impulse to all good inclinations. Though Ruth was not what is termed handsome, — that is, her features were not so regular and finely chiselled as they might have been, nor her complexion as white, nor her cheeks as red, as powder and *rouge* would have made them, — yet most people termed her pretty, which should be enough to satisfy you that she was far from being homely, and also prove that little Ruth was one whom none could know without loving, for there was something most pleasing in her appearance; and whether it was her manner, her voice, or her words which most did captivate, it would be hard to tell. No one could look upon her face without being aware that she possessed a most loving heart; for if the eyes are an index of the soul, then truly was it so with Ruth, for there was more of love beaming from those blue eyes of hers than would fill the hearts of half a dozen city belles of these days. In sad sooth it is most true that many women now, instead of living to be loved, — living for home and home joys, — seek rather to be thought cold-hearted and free from those sentiments which should be woman's greatest pride, — affection and respect for her husband, and love and care for her children. They too often forget that 'the training and bearing of a child is woman's wisdom;' and they seek in the frivolities of fashionable life for that entertainment which can only be obtained at home."

"Another libel, my children," said Mrs. Gray, "on your mother, and Miss Floy, and yourselves, and indeed all who are of the gentler sex. Your papa appears to be in a most amiable humor to-night, and I fear that something has gone wrong with him in town."

Making no reply, and only shaking my head at my wife, I continued: —

"Had it not been for Ruth, her father, jolly old Captain Tim, would have found his home most irksome; but when with her he felt that he had brought his ship into a good anchorage ground, — a quiet, retired bay, where no waves or winds came to disturb his repose. Never a loud or a cross word did his wife give unto Ruth, and even when she spake chidingly to her husband before Ruth, which was but seldom, her voice, modulated and softened from its usual severity, sounded more like those old winning tones which he had hearkened to of yore; and his sturdy heart — for he had a sturdy, brave old heart within his breast —

would beat to the measure of happier days. Often had little Ruth, when a child, sat for hours together on the old man's knee, with her small delicate hands clasped in his rough and horny ones, eagerly listening to stories of his seafaring life; and when he told of the many dangers he had gone through, of his shipwrecks and providential escapes from death, she would cling closer to him, and placing her soft arm around his neck, impress a kiss upon his weather-beaten cheek, and make him promise that he will never again venture upon that treacherous sea, but will always stay at home and tell stories to her. Then, when she grew older, seated in her chair by his side, she would read aloud to him — for his eyes were growing dim and he could not see clearly for any length of time — from that well-worn and long-treasured book, the Bible; and thus many a long afternoon in summer would she make short, and many a dreary one in winter pleasant, by her attention and care for his comfort."

"That was nice, papa, in her, was n't it?" asked Miss Em.

"Yes, my child," I answered; "and it is what all good little girls who love their papas ought to do. Is n't it, mamma?"

"Yes," said mamma.

"Now, it is not to be expected," I continued, "or even desired, that little Ruth, who had arrived at the sunny age of eighteen, should be without admirers; nor was it so, though I know not how many, but at any rate a goodly number of the young men who were then residents of the quiet little city, had long looked upon Ruth with feelings very much akin to love. It is true that none had as yet dared to tell her so, nor had she ever shown a preference for any of them; but, nevertheless, it was most certain that many of the young men worshipped, in the secrecy and silence of their own hearts, the modest little Quakeress, Ruth Coffin. But there was one thing which puzzled little Ruth most sadly: why was it that among all the young men about her, who were so anxious to do her bidding, there should be one of the number who had never offered his services to her in any way; he would stand quietly by and see others do that for her which would have been most easy for him to have performed; nor had he ever asked her to accompany him to any of the picnics and merrymakings which so often took place. All this to Ruth was quite a mystery and one which she could not understand. She did not dream for a moment that this very inattention to her sprang from a feeling of love, and that his seeming coldness was anything but natural. How could she know that he would have perilled his life for her had it been necessary? or why should she imagine that he loved her? he had never whispered to her any of the delicate flatteries of which the others were so bountiful, and which are at all times so pleasing to a woman's vanity, even though she may know at the time that they mean nothing. No, little Ruth was not as wise as are many of the maidens of these days, who would have seen that this seeming indifference was only the outer circle of love, which was to guard and hide that love from sight, — to keep it sacred from the prying eyes of the world, and only to be acknowledged to her at the proper time. She did not think of this; and so many a night she wept herself to sleep, because she feared that Charlton Mitchell, whom she had known from her childhood, who had been her playmate and companion for many years, and her warmest admirer, up to the very day he had gone away to that hateful college, where he had become so changed, and had come back such a different person from what he formerly was, no longer loved her. He was but a boy when he left, and four years had made a man of him; still she could not see why he should have altered in his relations to her. Therefore she wept, because she thought he no longer cared for her as he once had. Now I must acknowledge that it would have been very foolish for Ruth thus to have grieved, had it not been that she in good sooth really loved him; and though she did not acknowledge it, even to herself, and moreover was scarcely aware of it, yet am I quite certain that it was so — else why did her little heart beat so fast when she heard his footsteps, which she had learnt to distinguish from all others? why did she bow her head to hide her blushes, when his name was casually mentioned? why did her bosom heave so rapidly when he spake to her? why did such a full tide of joy rush over her whenever he clasped her hand? and why did the tears start to her eyes when he turned away from her?

"Though I never knew, my children, what it was," I said, pausing in my story, "to have a woman love me, until I met your mother," — "Oh!" said my wife, interjectively, — "yet I had often witnessed a woman's love for another, and quietly marked the effects, which were the same as those that little Ruth experienced.

"How it came to pass," I proceeded, "that Ruth discovered Charlton loved her was in this wise: She had, for a long time, found, every morning when she arose, a bouquet of wild flowers placed upon her own chair in the arbor, though she could not imagine who had laid them there. Morning after morning she arose with the sun, so that she might discover the mysterious giver; but she always found the flowers there before her, till one morning, earlier than usual, just as she drew back the bolt of the outward door, who should she see with the newly gathered flowers in his hand but Charlton Mitchell. It was too late to retreat; he was fairly caught; so he quietly gave the flowers into her own hands, at the same time murmuring something of which only the words "Ruth" and "childhood" were distinguishable. She simply uttered his name, while her bosom heaved and her heart beat to a happy measure. He took her hand in his and she withdrew it not; he looked upon her blushing cheek and marked her downcast eyes, and as he pressed his lips upon her soft smooth cheek, her large blue eyes looked up in wonderment. Then, a few whispered words — a pause — and a half-uttered trembling "yes" fell upon his ear, and then, why then — he had won her."

"Oh! I'm so glad," exclaimed Miss Em. "I was afraid that something awful would happen to her."

"Why?" I asked.

"Well,"— and Miss Em. hesitated, — "because you seemed — so mamma said, you know — in such a bad humor, and told such naughty things about us women-folks."

"'Us women-folks' is good, little girl; you are getting over girlhood rapidly," I said.

"Well," I continued, to come to the end of the story, for I see mamma is weary of it, and as for Miss Floy, she has been reading a book all the time I was telling it, while you little ones are just as sleepy as you can be."

"Oh, no, we're not, papa," they exclaimed.

"Do make it as long as you can," said Em. "I like it so much."

"And me, too," said little Mary.

The boy, however, rolled over on the rug before the fire, and though he opened first one and then the other eye, said nothing, and immediately thereafter dropped again to sleep.

"No, it won't do," I said, "to make it much longer. I could tell, if I chose, — but I will not, — how jolly Captain Tim — Quaker though he was — danced at the wedding. What long stories he told, and how merry he got. I could describe every article of his dress, from his broad-brimmed hat — which he persisted in wearing throughout the ceremony — down to the round-toed shoes, with their silver buckles, which covered his feet. I could inform you how his wife, Long Sally, forgot to scold him for a whole week thereafter, and in the joy of her heart, did that which she had not done before in twenty-five years, — kissed him, till the tears gushed from his eyes, and he made a vow, that would have gladdened the heart even of Uncle Toby, that his wife was the best of women and the model of a housekeeper. I might also relate how the bride appeared, in a white muslin dress, and a lace cape over her shoulders; how her glossy hair was braided, and a white rose-bud placed amid it, much to the scandal of her mother. In short, I might tell all about the wedding, — the smiles, the tears, and the kisses, the words of congratulation offered, and the kindly thanks returned. But I will say no more, leaving it to you, mamma, and to you, Miss Floy, and to you, little ones, to imagine it all as best you may. I will simply add that many years have passed since that happy day, and jolly old Captain Tim, with his long stories and odd jokes, is dead. His wife, Long Sally, has also gone to her long account. But Charlton Mitchell, and his little Ruth, are still in the land of the living, though many a weary day's journey from Woodbine Cottage; and though time must have silvered his head, and left a few lines upon the once smooth brow of little Ruth, yet their hearts, I dare say, are as young now as they were thirty years ago; nor have they forgotten, I am sure, the pleasant period of their youth."

"And now, my little ones, this closes our Christmas Nights in the Library; so kiss us all good-night, and go to bed, and peace be with you."

And they kissed good-night, and departed.

CHAPTER XLI.

My Old Lady asks me to Tea. — How Mrs. Gray dressed me for the Occasion. — What we had for Tea. — Touching an olden Chord. — A China-closet. —A Punch-bowl. — A Nosegay. — Birds. — Keeping Goats and Bees. — The Twenty-third Psalm.

Y old lady of black-matan memory sent me an invitation, a few days since, to visit, and take tea with, her. Of course I accepted her invitation. It is regarded, I understand, by her acquaintances a high honor to be asked by her to tea, as it is a repast which she always herself prepares in her own room. Being a widow, she lives with a married daughter, but has her own apartments, of which she takes the entire charge. Tea is the only meal she takes apart from the family, and it invariably is ready at exactly four o'clock, both in summer and in winter. As it is only the privileged few whom she invites to these entertainments, I was much flattered at receiving an invitation. Even Mrs. Gray was not included in the request. When I told my estimable wife of it, she declared I was a most fortunate individual, and she quite envied me the invitation. I think Mrs. Gray perceives that I am a favorite with the ladies, — especially with old ladies, — and, doubtless, she wonders if I will ever take to flirting with them. ·However that may be, she was very anxious, on this occasion, that I should appear as well as possible. She made me change my collar three times, before I found one that, in her eyes, " set well." Then she tied my cravat with her own hands ; and playfully suggested to me, while doing so, the propriety of my wearing a white one, such as, no doubt, the old lady's husband

had worn when he courted her. Mrs. Gray mischievously thought it might be pleasantly suggestive to my venerable friend.

Aware of the old lady's regard for punctuality, I entered her rooms precisely at the moment the ancient clock standing in the corner struck four. At the same instant the maid appeared, bearing the tea-urn, which she placed upon the table; while the venerable dame, with stately courtesy, received me, and motioned me to a seat at the table. I was the only guest, and as I looked at the prim old lady of over sixty years, and remembered that many gentlemen of the old school had from time to time assembled at her hospitable board, I confess I experienced a little anxiety lest I might not appear to advantage. I felt very grateful to Mrs. Gray for the pains she had taken in fastening my neck-tie, and in brushing the lint from my coat, when I kissed her farewell in the hall.

The appearance of the table was charming, and the meal itself most delicious. The purest of damask linen covered the table, and the urn, sugar-bowl, and cream-jug were of silver, engraved with her family's crest. The biscuits were light and white, and, though I did not inquire, were, I think, made by the old lady herself. There were, as delicate appetizers, thinly shaved smoked beef and grated cheese. There was a variety of preserves, including East India ginger, which is my especial favorite. The tea possessed an exquisite flavor, and was poured into little white china cups, of antique shape, with blue and gilt edges, and golden spots, like stars, studded over them. The monogram "W. & P. C.," in gilt, in the centre of each piece, was surrounded by a blue border. The old lady informed me that this china, which she only used on notable occasions, had been brought from China as a wedding gift, more than fifty years ago, by her late husband, who commanded an East India merchantman. "Poor, dear William!" she continued; "ten days after our marriage he sailed for China, and I never saw him again. The ship was not heard from after she left port; but whether she foundered at sea, and all on board perished, or was attacked by pirates, and my husband and the crew murdered, I never knew. But the hour cannot be far distant when, I trust, kind sir," she said, "the mystery will be solved to me, and, in the other world, I shall rejoin him from whom I have so long been separated."

"Oh," I said, "don't speak so discouragingly. You are not so very old; and who can tell, perhaps you may marry again?"

"No," she replied, "that can never be; though, to be sure, stranger things sometimes happen, and if an old beau of mine, my husband's cousin, should ask me again to be his wife, it might come to pass."

And the old lady sighed, and the color came to her faded cheeks. Without meaning to do so, I had evidently touched a chord in her breast which trembled with bygone memories.

After tea, she opened her china-closet, and showed me the treasures it contained. She apparently takes much pride in her store of old china; and, I learn, is continually dusting and rearranging it. It consists of several sets of tea, coffee, and dinner services. Many pieces of each, however, have been broken; but their value, in her opinion, seem to have increased as they gradually have been broken and destroyed. The good dame possesses a wonderful memory, and gave me the history of the destruction of each piece. Most of these disasters were caused by the carelessness of servants to whom she had foolishly, she said, intrusted them to be washed and put into their places.

The principal attraction, however, in her china-closet — to me, at least — was an immense punch-bowl, capable of holding several gallons of that delectable mixture. The figures on it — which could only have originated in the mind of a Chinaman — consisted of outlandish-looking birds, red, blue, and yellow, almost as large as the fantastical pagodas over which they were represented as flying, having evidently been urged to perform this act by sundry genteelly dressed ladies, with round faces and little feet, that they — the ladies, I mean — might have space to open the very large parasols they held over their heads, and of which the handles apparently were a mile long. A very jolly looking sun, on the point of going down behind a blue hill, shone, notwithstanding the umbrellas, full into the faces of the ladies, and must have caused them much annoyance. Several green fishes were swimming around in the atmosphere, the classification of which would, perhaps, puzzle even my friend Genio, the fisherman. This bowl, the old lady said she would leave to me at her death, which I think very kind in her. I shall prize the bowl, doubtless, as much as she does. I have not failed to notice that china purchased at the warehouses never acquires such value in the eyes of its possessor, as that brought home from the East by a husband, a brother, or a dear friend. I am disposed to believe, therefore, that the pride the old lady has in her china, is less on account of its intrinsic value, than for being the gift of the husband who sailed for India and never returned.

The old lady has also a great partiality for plants. Next to her china, she devotes her attention chiefly to the cultivation of flowers. She has a plant-room adjoining her parlor, containing more than a hundred different plants, growing in jars. She took great pleasure in pointing out the choice varieties, and plucked for me a nosegay of the sweetest flowers in bloom. She gave me the history of many of the plants, and mentioned their names, — most of which, however, I have forgotten. I remember, though, the pomegranate, with its red, waxlike cup, and its flower of the same color. I noticed that the old lady liked best those flowers whose perfume was the strongest, such as the Cape-jessamine, tuberose, and hyacinth. She had a partiality, she said, for tulips, lilies, and poppies, which are worthy garden flowers, as is also the rose, which is the queen of all others. She was old-fashioned enough, too, she declared, to like hollyhocks and sunflowers, lilacs and syringas. Then she narrated some strange stories concerning the instincts her plants possessed; and she solemnly declared that several knew when she approached to water them, and would recognize her by folding their leaves. I think she said these were called sensitive-plants, which, I doubt not, they are.

Besides her china and flowers, the old lady has still other pets, in the shape of birds. Ten or twelve cages hang in her plant-room, each of which contains one or more birds. Most of these are canaries, though robins, mocking-birds, and Java sparrows are to be found there. Parrots are her abomination. She has several stuffed birds in glass cases, — old favorites, she said, raised by her from the nest. She did not take as great an interest now in her birds as formerly; they required so much time and care. She used to have as many as fifty birds, she declared; but twenty was all she had at present. She thought sometimes that she would give up all her birds, and only keep her plants and china. "But," she continued, "I hope this will never come to pass, and that I may in the end gently fall asleep amidst my birds, so their singing may remind me of the songs which emanate from angels in that better land, where I pray to go when my life here is ended."

After a short pause, during which she sat with folded hands, she said, briskly, that she missed the black-matan dog; but now that the goat was gone, — "And, kind sir," she asked, "how do you get along with that goat?" — she did not know that she regretted having disposed of him to me.

"As far as the goat is concerned," I said, "she is most

salubrious; and now that the cold weather has set in, and there is little temptation for her to scale fences in pursuit of provender, she is much less addicted than she was to raids of that nature."

"She is a good goat," said the old lady, "and yields her milk freely to any hand that knows how to milk her. Have you learned to milk her, kind sir?" she asked.

"I have, most estimable old lady," I replied, "but I cannot say that I am partial to the operation. I have tried now both keeping goats and bees; and though the employment may be of a pastoral character, and you may even quote Scripture in praise of it, yet I do not think I envy the person whose lines have fallen to him solely in a land flowing with milk and honey."

Thereupon the old lady said that she thought I was right, and she hoped that my lines would not fall in such a land. It being by this time nearly nine o'clock, and as I knew that the old lady was addicted to early hours, I rose to depart. But she begged me to be seated, as she had one request to make of me, which she trusted I would not refuse.

I said that I thought she might safely depend upon my obliging her.

So, after bringing forth a dish of apples, and some hickory-nuts, and a pitcher of cider, of which we partook together, she asked me to read aloud to her the Twenty-third Psalm, which I did, and then bidding her good-night, I took my leave. As I went down the stairs I heard her repeating to herself, — "Yea, though I walk through the valley of the shadow of death, I will fear no evil; for thou art with me; thy rod and thy staff comfort me."

CHAPTER XLII.

Growing Old. — Youthful Follies. — " In a Vineyard." — Fifty Years ago. The Old Homestead. — The Garden. — The Garret. — Swallows. — Indignant.

MRS. GRAY, my estimable wife, has recently hinted to me the disagreeable fact that I am some years older than when I married her. She says sly wrinkles are creeping around my eyes, and gray hairs mingling with my flowing locks. I fear that it is even so, and that, with an increasing fondness for solid, family dinners, and quiet morning calls, and a growing dislike to picnics and crowded evening parties, I am in a fair way to be set down, before the season is over, by dashing belles and fast youths, as a respectable, middle-aged gentleman.

The thought of this, I must confess, is somewhat humiliating. To give up these things — the picnic, the ride, the dance, and the evening promenade — of my own free will, because they have grown distasteful to me, is bad enough; but to be elbowed out, as it were, from all these youthful follies by younger and better-looking men than myself — or, worse still, purposely omitted or forgotten in the making up of parties — is, to such a sensitive being as myself, really cruel, and only to be remedied by the companionship of my savage literary friend over a bottle of champagne and a box of cigars. This is an unfailing source of consolation, and often serves to call forth pleasant reminiscences of times past, when youth and pleasure went hand in hand. Sometimes, under the spell of the blood of the vine, I write such rhymes as this, which my friend and I sing joyfully together.

IN A VINEYARD.

I 'VE drank all wines that earth can boast,
And of them all I love the most
Champagne that brightly gleams;
The laughing, sparkling wine that flows
From grapes Charles Heidsieck only grows,
In vineyards close by Rheims.

In the delicious harvest-time,
I wandered through the mellow clime
Of France, so warm and bright,
And marked, within a vineyard's bounds,
The lusty gatherers go their rounds,
From early morn till night.

As crowns, upon their heads they bore
Great baskets, heaped and running o'er
With grapes of purple hue;
Beneath which shone, through waving curls,
The blooming cheeks of peasant girls,
With eyes of black or blue.

And merry, stalwart, sun-bronzed men,
Drawing full wains, would, now and then,
Shouts songs in Bacchus' praise.
Oh, rare the wine that then was made,
And blest the vineyard's sun and shade,
In those delightful days!

The wine was Heidsieck's best champagne,
And o'er the vineyard did he reign,
Its owner and its lord:
Then, drink the gallant Frenchman's health —
May never fail his crops nor wealth!
Hip! hip! with one accord.

After reading the above to Mrs. Gray, she wished to know when it was that I visited France, for she never had heard me speak of it before.

"It is many years ago," I replied; "long before I knew you, Mrs. Gray, and when there were no wrinkles or gray hairs to annoy me."

" How many years since did you say, Mr. Gray ? " she inquired.

" Less than fifty, my dear," I answered ; " but to look back to those days always fills me with regret."

" Why so, Mr. Gray ? "

" Because you, my dear, was not with me to enjoy them."

Mrs. Gray shook her head at me, and gave me to understand that she regarded me in the light of a humbug. Dear woman ! I fear she has not that confidence in my veracity which as a wife she ought to possess.

" Speaking of fifty years ago, Mr. Gray," she added, after a pause, " reminds me that you promised to tell me something concerning your early life and home. Can you not relate this to me now ? "

" Certainly, my dear, if you desire it," I replied ; and then, giving the fire a thrust with the steel poker, till the sparks flew up the chimney, and the ashes out into the room, I gave my wife this description of my old homestead : —

" Many years ago, Mrs. Gray, — so many, indeed, that it would sadly puzzle your youthful head to remember, — there stood, a little back from the main street of my native village, an old wooden tenement, whose faded paint, broken windows, and unhinged shutters spoke plainly of desertion and decay. The walk leading from the street up to the wide hall-door was grass-grown, and rank May-weeds forced their way through the crevices in the pavement. The thick growth of trees and bushes that surrounded the house, and the full-leaved woodbine that clambered over its southern exposure, even to the tops of the chimneys, gave a somewhat cheerful aspect to an otherwise gloomy mansion. A heavy cornice, worm-eaten and broken, ran around the top of the building, which was surrounded by a balustrade, ornamented with wooden urns and balls. The house was two stories high, and built after the manner of country houses a hundred years ago, with a wide hall running through the centre, flanked on each side by two large square rooms. Additions, however, had, as the years moved on, been made by the generations that successively occupied it, and wings had been added to each side at different times, and to the rear out-houses innumerable had been attached.

"This house my grandfather had built, and in it both my father and myself were born. Shortly after my birth, however, my mother, who was still youthful, — a little older, perhaps, than you, Mrs. Gray, are now, — persuaded my father to erect at the further end of the garden — which extended back some two hundred feet, unto a new and fashionable street — another and more modern mansion than the old one. There, within sight of the time-worn homestead, and only separated from its grounds by a low picket-fence, was my boyhood passed. After I got to running alone, it became a common occurrence for me to make my way to the old house, and climbing through a low window, ramble for hours in the deserted rooms, and up and down the creaking staircase. Often, when night came, and my absence from the nursery was noticed, and all search for me about the new house had proved unsuccessful, I would be found stretched upon a dusty chest, in the garret of the old house, fast asleep.

"This rambling about the deserted mansion had a charm for me I could never understand; and the influence which those silent and solitary chambers exerted upon my boyish mind has been felt by me through life. Naturally of a retiring disposition, as you, my dear, are aware, and caring little for the companionship of boys, but loving better to indulge in solitary dreamings, these silent communings with my own childish thoughts, in the midst of dust, gloom, and cobwebs, failed not of having an effect on my life. They influenced me to keep aloof from my fellows, not from pride, but because I felt myself unfitted to enter cordially into their feelings. Half poet, half dreamer, I passed through life till I was twenty, knowing little of men or women. After the death of my father, which occurred when I was about twelve years old, my mother retired from the gayeties of life, and seldom visited or received visitors. Educated at home, and solely under her care till I entered college, it is not strange that I, at times, even now, shrink from mingling with mankind."

Mrs. Gray here interrupted me, and said she had never noticed such sensitiveness in my character. It is evident to me that my wife is still deficient in her knowledge of me. I continued: —

"From my earliest childhood, Mrs. Gray, up to the day I left my fond mother for my *Alma Mater*, the old homestead was my chosen resort; there I dreamed my childhood away; there I learnt my boyhood's lessons, and studied my Latin and Greek; there, too, I learned to write in rhyme, and there I wept silent tears over my youthful grievances, and bethought me of what I would do when I became a man. Ah! Mrs. Gray, that old homestead, though years have passed since I last saw it, is as clearly pictured in my memory as though it was only yesterday I left it. The swallows, even now, while I speak, are, doubtless, flying in and out of its garret windows and unused chimneys, as I have watched them do in the summer evenings long since past."

"Do swallows fly in December, Mr. Gray?" asked my wife, "in the part of the country where that old tumble-down house is located?"

"Perhaps not," I replied; "but they will, my dear, when summer comes." And then, indignant at Mrs. Gray, I refused to add another word.

CHAPTER XLIII.

My Wife receives a Present. — Captain Coffin, of the Ship *Fleetwing.* — The Vale of Cashmere. — Shawls. — Going to Church. — "Ship ahoy." The Cabin. — A. C. H. Official. — Old Jamaica cold *vs.* Old Ja-maica hot. — Ham, Turkey, and Olives. — Kittens. — India Shawls. — His Daughters not my Wife. — That Monkey. — A Bengal Tiger. — Our Menagerie. — *Simia Sinica.* — The Bonnet Monkey. — Going Home. Call a Coach. — A Delight. — A Disappointment. — An Iconoclast. — Nuts and Candies. — A Surprise. — An old Battered Hulk. — A dear, good Old Man. — Stopping Grog. — Astonishing. — Household Pets.

MY wife received, recently, a present. It came from a gay and festive sea-captain, a widower, a second or third cousin of mine, whose ship just arrived home from India. The captain's name is Coffin, and he hails from Nantucket; at least he did hail from there when a lad; but that was fifty years ago, and now he "stops," when on shore, — which, however, is but seldom, for his life is chiefly spent "on board ship," — in New York. When his ship came alongside the pier, No. 40 East River, one day last week, he sent a messenger to me to give me notice of his arrival, and to inform me that he had brought a present from India for Mrs. Gray.

When I went home and told my wife of the old sea-king's arrival, and that he had brought her home a present, she immediately said it must be a shawl, an India shawl, from the Vale of Cashmere.

"Ah," I said, "I have heard of the Vale of Cashmere, —

'With its roses the brightest that earth ever gave,
Its temples, and grottos, and fountains as clear
As the love-lighted eyes that hang over their wave;

but I don't know much about its shawls."

"Now, I do," said my wife, "and the shawls made in that valley are the finest known. They are manufactured of the inner hair of the goat raised on the table-lands of Thibet, and are worth their weight in gold."

"Good!" I exclaimed; "but what makes you think that the captain has brought you one of these shawls?"

"Because," replied the dear woman, "when he was here, three years ago, he said I ought to have one."

"Well," I said, "I hope you will not be disappointed; but you build your hopes on a very slight foundation. However, we will see."

The next day being stormy, I had decided not to go to town; but my wife urged me so strongly to go, so that I might bring her shawl home that afternoon, I consented. She said she was fearful that the captain would give it away to one of his daughters, if I neglected to go for it.

Besides, she had an idea that he had come home now to stay for good; "and when captains," she continued, "who have been all their lives at sea, come home to remain, what is it a sign of?"

"Why, that they are not going to sea again," I answered.

"True," she replied, "and it further is a sign that they are going to get married."

"Nonsense!" I said; "what put that into your head?"

"Because, the last time he was home, he said he believed he would make one more voyage, and then settle down in life."

"Oh, that 's nothing," I replied. "He meant nothing by that."

"Well, you 'll see," she said, "and I 've made up my mind who his wife will be."

"Who?" I asked.

"Never mind who," she said; "but you 'll see, and that before many days have gone by. But don't you fail to go to town to-day to get that shawl, or he 'll be sure to give it to Mrs. —— I sha'n't tell you who — but somebody."

I think the truth was, that, as it was Saturday, my wife wished the shawl to wear to church the following day.

"If," I said, "that honest old captain has brought home a shawl for you, he will not be likely to give it to any one else."

"Not to either of his daughters, think you," she asked, "if she should say she desired it?"

"No," I replied; "for, the probability is, that they each have one already, or that he has also brought some home for them. Besides, the captain's daughters, as I happen to know, are living in Nantucket, and could not readily get to New York before next week. But, notwithstanding that, I will go in town, since you wish it, and pay the captain a visit on board his vessel. Still, you must not be greatly disappointed if I come home without the wished-for shawl."

I went to town. In the afternoon I waded down to the pier through the mud and slush, and, after much trouble, found the good ship *Fleetwing*. Why are ships always termed good? Being a stormy day, the process of unlading was not going on, and comparative quietude brooded over the old vessel, as if she were resting from her long voyage. The captain, however, was pacing to and fro on the upper deck, in a somewhat meditative mood, keeping an eye, however, on the scudding clouds, the fickle wind, and the Custom-house officer engaged in drinking old Jamaica, down in the cabin. The captain failed to see me until, passing up the gang-plank stretching along the side of the ship from the wharf to the deck, my form appeared above the bulwarks. As our eyes met, —

"Ship ahoy!" I cried.

"Ship ahoy! yourself, you lubber," he answered. "Bother me," he continued, wringing my hand with a grip of iron, "if it is n't curious! Here was I, this very moment, wishing for you, and wondering what kept you away. Come, let 's go below."

The cabin of the *Fleetwing*, though small, is comfortable, and even handsome. There is much panelling in it of polished bird's-eye maple, surrounded with gilt beading, and lighted from above with stained glass skylights. Through the doors of several state-rooms opening from it I saw, draping the berths, yellow satin curtains, looped up with great yellow twisted silk tassels, and revealing between them the white counterpanes covering the beds. An air of neatness and cleanliness pervaded the cabin, and on the rack above the mahogany table at which I seated myself was a display of gleaming goblets, suggestive of many pleasant drinks. On the table a cold boiled ham and a roasted turkey, a dish of sardines, some olives, and bread and butter, were equally suggestive of a pleasant lunch. The fact is, the captain, when in port, always keeps his table spread "with a plate ready," as he says, "for any guest who may come alongside."

The Custom-house official, who appeared to be a good honest fellow, excused himself for not rising by candidly stating to me that he considered himself incapable of so doing, as he had, by the express orders of the captain, been sitting at that table since eight o'clock, indulging in ham and Jamaica cold. Considering the number of empty bottles which stood before him, I came to the conclusion that but few men, under like circumstances, could have made as sensible a remark as he did, and who would not have been found under, instead of sitting at, the table, after so many hours had elapsed. His time came, however, immediately after drinking a couple of Old Jamaicas hot and spiced, which the captain ordered, when he retired in good order, assisted by the cabin-boy, to the nearest state-room.

"That fellow," said the captain, confidentially, "is a pretty fair drinker, considering he has been in the Custom-house only three or four years; but he don't do it scientifically. He eats too much ham, and don't swallow enough olives. Let me give you another slice of turkey, my boy. I won't crowd you on the Jamaica, — though I think you had better take another glass, — for I know your good wife and children will expect you home to-night. And that reminds me I have a present for your wife. I had a good deal of trouble in getting it here, for everybody on board ship wanted it; but no, I said, that is for my cousin's wife, who knows how to appreciate it. I had n't forgot, you see, those lively little kittens with which your wife and the children used to play so cheerily when I was last in port. And when I saw how their antics amused her, I made up my mind that I would bring her something from foreign parts that would take the fur off of those kittens in no time." What an India shawl had to do with our kittens, which became cats long ago, I could n't imagine; but, as a wise man should, I held my peace.

Thereupon the captain called the cabin-boy and ordered him to bring to him something; but what it was I did not hear.

"Now," said the captain, "go with me into my state-room, and let me show you some pretty things I have in my chest." And we went.

Then the captain drew forth from the inmost recesses of his chest a carefully folded package, and, upon opening it, revealed several India shawls, rich in pattern and of a fabulous price.

"There," said the bluff old captain, "are three shawls, which I brought home for three of the best women in the Union, — my three girls."

"His daughters!" I thought. "Alas! how disappointed my poor wife will be."

My interest in the shawls greatly abated when I learned for whom they were intended.

"But which one," asked the captain, "do you think the handsomest?"

I pointed it out.

"The very one," he continued, "which I selected for Jennie, who was named after my poor wife. But here comes the boy with the present for Mrs. Gray. Talk about the fun in kittens! Why, that monkey will beat them all."

"A monkey!" I exclaimed, in despair; "that will be a nice thing to take home to my wife."

"I'm glad you like it," said the captain; "for, to confess the truth, I was a little doubtful as to whether you and your wife would appreciate it."

"Appreciate it!" I echoed. "My dear friend, nothing, of course, could have pleased us better, except, perhaps, a regular Bengal tiger, fresh from his native jungles."

"You don't say so?" cried the captain, innocently, and in a self-reproaching tone. "My dear boy, drown me if I don't bring you one on my next return voyage."

"For Heaven's sake!" I said, "don't put yourself out to get one. I think we will get along well enough, at Woodbine Cottage, with the monkey, without troubling you to add to our menagerie."

"No, no," said the captain, "I'll do it for you; and when Captain Coffin gives his word, you may be certain he'll never break it. That kind of thing don't run in the family."

All this time the monkey stood in the cabin chattering and snapping at the boy, who held him by a chain, and against whom, as I afterward learned, he entertained the utmost dislike, on account of sundry cruel acts of the boy towards him.

The moment, however, that he heard the captain's voice calling him "Bonney," — a name given to him on account of his having what appears like a sort of bonnet, and which was an abbreviation of that word, — he became quiet, and the boy loosing him, he sprung toward the captain, jumped upon his shoulder, and commenced pulling his whiskers.

The species of this monkey or ape is the Macaque, and is known among naturalists as the *simia sinica.* His color is brown, but on the upper part of the head is a portion of white, which diverges outward in a raylike form. The face is flesh-colored, and the under surface of the body white. He is only about a foot and a half in height, and is, so the captain assured me, most teachable as well as mischievous.

The captain caused him to go through many of the tricks which he had taught him, until at last, notwithstanding my disappointment, I began to get quite interested in the little rascal, and consoled myself by thinking that the children, at least, would be more delighted with that monkey than if their mother had received the costliest of shawls.

As it was getting late, I told the captain I would have to go, and that I would try to send for the monkey on Monday, as it would be impossible for me to take him myself.

"Nonsense!" cried the captain; "I had a nice little tin cage made for him, into which you can put him, and then, tucking it under your arm, walk off."

"No," I said; "it's snowing, and that monkey will catch his death-cold, if exposed to the night air."

"Bosh!" exclaimed the captain; "I'll call a coach, and then you can both ride up to the cars in comfort."

"Why," I said, half to myself and half aloud, "do captains in port always call coaches if they want to go a block or two?"

"I suppose," said the captain, in the same aside voice, "it is because we have always our sea-legs on, and we don't like to expose our professional character to landlubbers."

The coach was called, and then, to my surprise, the captain insisted upon seeing me safely home to Woodbine Cottage. I think he was afraid that I would make away with, or in some manner dispose of, that monkey before I reached home, unless he accompanied me as a kind of special policeman. It could not be that he regarded me as being under the influence of Jamaica hot and spiced, for my libations in that line had been neither frequent nor deep. As I showed by my manner that the present was not over acceptable, he thought, perhaps, that I might dispose of his pet to some itinerant organ-grinder.

So home we together went. The old captain in the jolliest of spirits, and I somewhat disposed to be snappish. I knew that my wife had set her heart upon having a shawl, a real Cashmere, and now to appear before her with a monkey instead, did n't seem to me to be a pleasant thing.

Had I gone to the cars alone, I should probably have stopped in Broadway and bought some little gift for my wife; but, somehow, with the captain beside me, spinning all kinds of sailor yarns, and the monkey chattering on the opposite seat, this good intention of mine was quite forgotten, until we were entering the door of my house. Of course it was then too late.

My wife met us in the hall. She received the captain warmly, and allowed the old rascal to kiss her cheek. When the monkey was brought forward, the little ones were delighted with him, and soon had him out of his cage; but immediately, frightened by the unaccustomed noise, he sprung to the top of one of the bookcases, knocking down, in so doing, a couple of Rogers's statuettes, which were broken to pieces on the floor. There he sat, chattering and grinning, until coaxed down by the captain, who, for safety, put him back into his cage. Then my little boy stuck a finger through the bars, and the monkey nipped it. Then the boy cried, and the captain scolded the monkey, interlarding it with a sea-oath or two, and the monkey scolded back. Then my wife declared that she would n't have such a pest in the house, and hoped that the captain, when he went, would carry him back with him to town.

In the mean time, taking me quietly aside, the dear woman had asked me where was the shawl, and I was obliged to tell her that the captain had brought no shawl for her, but that the monkey was the present. The disappointment of my wife was sad to observe, but she bore up under it bravely; and though her eyes grew just a trifle moist, and the lips quivered just a little bit, she soon looked up at me smilingly, and the above observation of hers, in regard to the captain carrying the monkey back again to the ship, was all that she allowed herself to express of her disappointment.

Then we had dinner, and the captain felt very happy, and recalled former occasions when we had met, as now, about the social board. The monkey got quieted, and, after dinner, allowed the little ones to feed him, and, after a while, was let out of his cage again, without committing any serious act of mischief, except slinging the cat, who incautiously ventured into the room to take a look at the stranger, through a pane of glass, out into the garden.

When the little ones — who had eaten their fill of candies and nuts, which the captain obtained from the capacious pockets of his overcoat, hanging in the hall — had kissed all around and gone to bed, and only we three — for Miss Floy was in the nursery, hearing the children say their prayers, which they did as well as they could for the sugar-plums in their mouths — were seated before the blazing fire, enjoying the warmth and steaming cups of tea, and talking Christmas talk, the old captain made one more visit to his overcoat, and, returning therefrom, placed a package in my wife's hands, which proved, when she opened it, to be what ever since I had seen the captain striving to conceal it in the cars under his coat, I had hoped it would, — a shawl from the Vale of Cashmere, — the duplicate of the one I regarded as the handsomest.

My wife's eyes sparkled, her lips smiled, though she said nothing, but simply took the old captain's hand in hers.

"You old battered hulk, you," I exclaimed, "I might have known you were humbugging me. You are always teasing people in this way. What a life you must lead your sailors out at sea! I would n't be one of them for the world."

"And I would n't have you one of 'em for a good many worlds. What could you do aboard ship, I 'd like to know? I 'd have to stop your grog and rope's-end you every day through the entire voyage. You 'd do no more work than a monkey."

"Hang your monkey!" I said; "the best thing you can do for him is to take him back to Calcutta; for if you leave him here, I 'll send him to join Barnum's 'Happy Family.'"

"Not exactly, Mr. Gray," said my wife; "remember he is not yours to give away; he is mine, and we will keep him here, and call him Captain, after our dear, good old friend here."

"It is astonishing," I said, "what a difference the present of a shawl can make in the feelings of a woman. A few minutes ago you yourself had requested the captain to take him back to town."

"That was because he bit the little boy," she replied. "When he becomes acquainted with the children he won't bite or annoy them in any way, — will he?"

"No," answered the captain; "he 'll be quite like a lamb in a few days, and I know the little ones will be delighted with his antics."

And so it was resolved that the monkey should remain, and become one of the household pets. Although only a few days have passed since he came among us, he has already become the terror of our two cats, the enemy of the dogs Gumbo and Jack, Sinbad the Sailor's old man to the goat, the annoyance of our neighbors, and the iconoclast and something more to Woodbine Cottage.

CHAPTER XLIV.

Woodbine Cottage is invited to a Wedding. — The Happy Couple. — My Old Lady and the Captain. — Mrs. Gray's Suspicions. — Alongside. — The Cherub aloft. — A Black Bottle. — A Wedding Present. — Sunday Morning. — No Nonsense. — Silvery Locks and Youthful Hearts. — A Romance. — "Stern Parient." — The Wedding Day. — The Groom's Attire. — The Bride's Dress. — A Good Custom; an Improvement upon it. Cheer, Boy, Cheer! — Mr. Stricklebat's Success.— Miss Floy willing. — The Dinner. — Speeches, Songs, and Stories. — Amen! — A Dance. — A Merry Christmas and a Happy New Year.

THE inmates of Woodbine Cottage have recently attended a wedding. It is a pleasant thing to go to a wedding, especially if you are acquainted with the parties who are to be married. On the present occasion both my wife and myself had the pleasure of knowing the bride and groom. The latter had been a friend of ours for many years, though the former was an acquaintance only of a few months. To say that we were surprised when we received our invitation would but slightly express our feelings. I was not aware, until asked to the wedding, that either of the two knew each other, although my wife pretended that she knew all about it. I often think that women possess an intuitive knowledge of these matters. When, therefore, our friend, the captain, told us, as we sat around the blazing wood-fire the evening he came home with me, that he was going to be married, and, leaving the sea, and settling down in the country, become a neighbor of ours, I was greatly astonished; nor was my astonishment diminished when he informed us who he intended to marry. I will give my wife the credit of saying — after she learned the name, however, of the coming bride — that she had suspected, ever since the day I took tea with my old lady of black-matan memory, that she had an object in inviting me to her house which I did n't know, and now she was certain of it.

Of course, it was very easy for Mrs. Gray, after she knew that it was this old lady whom the captain was to marry, to state her suspicions as above; but that she had not previously done so I was certain, though I did not care to ask her why she had refrained.

"Yes," said the old captain, nursing his gouty leg upon his knee, and puffing forth a cloud of tobacco smoke, "I promised the old lady, when I was last in port, that, if I lived to return from this voyage, I 'd place my craft alongside of hers, and, in calm and in tempest, foul weather and fair, as long as this old hull kept above water, we 'd float together on the tide, steering clear of all rocks and sand-bars as lay in our course, until, finally, the safe haven of rest was reached. I feel good, my boy," he continued, still stroking his leg, "for ten years to come on this 'ere table-land; and, though we can't always tell as to how long we shall be permitted to weather the gale of life, yet, as I have n't lived many of my days on land, I have a notion that the cherub who sits up aloft to keep watch o'er the fate of poor Jack, as the song has it, is n't going to let me be put under hatches until I 've had a chance to try again the kind o' life which Adam used to lead in Paradise afore Eve went against orders.

"It 's a good many years," continued the captain, putting his unfinished cup of tea aside, and reaching out for the black bottle which was conveniently beside him, "nigh on to fifty, since I was first married, and, though I enjoyed my wife's society going on for five years, most of which time we were together, yet I knew little about living on shore, for I used to take my wife to sea with me wherever I went. She left me, one day, for that better land; and now that my daughters are all married and settled, I have an idea that I 'd like to end my days on the land, and possess, once more, the comfort of a home. I 've known the old lady ever since I was a boy, for we went to school together, and her husband and myself were mates, and sailed in the same ship many a year. He went to Davy Jones's locker long ago, and now I 'm going to marry his widow;" and the captain took a long pull from the black bottle, heaved a deep sigh, and looked up inquiringly into my face.

"Well, I don't know," I said, "that you could do better than marry my old lady. She is a nice body, very neat and particular as regards the appearance of her tea-table, and makes the lightest of biscuits and the strongest of tea."

"I don't feel," said the captain, "that I care much for tea; but if she takes kindly to Jamaica, hot and spiced, and don't object to my smoking, I think we may get along quite well together."

"Tobacco smoke," I said, "is a sure remedy for bugs on plants; and as she has a fine collection of geraniums, rose-bushes, japonicas, etc., you can tell her that you smoke almost solely for the purpose of keeping her plants in a healthy state. Then, too, she is very fond of pets of all kinds, and it would not be a bad idea for you to present her, for a wedding present, with the monkey you were so kind as to bring my wife. I am certain that, for such a purpose, she would willingly resign it to you again."

"No, no!" exclaimed the captain, "you shall not be called on to give up that monkey. He shall belong to you and yours for generations to come, and every boy and girl in your family will find much delight in his companionship."

The captain was evidently a little shy about visiting my old lady alone, and made me promise that I would accompany him thither the next day.

It was a bright, sunshiny Sunday morning when the

ATTACK ON THE CAPTAIN. BEARD.

captain and myself drove over to the Corners, to call on my old lady. As the captain left the house, the goat, probably not approving of the match, gave him a taste of her fighting powers, laying him sprawling in the dust.

"There will be no confounded nonsense," said the cap tain to me as we rode along, "between that old lady and myself when we meet. Hugging, and kissing, and that sort of stuff will do well enough for youngsters like you, but I'm too old a bird for that kind of work. It's enough for me to be tender-like with my daughters, without taking every old woman into my arms who comes along."

Remembering this speech of the captain's, therefore, I was somewhat surprised to see the warmth with which that old couple embraced when they met, and the affectionate glances which they cast one on the other. Still, it was a pleasant sight to see the simple, honest affection of those two old souls, and to know that, notwithstanding their silvery locks, youthful hearts were beating in their bosoms.

The old lady, in the innocence of her life, said: "You must excuse us, kind sir, for thus displaying our regard for each other before you; but we used to be sweethearts many and many a year ago, and though Providence willed it that we should not marry in our youth, yet I think we always thought of each other with kindness, and, perhaps, hoped that some day in the future would find us man and wife."

"An event," I said, "which now promises very soon to be consummated."

The old lady smiled, nodded her head approvingly, and folded her hands quietly upon her lap. The captain put an enormous quid of tobacco into his mouth, and then blew a stentorian blast upon his nose.

"From the way in which you speak, my dear old lady," I said, "there must have been something of a romance between you and the captain in your earlier days."

"Not much," she replied; "but you know 'the course

of true love,' as the playman has it, 'never did run smooth.'"

"Ah! I see," I said; "another case of a 'stern parient' interfering."

"That was it," she replied; "and though we sorrowed at first, and were very unhappy for a time, yet, as young hearts will, we lived through it, and enjoyed domestic happiness afterwards probably as well, kind sir, as most people."

"And now," I said, "after many years, early love is resurrected, and secret constancy rewarded by marriage."

"Humph!" ejaculated the captain.

As neither the old lady or the captain had any especial preparations to make for the occasion, it was agreed to have the wedding take place on the following Wednesday, and I was delegated to see the Rev. Mr. Stricklebat, and engage him to perform the ceremony. In the mean time the captain returned to his ship, the old lady resumed her knitting, and I went back to the bosom of my family.

On the day of the wedding the captain was in the most radiant of humors. He was arrayed in what, to him, was most gorgeous attire; a blue coat with gilt buttons, a buff waistcoat, a white necktie, a ruffled shirt, low-quartered shoes, and black-satin breeches, — the relic of former days, — completed the adornment of the outer man. He was constantly flourishing in air an India handkerchief, of red silk, studded with white spots, which added materially to his festal appearance.

My old lady wore a dove-colored silk dress, with lace mitts of the same color, and a tasty cap, trimmed with white ribbons. She was very quiet and thoughtful, and, just before the ceremony, passed around, with her own hands, to her guests a plate of thin, brittle cakes, filled with caraway-seeds, and small glasses of currant-wine, both of which she herself had made. This was a custom, she said, which had been followed in her family for many generations, and was observed, not only at weddings, but at christenings and funerals.

"And a very good custom it is, too," said the captain; and then aside to me, "though I think the cakes might be thicker, and the wine a trifle stronger, without injury to any one. Come with me quietly," he continued, "and I'll show you an improvement on this."

And the captain led the way to a closet off of the hall, where he produced a black bottle, still half full of Old Jamaica, and the remains of a cold duck.

"There," said the captain, "lay to, my boy, and help yourself. 'T will serve to keep your spirits up during this trying occasion. Don't be down-hearted, lad, 't will soon be over; and though the ceremony is something like going through the breakers, it will be plain sailing enough afterwards. I've gone over that track once before, and I know all about it. Cheer, boy, cheer!" and the captain softly whistled the air of a sea ditty, as we went back to the parlor.

To have heard the captain talk, one would have thought that it was I instead of he who was about to be married.

I have been present at a good many weddings, but at none have I been more deeply impressed with its solemn character than on this occasion. There stood two persons who, nearly fifty years before, had loved each other, but whom Fate had parted, and who now came together again, to renew and consummate the vows made in their youth. Many sorrows and many joys had doubtless been theirs. Children had grown up around them, and, marrying, had left them for homes of their own; and now, they being once more alone in the world, turned again to each other; and, though their once dark hair was strewn with white, their eyes had lost their brightness, and wrinkles had chased the bloom from their cheeks, the clasp of their hands was as warm as when they wooed and lost each other so many years ago.

It was conceded by all present that, in the performance of the ceremony, the Rev. Mr. Stricklebat did himself great credit, and that his address to the married couple was a model one of its kind. It seemed to me, after he had concluded it, that he looked inquiringly around the room, as if desirous of finding another couple to bind in the silken web of matrimony. Miss Floy being the only marriageable person in the room, his eye rested long and earnestly upon her; but, however willing she might have been to sacrifice herself, as there was no one present who could, without committing bigamy, stand up with her in marriage, the parson was fain to postpone, until another time, her victimization. After the ceremony, "Now," said the captain, feelingly, "let us have a gay old time." The bride said we might regard the occasion as her and her husband's golden wedding, to which the parson replied Amen! Then we went to dinner; such a dinner as comes only at Thanksgiving or Christmas time, when turkeys, boiled and roasted; and geese and ducks, savory with sage and onions; and chicken-pies, and boiled hams, and great rounds of beef, and plum-puddings, and apple and pumpkin and mince pies, flanked by tarts innumerable, grace the mahogany, and still and sparkling wines, and stronger compounds, flow in profusion.

After dinner, the captain, who grew more jolly as the hours passed, made a speech, which, though interlarded with an occasional objectionable sailor epithet, the parson, nevertheless, said Amen to. Then my savage literary friend sang the song of "Good Saint Anthony," and the parson still said Amen! Afterward, I told a pathetic story about a couple of old babes who got lost in a wood. Whereupon the parson, in his most lugubrious tone, again said Amen! The truth was, that the parson was satisfied with everything, and had been ever since I placed in his hands, as a fee from the captain, a fifty-dollar greenback. He forgot to say Amen to that, but made it up afterward by saying it when the dogs Gumbo and Jack got into a fight over the turkey bones, and both severely whipped each other.

The evening was wound up with a dance, and the captain and his old lady, — my old lady, alas! no longer, — as they footed it up and down to the tune of "Money-Musk," grew as light of foot and as gay of heart as when, a boy and girl, they had danced together fifty years before. With many wishes for the future health and happiness of the captain and the old lady, we all bade them good-by, and leaving them at home, went home ourselves.

And now, with this account of a wedding, — a fitting conclusion to this rural episode in my life, — I will bid farewell to those who have followed me through these pages, hoping to meet them again, under still more felicitous circumstances.

THE END.

www.ingramcontent.com/pod-product-compliance
Lightning Source LLC
LaVergne TN
LVHW020215110826
845151LV00003B/728

* 9 7 8 1 4 2 5 5 3 3 9 2 2 *